The Best of

Holidays & Seasonal Celebrations

Grades 1-3

Issues 22-26

Teaching & Learning Company

1204 Buchanan St., P.O. Box 10
Carthage, IL 62321-0010

This book belongs to

_____

Edited and compiled by Donna Borst

Cover photos by Images and More Photography and Rubberball Productions

Cover design by Jennifer Morgan

Illustrations by

Janet Armbrust	Chrissy Schofield
Gary Hoover	Vanessa Schwab
Becky Radtke	Luda Stekol
Shelly S. Rasche	Veronica Terrill
Mary Galan Rojas	Gayle Vella

Copyright © 2001, Teaching & Learning Company

ISBN No. 1-57310-299-7

Printing No. 987654321

Teaching & Learning Company
1204 Buchanan St., P.O. Box 10
Carthage, IL 62321-0010

At the time of publication every effort was made to insure the accuracy of the information included in this book. However, we cannot guarantee that agencies and organizations mentioned will continue to operate or to maintain these current locations.

Table of Contents

Winter . . . . 9.

Spring & Summer 198

Dear Teacher or Parent,

Here we are again—time for another great edition of our Best of *Holidays & Seasonal Celebrations* series. As I write this, it is 95 degrees out with no holidays in sight. However, as I browse through issues 22-26 of our magazine (grades 1-3), I find myself thinking about Halloween parties, Christmas decorations, Valentine crafts, Earth Day celebrations, and Easter eggs. All I need to do is flip through the pages of this book and I can find ideas and activities for all of these plus so much more. As a mom, as well as an editor, I can honestly say that you can find fun things to do for every season and holiday in this one resource. I use many of the ideas and activities myself at my kids' school. The teachers love me! The crafts are easy, the snacks delicious, and the holiday worksheets are just plain fun! And the school newsletters using the clip art found in *Holidays* have never looked better!

But just in case this is your very first "Best of" book, let me fill you in on what you can expect. We have taken our best ideas from issues 22-26 of *Holidays & Seasonal Celebrations* (grades 1-3) and have compiled them into one easy-to-use book filled with activities, worksheets, clip art, and much more to help you and your students celebrate the holidays and seasons. You will, of course, find crafts, activity pages, clip art, thematic units and projects for the more traditional holidays of Halloween, Thanksgiving, Hanukkah, Christmas, Kwanzaa, and Valentine's Day. In addition, you will also find activities for celebrating some of the lesser-known holidays such as Book Week, National Peanut Month, Candy Corn Day, Friendship Week, National Music Month, and Johnny Appleseed's birthday. Why not plan a celebration for the Autumnal Equinox or explore the life of a butterfly? We have end-of-school activities, a Birthday Bonanza, and Holiday Newspaper Fun. Everything you need is right here.

And if you are a veteran to *Holidays & Seasonal Celebrations*, you can be assured that all of the regular features you depend on are also here. Kid Space, Seasonal Science, Cooking with Kids, the Craft Corner, Holiday Sing-Alongs, and the Book Nook are all included. Plus we've thrown in some poems, songs, and holiday worksheets to help keep your celebrations fresh and exciting year after year.

Happy Celebrating!

Donna Borst, Editor

If you would like to contribute to future issues of *Holidays & Seasonal Celebrations*, please direct your submissions to:

Teaching & Learning Company
Holidays & Seasonal Celebrations
1204 Buchanan St., P.O. Box 10
Carthage, IL 62321-0010

A Year Full of Rhyme

Downhill sliding,
One lost mitten,
Snowflakes gliding,
Toes frostbitten.

Arrow sending,
Bright red rose,
Secret keeping,
Cupid knows.

In like a lion,
Lucky clover,
Out like a lamb,
Winter's over.

Puddle jumping,
Yellow galoshes,
Raindrops falling,
Splishes, sploshes.

Flowers blooming,
May Day basket,
Kite high flying,
Tisket tasket.

Barefoot walking,
Fishing poles,
Firefly chasing,
Swimming holes.

Castle building,
Cooling shade,
Ice cream melting,
Lemonade.

Sweetcorn picking,
Humid, hazy,
Summer's ending,
Last days lazy.

Pencil sharpening,
Brand-new books,
Football fields,
Teacher's looks.

Leaves falling,
Pumpkin patch,
Ghosts and goblins,
Scary masks.

Grandma's cooking,
Holiday fun,
Giving thanks
For everyone!

Gift giving,
Beautiful manger,
Joyful singing,
Blessed stranger.

by Debra Atkinson

Birthday Bonanza

Use the following creative ways to observe your students' birthdays.

Birthday Fun

On a child's birthday, have 10 friends write a brief statement about the birthday child on a 3" x 5" card. (Examples: Share about the time they rode horses together. Tell about how her mother makes cupcakes. Tell where he went on vacation this year.)

Have students select from the cards throughout the day and have the birthday child talk about what is on the cards. This simple activity gives special attention to the birthday child and develops public speaking.

by Jo Jo Cavalline

A Birthday Action Rhyme

Instead of, or in addition to, the traditional "Happy Birthday to You" song, have children say this action rhyme to celebrate each child's birthday. Stand children in a large circle with the birthday child in the center.

Time to
(Clap, clap, clap.)
Celebrate
(Stomp, stomp, stomp.)
Because today's
(Clap, clap, clap.)
A special date!
(Stomp, stomp, stomp.)
Jump up high!
(Jump up with hands raised.)
Shout, "Hooray!"
(Shout "Hooray.")
Today is *Bobby's
(All children join hands and raise them.)
Special day!
(Lean toward center of circle and stretch arms toward birthday child.)

by Mary Tucker

8

Pretend It's Your Birthday!

Use this activity to celebrate all birthdays at one time.

Make a Cake

1. Draw a cake.

2. Pretend it's your favorite flavor.

3. Color it with the frosting you like best (chocolate—brown, vanilla—white, strawberry—pink).

4. Draw as many candles on it as you will need for your next birthday.

5. Make a wish. (Don't tell anyone.)

Balloon Fun

1. Draw enough balloons to spell your name on them.

2. Put one letter of your name on each balloon.

3. Color the balloons in different colors.

4. Draw strings on them and let them sail on your paper.

Sing

Sing "Happy Birthday to Me" (in unison). Have children use their own names in the song.

Optional: It might be fun to actually have a cake and light the candles as you sing the birthday song.

by Dawn Avery Furey

Kid Space
School Yard Learning Adventures

Autumn Hike

Autumn is a wonderful time for hiking—the bugs are almost gone, it's not too hot, the underbrush is easy to make your way through, and the leaves and scents can be spectacular!

Symmetry Search

Help your students make discoveries about the meaning of symmetry and its prevalence in our natural and man-made world.

Discuss
- Something is said to have line symmetry if one side of the object is a mirror image of the other.
- Fold a piece of construction paper in half. Draw half a heart on the fold, then cut around it. Unfold the paper to show the full heart. Point out that each side matches the other perfectly. The two halves of the heart are symmetrical.

Directions
1. Take your students on an outdoor hike to search for symmetry.
2. Ask students to investigate items they find in the natural world.
3. What easy method will determine if items are symmetrical? (Folding as demonstrated.)
4. Students will find and fold leaves, blades of grass, flower petals and other plants.

5. Have students investigate and answer the following questions:
   - Do both halves match?
   - Does it matter which way the item is folded?
   - Can you find other examples of symmetry in nature?
   - Are you symmetrical?
   - Can you find examples of natural objects that are not symmetrical?
   - Can you find man-made things that are or are not symmetrical?

Leaf Symmetry
- Collect leaves and study them for symmetry.
- Fold your leaves in half. Do your leaves have matching sides?
- Fold your leaf another way. Is it symmetrical in this direction?

Teacher Tip
- After an outdoor hike, check children for ticks and "hitchhiking" seeds such as burdock.

by Robynne Eagan

10

Step to It!

Bring a little math into your hike!

You Need
- measuring tape
- trail markers

Directions
1. Mark a short trail from one end to the other.
2. Have each child determine the length of their step. This can be done by wetting the bottom of running shoes and then walking across pavement or by walking in soft earth. Children can measure the distance between each step and then take an average of those distances to find their average step. Children will record this measurement.
3. Have children estimate how many steps they think it will take for them to walk from one end of the marked trail to the other. Children will record these estimates.
4. Have children count their steps while they hike the trail. Children will record the actual number of steps it took to walk the trail. Discuss the relationship between their estimate and the actual number of steps taken.
5. Ask older students if they can find the length of the trail using the information they have gathered. The length of their step multiplied by the number of steps will give the length of the trail.

Pace is a term that refers to two steps. Some hikers talk about steps, some about paces and some about miles or kilometers.

Mushroom Markings

The cool, damp fall weather sets the scene for mushroom studies.

You Need
- moist, shaded area where mushrooms are known to sprout
- collecting basket, bucket or bowl
- sheets of white bond paper
- masking tape
- paper plates
- acrylic paint
- clear glass cup or jar
- sharp knife (to be used by adults only)

Directions
Collect mushrooms to take back to class for further study.

Activity 1: Mushroom Prints
1. Tape paper to your work surface.
2. Pour paint onto paper plates.
3. Remove the mushroom stem and dip the gills gently into the paint.
4. Press the gills gently onto the paper to make a mushroom print.

Activity 2: Take a Closer Look
1. Gently remove the stem from the mushroom and trim the bottom of the cap to expose the gills more fully.
2. Place the mushroom on the paper flat-side down and cover the mushroom with an inverted glass. Let sit for at least one hour.
3. Remove the glass, lift the cap and observe the intricate spore pattern.

Discuss
There are many species of mushrooms; some are edible and some are very, very poisonous. It is difficult to tell mushroom species apart, so you should never eat mushrooms that you find growing in nature. Mushrooms reproduce by tiny spores that are dropped from mature mushrooms. These tiny, light spores containing living matter inside a membrane, are carried by the wind. Single spores are so tiny that they cannot be seen without a microscope, but a group of spores appears as colored dust. The color of the spore dust helps us identify the different kinds of mushrooms. You might find black, brown, pink, green, white, purple, or yellow spores or "dust."

Leaf Study

Color Conversation

Every fall the leaves of deciduous trees burst into color. Short warm days, and longer, cool nights limit the hours of light the plant is exposed to and cause the vessels that carry water and nutrients within leaves to become clogged. These conditions interfere with the production of the pigment chlorophyll. Chlorophyll makes leaves appear green because it reflects green light and absorbs all other wavelengths of light. Chlorophyll can absorb color more than the other pigments in the leaves can reflect it. As chlorophyll fades and the leaf begins to die, other pigments remain or are produced in the leaf causing the colors we see. Carotenoid pigment gives leaves a bright yellow appearance and anthocyanin causes the brilliant red we see in oaks and maples. Both red and yellow leaves eventually turn brown from the tannin that is stored in leaves and the bark of trees. When the leaves eventually die and fall from the tree, the tree is able to conserve the moisture it needs for the dry winter months ahead.

Take a Closer Look at Leaves
- Have your group collect a variety of colored leaves; then meet back together.
- Hold up the various leaves and ask for color descriptions of each leaf.
- Different children may see and describe each leaf color in a different way. Help children recognize various shades, tones, and combinations of colors.
- Can children find the veins that carried nutrients to the leaf?

Leaf Scavenger Hunt

Take advantage of the bounty of wonderful shapes and colors falling to the ground.

Find leaves that have
- green, red, yellow, or brown coloring
- prominent veins
- one, five, or eight points
- a rounded or oval shape
- a smooth surface or rough surface
- jagged or straight edges (or "margins")

Leaf Pile Play

Add some fun to traditional games by including a pile of leaves.

- Play dodge ball around a pile of leaves.
- Play tag in an area strewn with leaves.
- Play follow the leader through a leafy forest.

Leaf Pile Challenge

You Need
- 4 rakes
- 4 markers

Directions
1. Divide your group into two teams.
2. Collect a large pile of leaves. Place one marker by the leaves.
3. Place a second marker 10 feet (3 meters) from the first marker.
4. Have each team line up in pairs.
5. On the signal, two team members at a time must rake a pile of leaves behind the second marker. When the members have passed the marker, they must run the rake back to the next two players.
6. The first team to rake their leaf pile from one marker to the other wins the challenge.

Leaf Pile Pals

You Need
- bag of kids' clothing including footwear and hat
- plastic bags of various sizes

Directions
1. Have students fill bags and or clothes with leaves to shape bodies for Leaf Pile Pals.
2. Have children dress the body shapes and then pose the Pals among the leaves.
3. This display could be brought into the school foyer, front entrance or library for a seasonal sensation.

12

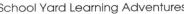

Apple Activities

October is Apple Month. Take advantage of the harvest to create some great outdoor learning opportunities.

Take a Trip

Take a trip to the apple orchard or a local market. Pick your own apples from the tree or a fruit stand. Discuss color, texture, size, shape, and taste. Make and taste some apple cider if you have the opportunity.

Hunt for Apples

Buy a bushel of apples and hide the apples around the yard. Have students burn off energy as they search for the apples to fill your bushel.

Pass the Apple

Play a version of Hot Potato using an apple instead. A portable CD or cassette player can be used for music. Players will form a circle and pass the apple around the circle while the music plays. When the music stops, the player holding the apple is "out" or receives a silly name of some sort.

Apple Over-Under Challenge

1. Divide your group into two equal teams. Have each team form a line.
2. Place a bushel of apples at the front of the line and an empty bushel at the end.
3. On the signal to begin, the first player passes an apple over her head to the next player who bends over and passes the apple under his legs. The next player passes the apple over her head and so on, alternately over and under until the apples have been moved from one bushel to the other.
4. The first team to transport their apples in this manner wins the challenge.

Apple Imagery

Create a guided imagery experience to teach about the growth of an apple. Have children sit outside, close their eyes, and imagine.

"Imagine you are a bud on the apple tree. It is springtime. The sunshine is warm. The rain is nurturing. You open up into a sweet-smelling blossom. A bee pollinates you. The wind blows your petals away. A tiny apple begins to grow. The sunshine warms you. The rain nourishes you. You grow and grow. The cool night air touches your skin. You can barely hold onto the branch, you are so big. You fall from the tree onto a bed of soft grass."

A Basket of Apples

1. Cut out about half of the inside of two paper plates as shown.
2. Color the plates to look like a basket; then glue them together back to back.
3. Color and cut out the apples below. Glue them inside the basket.

by Mary Currier

Sing About Fall

Colored Leaves

To the tune of "London Bridge"

Colored leaves are falling down,
Falling down, falling down.
Colored leaves are falling down
All around the ground.

Pick some leaves and throw them up,
Throw them up, throw them up.
Pick some leaves and throw them up.
Look at them fall.

Rake the leaves and pile them up,
Pile them up, pile them up.
Rake the leaves and pile them up,
Building a mountain.

On your mark, count 1, 2, 3,
1, 2, 3, 1, 2, 3.
On your mark, count 1, 2, 3.
Jump on the mountain.

Where Is Scarecrow?

To the tune of "Frere Jacques"

Where is scarecrow, where is scarecrow?
Standing here, standing here.
Funny little scarecrow, funny little scarecrow,
Full of fear, full of fear.

Here come the birds, here comes the birds,
In the sky, in the sky.
Flying over corn fields, flying over corn fields,
Will they try? Will they try?

Where is scarecrow, where is scarecrow?
In the corn, in the corn.
Wind has blown his hat off, wind has blown his
     hat off.
Birds are gone, birds are gone.

Tall Scarecrows

To the tune of "Twinkle, Twinkle, Little Star"

Funny, raggy, tall scarecrows,
Standing in the corn that grows.
When the birds come flying by,
Scarecrows watch them with an eye,
Moving when the wind does blow,
Keep the birds from flying low
And save the corn so it may grow.

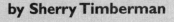

by Sherry Timberman

Autumn Antics

Autumn is a colorful and exciting time for youngsters. Here are a dozen projects, crafts, and experiments to get them into an autumn mood.

"Leaf" Me Alone!

Cut leaf shapes from colored construction paper or use leaf-colored fabric. On the surface of each leaf in fine marker, write a poem using the following format: first four lines are action words ending in "-ing" which describe falling leaves; last line is a concluding thought. Here are some examples from a sixth-grade class.

collecting	jumping	swirling
gathering	skipping	flittering
raking	hopping	fluttering
sweeping	flopping	skittering
autumn leaves piled high	children leap into the leaf pile	autumn leaves fall

It's Utterly A "Maze"ing!

Materials

leaf-colored construction paper
pencil
scissors
white glue
popcorn
dry tempera paint

Directions

1. On a piece of construction paper, trace and cut the shape of a cob of corn. Cut the husk from green construction paper.
2. Color popped corn with dry tempera paints. Place yellow, red, and orange dry tempera into separate plastic bags, add popcorn, and shake to coat.
3. Cover the surface of the cob with white glue.
4. Place popcorn onto the corn shapes.
5. Glue husks to the sides of the cobs.
6. Create a fall collage display using your corn as the center of interest.

The Stamp of Autumn!

Create autumn stationery, place mats, and book covers by using various autumn fruits and vegetables to make prints. Cut the vegetable or fruit horizontally and use the surface dipped in thick liquid tempera to create interesting prints. Add seeds, pressed flowers, or other autumn treasures for detail, gluing them in place with white glue.

by Gail Lennon

Don't Rub Me the Wrong Way!

Materials
leaves of different shapes and sizes, bark, nuts
thin paper such as onion skin, thin typing paper, or
tissue paper for rubbings
crayons, soft lead pencils
construction paper or white cartridge paper

Directions
1. Place a leaf, nut or bark on a smooth surface.
2. Put thin paper on top.
3. With the side of a crayon or soft pencil, make a gentle rubbing of the outline of the object.
4. Continue the process using diffcrent objects and colors for your rubbings.
5. Make an interesting collage by cutting out the rubbings and mounting them on a piece of paper to form a creative design. Create a fall poem or song to go with your rubbing. Mount the poem beside the rubbing, or write the poem on top of a rubbing.
6. Use rubbings to identify each of 10 or more deciduous trees. Mount the real leaf, the rubbing, and a brief paragraph telling about the tree.

Footprints of Autumn

Materials
Styrofoam™ meat trays
natural fall objects such as leaves, nuts, vegetables, fruit
white glue
hole punch
yarn

Directions
1. Collect natural objects such as seeds, dried flowers, nuts, fruit, and so on.
2. Arrange these things on a Styrofoam™ meat tray and glue in place.
3. If you wish to hang the completed collage, punch two holes at the top and string a piece of yarn for a hanger.

Falling Leaves
Create an audiotape containing songs and poetry about autumn and falling leaves. "Indian Summer" is a good example. Create an audio cover design and title to go with your tape.

Apple Head People

Materials

apples
knife
whole cloves
yarn
lace, ribbon, felt scraps
straight pins
craft sticks
rouge

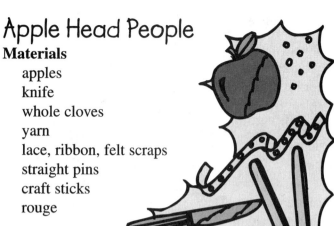

Directions

1. Peel apples.
2. Cut deep slices in the apple to create facial features—nose, eye sockets, chin, mouth. Create wrinkles by making more shallow cuts.
3. Press cloves into the slices to make eyes, nose, and mouth.
4. Place apples on cookie sheet and bake at 150°F (65°C) overnight. Allow apples to cool.
5. Push craft stick gently up the core of the apple face.
6. Use straight pins to attach yarn or fake fur hair. Decorate with felt hats, flowers, ribbon, lace collars, bow ties, and so on.
7. Add rouge to cheeks for face color.

Corn Husk Dolls

Materials

7 corn husks, dried
string or yarn
scissors
paper towels
bucket of water

Directions

1. Soak corn husks until soft. Drain, but keep the husks damp.
2. Cut six pieces of string each 6" (10 cm) long.
3. Roll one husk into a ball to create the head.
4. Layer five corn husks; then place the ball in the center.
5. Fold the five corn husks in half over the ball.
6. Tie a piece of string below the ball to make the neck.
7. Make arms by rolling one husk lengthwise and inserting it horizontally below the string holding the head.
8. Tie arms at wrists with two pieces of string.
9. Tie a piece of string below the arms to form the waist.
10. Below the waist, divide the corn husks into two legs and cut the husks vertically but not up to the waist.
11. Tie off legs at ankle. Allow corn husk dolls to dry.
12. Create facial features using permanent marker.
13. Add hair using yarn or corn tassels.
14. Arrange corn husk dolls as part of a display or as part of an autumn door decoration.

Candy Apples

Melt caramel-flavored candy in the microwave or in a double-boiler on the stove. Place a wooden dowel or craft stick into the center of medium-sized tart apples such as Macintosh. Dip apple (not dowel) into caramel substance and allow to drip back into the pot. Place apples on a sheet of waxed paper to cool.

The Amazing Painted Tree

Materials

    sponges cut into small squares
    brown, green, yellow, orange, and red tempera
    Styrofoam™ meat trays
    white construction paper
    brown crayon
    pieces of tree bark

Directions

1. Draw the outline of a tree on construction paper.
2. Use bark rubbing and brown crayon to create bark surface.
3. Sponge paint leaves onto the top of the tree using various fall colors and a different sponge and meat tray for each tempera color. You may wish to sponge paint some leaves onto the base of the tree trunk as well.
4. Read *The Giving Tree* by Shel Silverstein or *A Tree Is Nice* by Janice Udry while you are waiting for the trees to dry.

Leaf Stencils

Use real leaves to create leaf templates by cutting out leaf shapes from tagboard pieces. Use these to stencil leaf decorations on a book cover, place mat, stationery, or other items.

Nuts About You!

In preparing for winter, some animals and birds store food for hibernation; some add fat for the long, cold winter; and some add fat for the long migration south. Select an animal or bird that prepares for winter. Experiment with feeding it various foods. Keep track of how much is consumed and at what time(s) of the day. Be consistent in your experiment. Offer food only at specific time(s) and weigh what was left out and what remained to determine the amount eaten. Use your notes to analyze what you discovered over a two-week time period, offering the same foods at the set numbers of times. Share your results using graphs and charts to enhance your oral presentation.

Poseable Scarecrow

Materials

- 1 piece of white construction paper
- 2 pieces each of green, orange, or red construction paper
- 3 pieces of black construction paper
- 1 piece of tan construction paper
- scissors
- glue
- crayons
- 7 paper fasteners

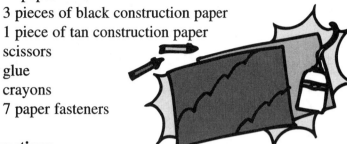

Directions

1. Cut a large oval from the white paper for the head. Draw facial features.
2. Choose green, red, or orange for the shirt. Attach one whole sheet to the bottom of the head with a paper fastener. Cut the second sheet in half lengthwise and attach to each side of the shoulder for the arms.
3. Cut one sheet of black paper in half widthwise. Glue one half to the bottom of the shirt for the body. Cut the other half into a triangle or other hat shape and glue to the head.
4. Cut the two remaining sheets of black paper in half lengthwise. These will be the upper and lower legs. Attach to the bottom of the body and at the knee with paper fasteners.
5. Cut the tan paper into six strips widthwise. With the scissors, fray each one halfway to look like straw. Glue these to the head for hair, and for the hands and feet.
6. Draw on patches, buttons, ties, belts, and other details.
7. As you're hanging your scarecrow, pose him any way you like.

Scarecrow Relay

Pick two teams and have a pile of clothing consisting of pants, shirt, hat, and some type of wig for straw hair for each team. Pick a scarecrow for each team and have the scarecrow stand on the other side of the room. On "go," the first runner grabs a piece of clothing, runs to the scarecrow, and helps him put it on, then returns to his team. They continue this until the scarecrow is dressed. The first team to dress their scarecrow wins. The clothing must be put on in the correct order—pants, shirt, hair, hat.

If you have more than five players on a team, you can add additional clothing, such as belt, scarf, glasses, and so on.

by Sherry Timberman

Name _____

Mixed-Up Scarecrows

One fall morning Meg woke up to find that the scarecrows had blown over in the garden. They were all mixed up. Use the clues to help her put them back in the right order.

1. The happy scarecrow with the cheerful smile was not first.

2. The scowling scarecrow with the menacing smile was between the happy scarecrow and the winking scarecrow.

3. The winking scarecrow was between the scowling scarecrow and the scarecrow with glasses.

by Nancy Ralston

21

Scarecrow Fun

Scarecrow Masks

Copy the scarecrow features for the children. Give each child a paper plate and the scarecrow features to color. Then have them cut out the scarecrow features and paste them on the plate to make a mask. You may prefer to cut out holes for eyes so children can look through them.

by Mary Davis

Scarecrow Song

Have children wear their masks as they sing this song to the tune of "Twinkle, Twinkle, Little Star."

Scarecrow, scarecrow, standing tall,
I see you waving every fall.
In the field of corn you hide,
Scaring birds with scarecrow pride.
Scarecrow, scarecrow, winter's here,
But I'll see you again next year.

by Sherry Timberman

Scarecrow Dolls

After reading the book *Barndance* by Jim Archambault and Bill Martin, Jr., ask students to cut scarecrows from wallpaper sample books. Provide basic pants and shirt patterns for them. Let them cut out their own shoes, hats, heads, and arms from various samples. Paste the scarecrows on orange and yellow paper and display around the room.

by VaReane Heese

Name _____

Back-to-School Backpack

The names of these school supplies are all mixed up. Unscramble and write them correctly. If you need help, use the picture clues below.

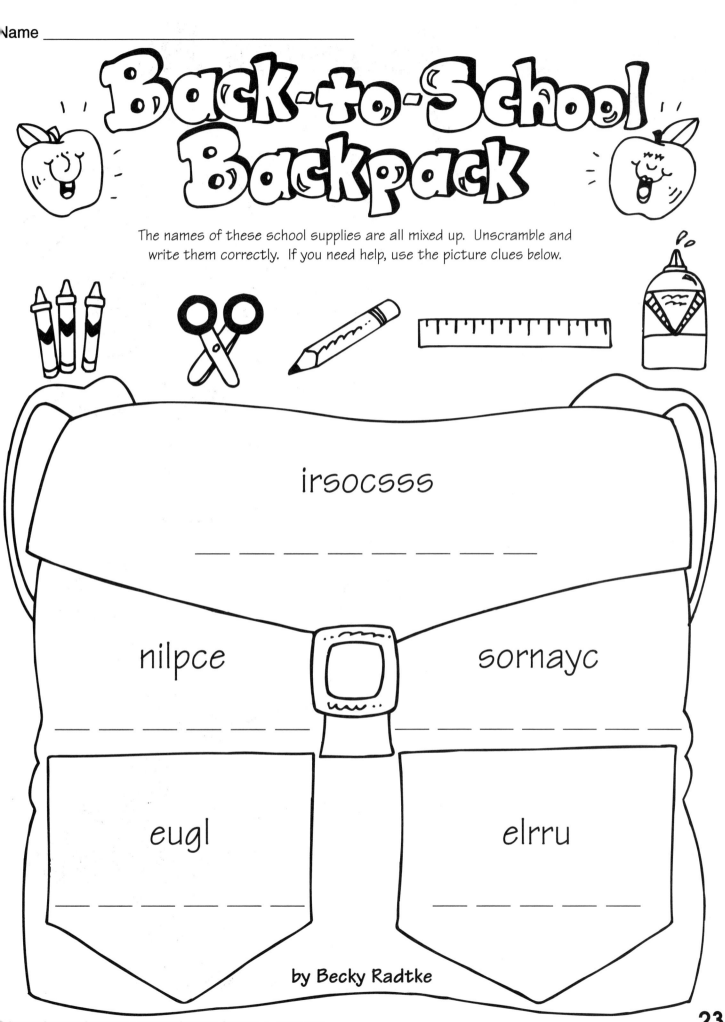

irsocsss

_ _ _ _ _ _ _ _

nilpce

_ _ _ _ _ _

sornayc

_ _ _ _ _ _ _

eugl

_ _ _ _

elrru

_ _ _ _ _

by Becky Radtke

Exploring Friendship

Encourage friendships and acceptance of others by making use of activities that allow children to interact with one another in a positive manner during Friendship Week, August 20-26.

Working Together

Friendship provides children with opportunities to communicate and learn to compromise. Help your children experience this aspect of friendship by pairing them up to create joint sculptures from a simple dough recipe (1 c. flour, 1 c. salt, and 1 c. water). Write the recipe on the board or on small cards. Let each pair of children work together to read, measure, and mix up a batch of dough. Have them use their dough to plan and build a sculpture project together. Allow the sculptures to dry thoroughly; then let the team players paint their works of art. Invite them to tell the class about their work.

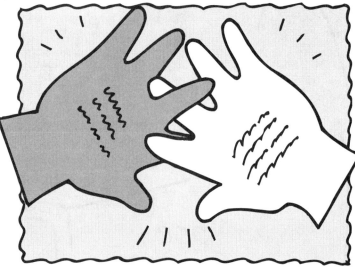

Join Hands in Friendship

Talk with the children about the characteristics of friendship. Note that friends are kind to each other, and that we share our friends with others. Help the students understand that friends offer companionship and support, as well as kindness. Prepare cardboard handprint shapes for the children to trace and cut from construction paper. Encourage them to think about what friendship means; then have them write poems about friendship on the palms of their paper hands. Join these hands in friendship by slightly overlapping the fingers and using them to edge a bulletin board. Read one poem a day from the board to remind the class of the value of friends.

by Marie E. Cecchini

Friendship in Action

Friends help each other in times of need. Use simple motor activities to help demonstrate this cooperative aspect of friendship. Arrange the children in pairs. Have them each hold one hand behind their backs. Now together, they must use their free hands to button both of their sweaters, or tie their shoes, or zip their coats, or pack up their backpacks, or clean their desks. In order for each pair to meet with success, they must work as a team and help each other.

In a Name

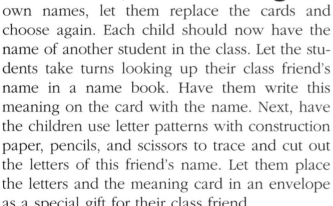

Invite the children to learn a little more about themselves and their classroom friends with this language activity. Have the students write their names on index cards. Place all of the cards together; then have each student choose a card at random. If they choose their own names, let them replace the cards and choose again. Each child should now have the name of another student in the class. Let the students take turns looking up their class friend's name in a name book. Have them write this meaning on the card with the name. Next, have the children use letter patterns with construction paper, pencils, and scissors to trace and cut out the letters of this friend's name. Let them place the letters and the meaning card in an envelope as a special gift for their class friend.

Friends Have Things in Common

Friendships generally evolve when people have at least some things in common. Yet each of us remains different in many ways. Use stamp pads and paper to demonstrate this to the children. Talk with them about the fact that even though we all have fingerprints, our fingerprints are different from one another. Let them press their fingers onto the ink pads, then the paper to make prints. Have them compare their prints with their neighbors. Use magnifying glasses to clarify the differences in lines and curls.

Friends Are Great

Have each student write his or her name on slip of paper. Collect the papers in a bag; then let each child choose a name. Each student uses markers and paper to draw and color a picture of the person whose name he or she has chosen. Below the picture, write the person's name and what he or she likes about this person. Is this person honest? Kind? Helpful? Nice? Bind all of the pages together into a book entitled *Friends Are Great* for the children to share.

Books About Friendship
Annie Bananie by Leah Komaiko, Scholastic.
Friends by Helme Heine, Macmillan.
Jamaica's Find by Juanita Havill, Houghton-Mifflin.
Matthew and Tilly by Rebecca C. Jones, Dutton.
The Rainbow Fish by Marcus Pfister, North-South Books.
We Are Best Friends by Aliki, Mulberry Books.

Bulletin Boards

September Stories

Each month, beginning in September, involve your students in writing seasonal stories or poems on the "shape of the month." Give each student a shape related to the month on which to write (September–leaf; October–pumpkin, ghost, or bat; November–turkey; December–Christmas tree or ornament, menorah or kanara; January–snowman; February–heart or Lincoln or Washington silhouette; March–shamrock or kite; April–umbrella, bunny or Easter egg; May–flower or bird; June–flag or tree; July–ice cream cone; August–sun or airplane). Put the shape stories on the bulletin board. When you take them down at the end of the month, place them in manila envelopes, one for each child. Near the end of the school year, pass out all the shape stories and have children make a *Season of the Year* book by pasting the shapes on sheets of paper, adding a border on each page, laminating them and binding the pages together.

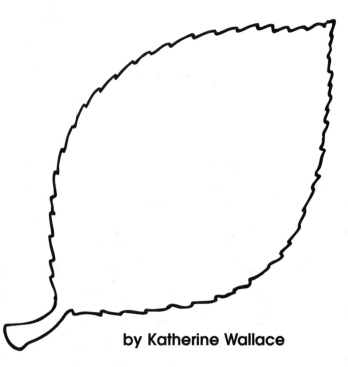

by Katherine Wallace

26

28

Autumnal Equinox

There are only two days a year when the hours of daylight are equal to the hours of night. September 22 is one of those days. It is the first day of autumn in the Northern Hemisphere. From this date on, the hours of daylight decrease in the Northern Hemisphere until December 21, the shortest day of the year.

Signs of the Season

Autumn sneaks in with gradual changes in temperature and the amount of daylight. Help children to be aware of these changes and other signs of the season with a bulletin board. Be sure to include birthdays and local or school events that occur in autumn.

Draw a tree trunk on bulletin board paper. Cut out colored leaf shapes. Write a sign on each leaf. Start with the Autumnal Equinox and keep adding leaves as changes become apparent.

by Linda Masternak Justice

Mystery Color Leaves

Materials
- coffee filters (one each)
- water-soluble markers
- water dropper or hollow coffee stirrer
- water
- leaf template cut from cardboard
- scissors

If using a coffee stirrer, dip one end of stirrer into a cup of water. While in water, cap other end with finger. To drop water, lift finger, and uncap. Practice—it's fun!

Directions

Cover the work surface with newspapers. Have children trace the template on coffee filters and cut out leaf shapes. Decorate the leaves with markers, making dots and stripes. Do not color the leaves completely. Don't be afraid to use black. Now place just a drop or two of water on one of the dots. Watch as it spreads and hidden colors appear mysteriously. When dry, hang them in the windows for all to admire.

What Happened?

The colors of the markers are made of a mixture of pigments. When these pigments are dissolved in water, they move along the fiber of the coffee filter. They separate in bands as a result of different degrees of solubility.

Leaf Print Tee-Shirts

Kids can wear colors of autumn. Ask each child to bring in a clean white or light-colored tee-shirt and several leaves. Leaves with prominent veins work best.

Materials
- acrylic craft paint in autumn colors
- plastic grocery bags
- foam meat trays
- newspaper
- sponge brushes
- paper towels
- textile drum (optional)

Directions

Place a section of newspaper inside a plastic grocery bag. Flatten it out and insert it inside a tee-shirt. This keeps the paint from bleeding onto the back of the shirt. Pour a bit of paint in a foam tray. Spread it on the vein side of the leaf with a foam brush. Place the painted side of the leaf on the shirt. Walk your finger over the back of the leaf. Remove the leaf. Repeat as often as desired. Don't be afraid to overlap leaves. Let them dry.

Sequence the Seasons

Help students understand the cycle of the seasons. Using seasonal pictures, have children arrange them in sequence. It doesn't matter where you start. Select a picture to display. What season comes before the picture? What season comes after the picture? What season is next? Scramble the pictures and allow children to put them in order.

Opposites of Autumn

While we are experiencing autumn in the Northern Hemisphere, the Southern Hemisphere is enjoying spring. Use a globe to show children the Southern Hemisphere. Identify Australia, South American countries, and the African nations. Point out that these countries are in the opposite hemisphere.

Brainstorm a list of opposites with your class. Here are some starters.

northern—southern
autumn—spring
cooler—warmer
days are shorter—days are longer
drying plants—growing plants
harvesting crops—planting seeds

Go Fly a Kite!

Traditionally March is a windy month and spring is kite-flying time in the United States. But autumn is also a windy season.

Read *Dragon Kite of the Autumn Moon,* by Valerie Reddix. It is the story of Tad Tin, a young Taiwanese boy, and his grandfather. Grandfather is ill and Tad Tin must decide whether or not to release his beloved dragon kite to carry away all their troubles.

Design model dragon kites to encourage cultural awareness and creativity. Dragon kites are named after their shapes. They may have tails more than 18 feet long. Duplicate the pattern on page 33 for each child. After drawing, coloring, and cutting it out, attach a three-foot long paper tail and streamers. Use the kites to decorate the classroom.

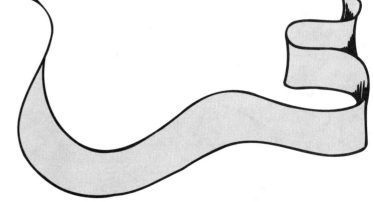

Dragon Kite

Color and cut out the dragon pattern.

Make a paper tail 5 inches wide and 3 feet long. Attach it to the dragon head.

Attach two or three streamers on each side. Make steamers from ribbon, paper or yarn.

Punch hole and tie on streamers.

Grandparents Are Great!

Involve your students in the following activities to celebrate Grandparents' Day.

Favorites

Give each child a one-page survey (one for each grandparent) made up of questions about their favorite things: food, song, movie, book, singer, clothes to wear, pet, car, and so on. Have children take the surveys home and ask the questions of their grandparents (in person or by phone), writing their answers on the survey to share with the class the next day. Compile the survey results to see if any overall favorites emerge. Your students will be interested to see what their grandparents' generation agrees on as favorites. Chart the results and give copies to the children to share with their grandparents.

My grandma has a dog named "Pickles"!

Grandparents' Rap

Teach this rap to your students and practice it so they can perform it for their grandparents when they come to visit the class.

Grandparents are cool!
(Clap, clap, clap)
Grandparents are fun!
(Stomp, stomp, stomp)
Lots of grandkids?
(Hold up fingers: 1, 2, 3.)
They love everyone!
(Kiss fingers: smack, smack, smack).
They love to spend time
(Clap hands over head.)
Just being with you.
(Clap hands in a circle.)
They're always proud
(Trace grin on face.)
Of whatever you do.
(Hold finger and thumb in OK sign.)
Grandparents are great!
(Clap, clap, clap)
Grandparents are fine!
(Stomp, stomp, stomp)
I sure wouldn't trade
(Shake head no and shake forefinger.)
Any of mine!
(Spread arms wide.)

by Mary Tucker

Grandparents Are . . .

Print the word *GRANDPARENTS* vertically on the chalkboard for children to copy down the side of a sheet of paper. Challenge them to create an acrostic to describe grandparents. Each descriptive word must begin with a letter in the word *GRAND-PARENTS*. If they need help getting started, give them one word (such as *great, patient,* or *affectionate*). Let them share their ideas when everyone is done.

If you work with younger students who have trouble spelling, you might want to do this activity as a class, coming up with words together.

I remember . . . when we traded hats!

Sharing Memories

Ask each child to think of a special time with grandparents and share that experience with the rest of the class. Get them started by sharing a favorite memory of your own with your grandparents. Explain that if a child has no grandparents, the class would like to hear of a favorite experience with aunts or uncles or older friends. Encourage each child to share, even if it's only a sentence or two.

Name _____

Dinner at Grandma's

Stacy is celebrating Grandparents' Day by having dinner at her grandma's house. Stacy brought her grandma some gifts. Can you find the gifts hidden in the picture? Look for a necklace, a scarf, a book, a flower, and some candy.

Johnny Appleseed Mini Book

Complete and color the pages, cut them apart, fold them in half, and staple together to make a book about Johnny Appleseed whose birthday is September 26.

After a while, apple trees were everywhere! The settlers were glad for the fresh fruit and the special treats they made from it: pies, cakes, applesauce, and jelly. Can you think of others?

7

_____

Your Name

The settlers were glad to see him. He brought news and told stories. They called him Johnny Appleseed. How many things in the picture start with the letter "b"?

5

John decided to walk west, planting apple seeds along the trail so the settlers could have apple trees later on.

2

by Mary Currier

John Chapman lived in Ohio in the 1700s when many people were moving west. Follow the maze from his house to the covered wagon.

1

As the seeds he planted grew into trees, Johnny traded the young trees for clothes and food. Circle the tree that is different.

6

_____   _____
REDE   RABE

_____
XFO

_____   _____
WOL   CARNOOC

John traveled alone, often sleeping on the ground with wild animals around him. Unscramble the names of the wild animals.

3

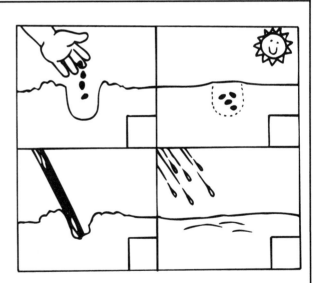

Wherever he went, he kept planting apple seeds. Number the pictures in the correct order.

4

Name _____

TAKE-HOME CHECKLIST

MY FIRE SAFETY CHECKLIST

☐ I practiced "Stop, Drop and Roll."

☐ I know my home and school fire escape plan.

☐ I never play with lighters or matches.

☐ I know how to call for help in an emergency.

☐ I know that all the smoke detectors in my house are working.

☐ I shared what I learned about fire safety with a parent.

BY VERONICA TERRILL

Name _____

Fire Safety Week

WORD SCRAMBLE

Unscramble the words below and use them to make a sentence about a fire safety rule.

LPYA _ _ _ _

IWHT _ _ _ _

HAMCTSE _ _ _ _ _ _ _

NOTD _ _ _ ' _

Fire Safety Rule: _____

_____

BY VERONICA TERRILL

Columbus Day Math Page

Celebrate Columbus Day by solving the problems below.

$$2 + 9 + 1 = \underline{\qquad}$$

$$3 + 4 + 5 = \underline{\qquad}$$

$$6 + 1 + 2 = \underline{\qquad}$$

$$10 + 5 + 3 = \underline{\qquad}$$

$$4 + 4 + 2 = \underline{\qquad}$$

$$8 + 6 + 3 = \underline{\qquad}$$

$$5 + 9 + 4 = \underline{\qquad}$$

$$6 + 1 + 6 = \underline{\qquad}$$

$$1 + 7 + 5 = \underline{\qquad}$$

$$4 + 8 + 3 = \underline{\qquad}$$

$$9 + 9 + 4 = \underline{\qquad}$$

by Veronica Terrill

National Candy Corn Day!

October 30 is National Candy Corn Day. We love candy corn! Americans ate 20 million pounds of it in 1996. Why not use candy corn to motivate a handful of corny learning experiences?

You Said a Mouthful!

Have students brainstorm a list of words that have the same initial consonant sound as *candy corn*. Then challenge them to write tongue twisters on a candy corn shape using as many of the words as they can. They can trade with a friend and try to rapidly read each other's tongue twisters. Copy the candy corn shape for students to write their tongue twisters on.

by: _____

BY LINDA MASTERNAK JUSTICE

Candy Corn Combinations

Duplicate the candy corn patterns at the right on white, orange, and yellow paper. Give each student two candy corns of each color. Have them cut out the shapes on all solid lines so that each kernel is in three parts. Then challenge them to put the kernels back together using only one stripe of each color in each kernel. How many combinations can be made using all three colors and changing the position of the colors? They may glue their combinations on a sheet of art paper.

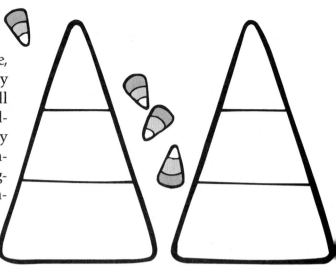

Need more challenge? How many combinations can be made using only two colors in any position? Ask them to draw their solutions or provide more candy corn to cut up and manipulate. Each child would need six of each color.

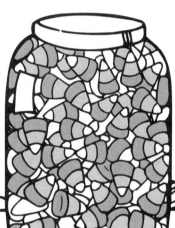

Candy Corn Contest

Develop estimating skills with a candy corn contest. Duplicate an entry form in the shape of a kernel for each student. (See the patterns on page 43.) Put candy corn in a plastic jar. Glue a piece of paper over the opening and replace the lid. Place the jar on a table with the sign at the right. Allow children to pick up the jar, turn it over, weigh it, and even try to count the kernels. Students write their official estimates and their names on entry kernels and place them in another plastic jar. At the end of the day, have a candy corn counting ceremony. Dramatically break the official paper seal. Remove the candy corn kernels one by one as the class counts in unison. The student with the closet estimate wins the candy corn. Have some extra candy corn around for consolation prizes.

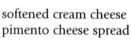

Corny Contest

Correctly estimate the number of candy corn kernels in the jar and win! Write your estimate on the official kernel entry form and place it in the jar.

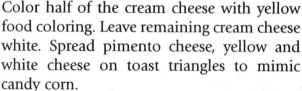

Corny Snack

softened cream cheese   yellow food coloring
pimento cheese spread   toasted bread triangles

Color half of the cream cheese with yellow food coloring. Leave remaining cream cheese white. Spread pimento cheese, yellow and white cheese on toast triangles to mimic candy corn.

Candy Corn Contest Patterns

Copy enough for one kernel per child.

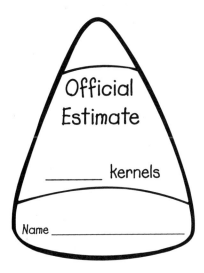

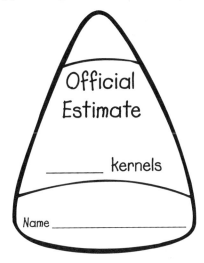

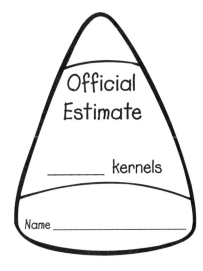

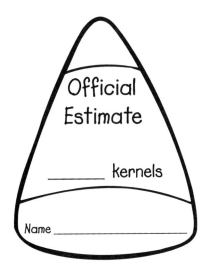

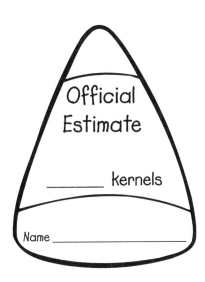

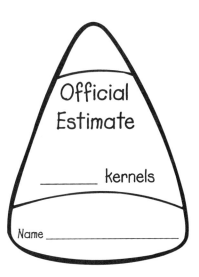

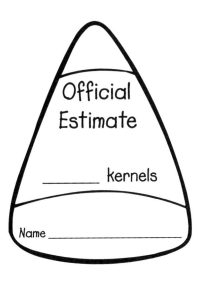

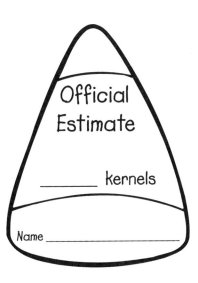

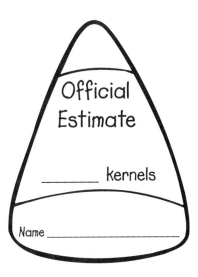

CANDY CORN TRIANGLE

How many triangles can you find in this triangle of candy corn?

Look carefully and count all the triangles!

I found _____ triangles.

Boo Times Two

One lonely witch feeling sad and blue.
Double it, double it and you have two.

Two black cats hissing by the door.
Double it, double it and you have four.

Three fat pumpkins out in the sticks.
Double it, double it and you have six.

Four mean mummies out by the gate.
Double it, double it and you have eight.

Five white skeletons giggle now and then.
Double it, double it and you have ten.

Six furry spiders for bugs dig and delve.
Double it, double it and you have twelve.

Seven scarecrows looking none too clean.
Double it, double it and you have fourteen.

Eight big monsters ugly and green.
Double it, double it and you have sixteen.

Nine vampire bats peeking through the screen.
Double it, double it and you have eighteen.

Ten trick-or-treaters eating food a plenty.
Double it, double it and you have twenty.

Zero ghosts out having fun.
Double it, double it. You still have none!

by Ellen Javernick

It's Pumpkin Time

*J*ack-o'-lanterns made from pumpkins are a popular Halloween item, and this is an ideal time to talk about pumpkins. This orange vegetable grows on the ground on a long vine that has broad, prickly leaves. Pumpkins come in many sizes and are usually round (though some are lopsided). Here are some ideas for pumpkin fun!

Field Trip

If possible, take your class to a pumpkin farm, market or grocery store. Observe the various sizes and shapes, hard shell with ribs, coarse stem. How does the pumpkin feel? Is there a smell? Which is the biggest? Smallest? Roundest? Perhaps the owner or manager will give you a pumpkin to bring back to school.

Pumpkin Science

Observe a pumpkin in the classroom. Shake it. Can you hear anything? Cut off the top and scoop out the inside pulp. How does it look? Feel? Smell? Taste? Put the seeds on paper towels to dry and use later. Plant some seeds and watch them grow. Talk about what is needed for growth and the various stages (seed, leaves, flowers, green pumpkin that later turns orange). Keep a chart to record each observation. (This can be done as a classroom or individual project.)

Make a Real Jack-O'-Lantern

Using a marker, let each child draw a feature on the pumpkin. These can be colored in, or you can carve out the features.

by Judy Wolfman

Pumpkin Art

Have the children trace around a pumpkin pattern on white construction paper. Color the pumpkin orange and the stem green. Facial features can be drawn on or cut-out black features can be glued on.

Mini Pumpkins

Mini pumpkins make cute individual jack-o'-lanterns or a "family" group. They can also make candle holders. Just cut off the top, leaving a hole about the size of a quarter. Remove the seeds and place a candle in the hole.

Pumpkin Music

While creating a jack-o'-lantern, recite the following poem: or sing it to the tune of "Did You Ever See a Lassie?"

Once there was a pumpkin, a pumpkin, a pumpkin.
Once there was a pumpkin with no face at all.
With no eyes and no nose,
And no mouth and no teeth.
Once there was a pumpkin with no face at all.
So I made a jack-o'-lantern, jack-o'-lantern, jack-o'-lantern
So I made a jack-o'-lantern with a big funny face.
With big eyes and big nose,
And big mouth and big teeth.
So I made a jack-o'-lantern with a big funny face.

Pumpkin Math

Paint or write a number on each pumpkin. Have the children place them in numerical order. While a child closes his eyes, remove a pumpkin and let him guess which number is missing. Select two pumpkins and have the children tell you which number is more or less. Select two pumpkins and have the children add or subtract, using those numbers.

47

Pumpkin Muffin Snack

Children enjoy cooking and can help measure, stir, pour, and eat these delicious muffins. Blend together (with electric mixer) 1 cup canned pumpkin, ½ cup packed brown sugar, ½ cup melted butter or margarine, and 2 eggs. In a separate bowl, combine 2 cups of flour with 2 teaspoons baking powder, and ½ teaspoon salt. Add the dry ingredients to the pumpkin mixture and blend well. Spoon the batter into a muffin tin lined with paper liners. Bake in a preheated oven (375ºF) for 20 minutes. This recipe makes 10 to 12 muffins.

Pumpkin Games

Using numbered pumpkins, have the children stand behind a line and toss a Hula Hoop™ over them. Give each child two or three chances and total the score. The highest score wins. Create a big pumpkin on poster board or mural paper with no stem. Give each child a cut-out stem. Place a blindfold over the eyes and let each child try to pin the stem on the pumpkin (similar to Pin the Tail on the Donkey). You can vary this game by letting them pin on the eyes and mouth.

Pumpkin Seed Art

Because they are flat, pumpkin seeds are easy to glue on paper plates, oak-tag, or construction paper. First, dry the seeds on a paper towel. Children will draw a picture or design and trace over their lines with craft glue. The seeds are glued over the lines, or can be used to fill in the spaces. For more color, add other dried seeds from fruits and vegetables, or color some pumpkin seeds by dipping them in tempera or coloring them with markers; or color the background with markers or crayons.

Literature

The Perky Little Pumpkin by Margaret Freskey (Children's Press 1990).
The Magic Pumpkin by Bill Martin Jr. and John Archambault (Henry Holt, 1989).
Pumpkin Fiesta by Casryn Yacowitz (HarperCollins, 1998).
The Pumpkin Fair by Eve Bunting (Clarion, 1997).

Holiday Sing-Alongs

by Mabel Duch

Just for Tonight

To the tune of "Mary Had a Little Lamb"

Just for tonight, I can be,
I can be, I can be.
Just for tonight, I can be
Almost anything.

Just for tonight, I can be,
I can be, I can be.
Just for tonight, I can be
An ancient mighty king.

Just for tonight, I can be,
I can be, I can be.
Just for tonight, I can be
A witch in a pointed hat.

Just for tonight, I can be,
I can be, I can be.
Just for tonight, I can be
The witch's big black cat.

Just for tonight, I can be,
I can be, I can be.
Just for tonight, I can be
A child from outer space.

Just for tonight, I can be,
I can be, I can be.
Just for tonight, I can be
A man with a tattooed face.

Just for tonight, I can be,
I can be, I can be.
Just for tonight, I can be
A happy circus clown.

Just for tonight, I can be,
I can be, I can be.
Just for tonight, I can be
A queen with a golden crown.

Just for tonight, I can be,
I can be, I can be.
Just for tonight, I can be
An elf in forest green.

Just for tonight, I can be,
I can be, I can be.
Just for tonight, I can be
Because it's Halloween.

Background
After singing the song through, have individual children or small groups of children sing the last lines of verses 2 through 9, one child or small group to a line.

Then, if you like, have individual children take turns substituting what they will be wearing on Halloween for the costumes mentioned in the last lines of verses 2 through 9.

49

Discussion

1. Why is it better to have stick-on tattoos or face paint rather than a mask? (Masks can obscure vision.)

2. What other precautions should you take on Halloween, especially while trick-or-treating?

Help your children draw up a list of trick-or-treating safety rules. Such a list might include:

1. Trick-or-treat at only the houses of people you know.

2. Have an adult or a teenage sibling or teenage friend with you.

3. Wear light clothing or clothing with reflective strips, and carry a flashlight if you trick-or-treat at night.

4. Instead of a mask, wear face paint or stickers.

5. Be sure your costume is short enough so you can't trip on it.

6. Be very careful when crossing streets.

7. Don't eat unwrapped candy.

8. Don't eat all your candy at one time.

Sometimes communities or service clubs have Halloween parties for children. Find out and encourage your children to attend these.

Activities

1. Invite children to illustrate one or more of the trick-or-treating rules. Label and post the pictures before Halloween.

2. Let them design dream costumes, what they would wear if they could. (Probably some will draw what they are going to wear.) Cut out the pictures and make a bulletin board of children trick-or-treating in their dream costumes.

3. If you are having a Halloween party at school, take a picture of each child. Get double prints, one to take home, and one for posting (and for you to keep as a memento of a Happy Halloween).

50

Name _____

Trick-or-Treat Math

Part A: Complete this part in school.

1. I estimate I will receive _____ pieces of candy when I go trick-or-treating.

Part B: Complete this part for homework.

2. Count your Halloween candy. Write the number of pieces here. _____

3. Look at the numbers you wrote in the blanks for problems 1 and 2.
   Write the larger number on the top line.
   Write the smaller number on the second line.
   Subtract the smaller number from the larger number.

    _____
  − _____

    answer _____

4. Look again at problems 1 and 2.
   Compare your estimate with the actual number of candies you received. Complete the statement below by circling the correct word to make the statement true.

   My estimate was higher/lower than the actual amount of candies I received.

by Sally Stanley

Fall Sensations

Delight your youngsters with the most "boo"tiful season ever with the array of craft ideas and recipes in *Halloween Treats* by Donata Maggipinto (Chronicle Books, 1998). Your children will love creating their own paper bag pumpkins or writing secret messages with invisible ink. Whip up a batch of Cocoa Cobweb Cupcakes, Jack-o'-Lantern Cookies, or Jiggle Pumpkins and Wiggle Bats.

Need perfect snacks for the seasonal party or special event? Then *Silly Snacks* (Better Homes & Gardens, 1998) is the book for you. This book features such holiday delights as Silly Season Circles, Graham Cracker Cabins, and Uncle Sam's Pizza. Some of the spooky foods in store for you include Witch's Warts, Creepy Kettles, and Bloody Good Phantom Faces.

For everything you've ever wanted to know about pumpkins, read *The Pumpkin Book* by Gail Gibbons (Holiday House, 1999). Follow the growth cycle of the plant, learn about the different varieties of pumpkins, tips on how to decorate them, and direction for drying their seed. And that's not all—discover the history and other interesting trivia bout this popular autumn plant.

The Pumpkin Fair
by Eve Bunting
illustrated by Eileen Christelow
Clarion Books, 1997

Autumn means pumpkin time and here's the perfect book to celebrate the season. Join a little girl and her family as they enjoy a pumpkin fair. Some of the "pumpkin-tivities" in store for the participants include contests, pumpkin bowling, basketball, and other games. And best of all, give a cheer when the little girl wins a blue ribbon for having "the best loved pumpkin."

- Which "pumpkin creature" in the book did you like best? Tell why.

- Design a pumpkin creature of your own. Think of a name for your creation.

- Some of the treats served at the fair included pumpkin cookies, ice cream, pies, and cakes. Think of a new pumpkin dessert that everyone would rave about. Draw a picture of your dessert and write the directions for making it.

The Stubborn Pumpkin
by Laura Geringer
illustrated by Holly Berry
Scholastic, 1999

Here's another pumpkin story that's sure to tickle your funny bone! A farmer grows a gigantic pumpkin that's so big, he can't pull it off the vine. He enlists the help of everyone—his wife, daughter, cow, dog, and cat. The stubborn pumpkin won't budge until a tiny mouse comes to the rescue.

- Put on your inventor hat! Invent a new state-of-the-art machine for picking pumpkins off the vine. Draw a picture of your amazing machine and label the parts.

- Pumpkin chit chat! Draw two pumpkins. Write what each pumpkin is saying.

- Be an author! Write a story about a farmer who grows a giant carrot.

Amazing Bats
by Frank Greenaway
Alfred A. Knopf, 1991

Did you know that there are about 1000 different kinds of bats? Find out all about this mysterious flying animal in this fascinating book.

- Draw a picture of a bat and label the parts of its body.

- Be a bat detective! Conduct some research about your favorite kind of bat. Create a poster report featuring facts and pictures about your selection.

- It's game time! Make your own bat trivia game, using some of the interesting facts you can find in this book.

by Mary Ellen Switzer

Book Nook

John Pig's Halloween

by Jan L. Waldron
illustrated by David McPhail
Dutton Children's Books, 1998

"Pig out" this Halloween on a rollicking and funny pig tale! When John Pig stays home from trick-or-treating, he expects to have a long, quiet evening. However, his plans quickly change when a witch comes to visit and helps him prepare a tasty feast of cakes, pies, and cookies. Soon some monsters stop by and John Pig ends up throwing a Halloween party he'll never forget.

• What monster in the book do you think was the scariest? Write two sentences to describe the monster and draw a picture of it.

• John Pig served cakes, pies, and cookies at his Halloween party. Plan the perfect menu for a Halloween party you'd like to have.

• Design a new book cover for *John Pig's Halloween*.

The Bookstore Ghost

by Barbara Maitland
illustrated by Nadine Berrd Westcott
Puffin, 1998

What's the Halloween season without a ghost story? Don't miss this delightful tale about Mr. Brown, a bookstore owner who sells only ghost books. When mice are frightening his customers, he enlists the help of his cat to get rid of the pesky mice. The cat and the mice are friends, so they think of a clever plan to attract more customers to the bookshop. Will their plan work?

• Welcome to the Blackcat Bookstore! Design a billboard to advertise Mr. Brown's unusual bookstore.

• Think of another plan that the cat and mice could have used to attract more customers to the bookstore. Write a paragraph explaining your plan.

• Make a list of some of the book titles that Mr. Brown sold in his store. Now put the list in alphabetical order.

• If you owned a bookstore, what kind of books would you sell? Why?

The Reptile Ball

by Jacqueline K. Ogburn
illustrated by John O'Brien
Dial Books for Young Readers, 1997

You are cordially invited to an autumn extravaganza of slithering creatures at the elegant Reptile Ball. You will meet some unusual guests as you read these lively poems, such as Komodo dragons, chameleons, iguanas, and crocodiles. Included in the book is a glossary, listing the names and descriptions of the animals featured in the poems.

• Reptile roundup! Create a picture book with pictures and facts about some of the reptiles in the poems.

• Challenge yourself! Write a list of all the words you can think of using the letters in *reptile ball*.

• Pretend you traded places with a reptile for the day. Write a journal entry about your most unusual day.

Halloween Fun

Halloween Sights

Choral speaking is an effective way for children to recite poems, be expressive, be creative, and have fun. After several recitations, the children will know the teacher's part well enough to exchange roles. Parts can be performed by the entire class, small groups, or individuals, and the lines can be cleverly "acted out."

Children: What do you see on Halloween?
What do you see on Halloween?
Teacher: I see a white ghost as it floats by.
I see a witch flying in the sky.
Children: What do you see on Halloween?
What do you see on Halloween?
Teacher: I see a black bat flapping around.
I see orange pumpkins on the ground.
Children: What do you see on Halloween?
What do you see on Halloween?
Teacher: I see costumed people in the street.
I see children as they trick-or-treat.

by Judy Wolfman

Frightful Activities

• Use holiday stickers to create rebus sentences, such as: Daddy helped me carve a 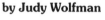 .

Are you afraid of  ?

• Cut practice paper into holiday shapes. Large simple shapes are best: hearts, pumpkins, ghosts, bells.

• Have a group of students make a scary witch to display. Ask the class to name the witch, and make up a story about her. Tape-record the story and play it during your Halloween party.

• Ask students to write the first sentence of a holiday story, like "Even the other ghosts were frightened" or "The farmer noticed something very, very strange about the pumpkin he had just picked." Exchange papers, and write the rest of the story.

• Distribute newspapers, and ask students to clip any words which pertain to the holiday. Give a prize to the student who finds the most words, and also to the one who finds a word that no one else does.

by Isabel L. Livingstone

Pop-Up Ghost

Materials

1 white paper or Styrofoam™ cup
1 drinking straw
1 cotton ball
1 white handkerchief
black marker
pencil
glue

Directions

Carefully poke a hole through the center of the cup bottom. Push a straw up through the hole. Glue a cotton ball to the top of the straw. Drape a handkerchief over the cotton, straw, and cup, and glue the center to the top of the cotton. Let it dry. Draw two eyes and a mouth.

Pull the straw down to hide the ghost inside the cup. Push it up to pop up the ghost.

by Sherry Timberman

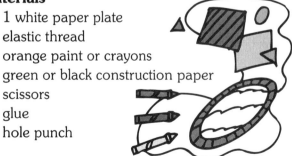

Mini Lanterns

Materials

paper egg carton
scissors
yellow and black paint
brush
glue
paper clip

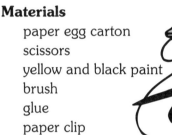

Directions

1. Cut two cup sections from the egg carton, leaving small feet on the edge to glue.
2. Cut half circles out of three sides on each cup.
3. Paint the inside of both cups yellow. Paint the outside of both cups black.
4. Unfold the paper clip and make it straight. Carefully bend it into a rounded handle. Poke both ends down into the bottom of one cup, and bend the ends to hold it in place.
5. Glue the two cups together at the feet, matching the openings.

by Sherry Timberman

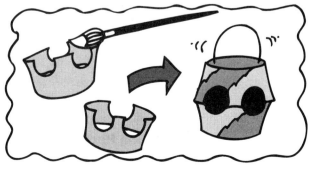

Pumpkin Masks

Materials

1 white paper plate
elastic thread
orange paint or crayons
green or black construction paper
scissors
glue
hole punch

Directions

Color or paint the plate orange. Cut out the pumpkin features. Cut a green stem or a black hat and glue it to the top of the pumpkin. Punch a hole in each side of the plate and attach a length of elastic thread.

by Sherry Timberman

Andy's Special Pumpkin

Andy Wentworth closed the freezer lid, satisfied with his work. If he hurried, there was time for a bike ride. He whirled around, only to come face to face with his little sister.

"Andy," whined Melanie, poking him in the ribs, "I saw you."

"So?"

Melanie put her hands on her hips. "I'm gonna tell Mom about the pumpkin."

"Pumpkin?" asked Mom, coming up beside Melanie.

"Remember?" said Melanie, sticking her pointy chin out. "The one that was our jack-o'-lantern."

"Oh, that one," Andy replied, pretending to be surprised. "I put him in the freezer to keep him fresh. You know, preserve him."

Mom opened the freezer. "There's not enough room in here for a week-and-a-half-old jack-o'-lantern, Andy. Halloween is over." She plopped the basketball-sized pumpkin into his arms. "It's time to get rid of it."

"Yeah, Andy," said Melanie, as she flounced outside. "It's time."

Andy tightened his grip on the big vegetable. "I guess it's stupid to want to keep him."

Mom smiled and ruffled his hair. "No, it's not stupid. When I was your age, I didn't want winter to end. So I stuffed a snowman in our freezer. Grandma had a fit when she peered in and saw a face staring back at her."

Andy smiled. "Can he stay a few more days?"

Mom nodded. "Take him out of the freezer and you can keep him until Friday."

Andy sighed and trudged to the porch, where he set the jack-o'-lantern on the top step. The pumpkin seemed to be watching over the yard. It was special, with its jagged smile and stick-out ears made from extra pieces of the shell. He and his friend Jamie had carved it. They laughed so much that Mom said they sounded like a gaggle of geese. It was the last thing they did together before Jamie had moved to another city, far, far away. Andy didn't want to lose the pumpkin, too. He needed to do something before Friday.

The next day after school, Andy lugged the jack-o'-lantern upstairs and hid it in his room. Not even Melanie would find it. All was well until dessert time. Tar, their big black dog, came racing down the stairs and careened into Andy's mom, who was carrying a tray loaded with servings of butterscotch pudding. Mom tripped, launching the little dishes across the room. They landed in caramel-colored heaps on the rug. Andy's dad shouted, "What's gotten into that dog?"

"Maybe he heard a raccoon in the woods," offered Andy.

"No, he came from your room," said Melanie, stepping over the piles of pudding. "Come on, Tar."

They followed the dog upstairs, with Andy lagging behind as though his feet were in cement. Tar scrunched under Andy's bed, woofing like crazy, his tail wagging like a cyclone. Mom commanded, "Here, Tar." The wagging stopped, the woofing quieted, and slowly Tar backed out from under the bed. He sat proudly, an orange stick-out ear hanging from his mouth.

by Gail Hedrick

"Andy?" said Mom, tapping her foot.

"Yes, Ma'am," said Andy, trying to block Mom's view of the dog.

"Is that a jack-o'-lantern ear in Tar's mouth?"

Andy peered around, and said, "Yes, I think so."

"Does that mean the jack-o'-lantern is under your bed?"

Andy nodded.

Mom grabbed the dog, and Dad removed the ear. He handed it to Andy, and said, "This jack-o'-lantern was a good one. But it needs to go back outside."

Andy said, "Yes, Sir." He sighed and headed to the porch, thinking how he hated throwing the pumpkin away. But the top was shriveling. Soon, the jack-o'-lantern would look as caved in as a sand castle hit by a giant wave.

Andy tried not to think about the pumpkin for a few days. On Friday, he invited a boy from his soccer team to come home with him. As they got off the bus, Andy's mom greeted them. "I'm so glad to see you, Justin. If you two watch Tar until I'm finished raking, I'll fix a snack, okay?"

"Sure," they said together, and began planning their afternoon. Immediately, Melanie interrupted them. She skipped up, bugging out her eyes, and taunted, "It's Jack day; it's Jack day. Today's the day for Jack!"

Andy glared at Melanie and turned away.

Justin asked, "Who's Jack?"

Andy felt a lump in his throat, but only said, "Come on, I've gotta get rid of the pumpkin." He couldn't look anywhere but the ground. Gosh, he hoped he wouldn't cry.

They walked toward the porch, but when they had gotten far enough for only Andy to hear, Justin nudged him with a shoulder. "Don't you hate to throw him away?"

"Yeah," Andy said, amazed. Someone else felt like he did! "He reminds me of someone I don't want to forget."

Justin stared at the jack-o'-lantern for a minute, then said, "You had a friend who looks like this?"

Andy grinned. "Yup, and he did have pretty big ears."

"Let's get this over with and play some soccer," said Justin, picking up the pumpkin. "Where to?"

Andy pointed toward the trash cans, then said, "I'm going to do one thing first. Don't laugh."

Justin shrugged. "I'll try not to."

Andy jumped around a few times, then shook himself like Tar did after a bath. "There, I'm all set."

As he lowered the pumpkin into one of the cans, Justin asked, "You okay?"

"Just fine," said Andy, shutting the lid.

"So what was that jumping around business?" asked Justin, reaching down to pat Tar.

"Well, one time my grandpa said, 'I've got to move around some.' I asked him what for. He laughed and said, 'Shoot, child. I need some extra room in my heart for a good memory. I've got to wiggle around and shift things loose. Then there's room.'"

"That's what you were doing?"

"Yup," said Andy, looking around. "And it works."

"Wait one minute," Justin said. "I want to remember my old house." He pushed up the sleeves on his sweatshirt, and hopped on one leg. Then he waved his arms overhead like a windmill. Tar aimed his nose skyward and began to howl.

Andy shook his head, and his smile was as wide as the one on a jack-o'-lantern.

The Frightening Night

Nothing motivates students like Halloween, and it's fun to have holiday activities to celebrate across the curriculum. This reading lesson on silent consonants gh, t, l, k, b, is fun for younger children and a good review for older children as well.

People often talk about that frightening night. It all happened on Halloween in the hours before midnight. It was pitch black except for the bright lights coming from a few streetlights. The whole town was filled with little folks out trick-or-treating. The children carried their knapsacks to hold their candy. They walked past an owl on a tree limb. "Whooo!" said the owl. They dodged bats that swooped through the sky. They listened to black cats fighting. They saw a few pumpkins left in the pumpkin patch. To keep from getting too frightened, they whistled as they passed the tombstones in the graveyard. At the edge of the town they came to a stop. They did not know which way to go. Then they saw a sign that said, "Watch Out! Haunted Castle This Way." They crossed a ditch and climbed up a hill to the castle. A knight with a knife stood guard at the gate. Several skeletons were hiding behind a hedge. Ghosts floated in the garden. In the window they saw a witch combing her hair. The children were so frightened that their knees were knocking and their knuckles were white. They had knots in their stomachs. Then one of the children turned the doorknob and they all went in . . . to the Halloween party.

by Ellen Javernick

58

CRAFT CORNER

Back-to-School Bookmarks

Encourage reading and individuality when children make statements about themselves with an item that can be used throughout the school year.

Materials
8" x 2 ½" (20 x 6 cm) strips of card stock
flat decorative items: photographs, magazine pictures, stickers, nail polish, ticket stubs, stamps, and so on
drawing materials
craft glue and glue brush
lamination equipment or clear, self-adhesive sheets
hole punch
ribbon

Let's Make It
1. Give children advance notice to round up two-dimensional items that represent something about themselves. Suggest photographs, magazine pictures, ticket stubs, stickers, nail polish, or any other materials that can be pasted or applied to the card stock.
2. Once items have been gathered and brought to school, the creating begins! Allow children to select card stock strips in their choices of color for the background.
3. Children will plan the placement of their items on the bookmark and/or drawings that will be done.
4. Once the design has been planned, children will draw and/or paste the items to both sides of the bookmark.
5. Allow bookmarks to dry thoroughly and then laminate them using a laminating machine and lamination film or by using clear, self-adhesive sheets.
6. Have children punch a hole in one end of the bookmark and attach ribbon in a color of choice by folding the ribbon in half and threading the loose ends through the loop.

Halloween Silhouettes

Halloween celebrations began with ancient festivals when it was believed that spirits roamed the Earth on October 31 causing mischief. Today children dress in costumes to go "trick or treating."

Materials
Halloween shaped cookie cutters (bats, witches, jack-o'-lanterns)
fall magazines for cut-outs
black construction paper
pencils
scissors

Let's Make It
1. Have each child draw a Halloween shape, trace a cookie cutter, or find a theme picture in a magazine to cut out. Children trace the shapes on the black paper.
2. Children will then cut the shapes out of the paper to make silhouettes.
3. Decorate windows with the spooky silhouettes.

by Robynne Eagan

Back-to-School Buddies

Your students will be hanging out together all year. Start the year off by creating hang-out buddies to represent each child.

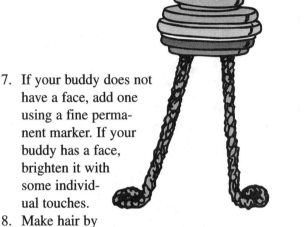

Materials

2 pipe cleaners one 12" (30 cm), one 6" (15 cm) long
10-15 medium sized buttons
1 large button
1 large wooden bead (with or without a face)
fine-tipped permanent marker
yarn (variety of textures and colors)

Let's Make It

1. Bend the long pipe cleaner in half. Thread each end of the pipe cleaner through the holes of the large button. Push the button all the way to the top to make a hat for the buddy.
2. Thread both ends through the bead "head." Slide the bead all the way up to the button.
3. Choose buttons of particular colors and styles to thread onto the pipe cleaner to make the body.
4. When the remaining ends are the correct length to make legs, twist the pipe cleaner, and shape the legs.
5. Wind the short pipe cleaner between two of the buttons to form arms.
6. Bend the ends of the arms and legs to represent hands and feet.
7. If your buddy does not have a face, add one using a fine permanent marker. If your buddy has a face, brighten it with some individual touches.
8. Make hair by cutting strands of yarn and tying the yarn between the hat and the top of the head. Untwist the yarn, braid it or cut it to give the look you want.
9. Hang a string somewhere in your classroom. Have each buddy cling to the string and "hang out."

Trung Thu October Moon

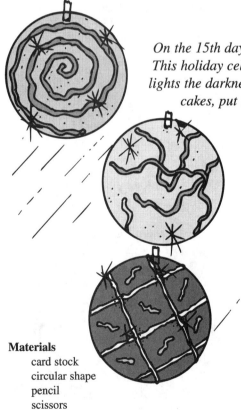

On the 15th day of the eighth lunar month, the Vietnamese holiday of Trung Thu takes place. This holiday celebrates the beauty of the bright, white October moon. The moon's brightness lights the darkness of the long October nights. On this holiday children wear masks, eat moon cakes, put out candle-lit lanterns, and take part in a procession through the streets.

Let's Make It

1. Children will trace the large circular shape on their card stock.
2. Children will cut out their circles.
3. A long piece of string will be provided for each child. Children will explore ways that they can cover the circle with the string. Patterns will vary from child to child.
4. Once a pattern has been designed, children will remove the string, apply a thick coat of glue to the surface of the circle, then place the string once again in the pattern designed.
5. Once the string has dried in place, dabs of glue can be painted on the surface and then sprinkled with silver glitter. The excess glitter can be shaken onto a tray and reused.
6. These moons can be taped to a window to represent the bright October moon.

Materials

card stock
circular shape
pencil
scissors
butcher's string
white craft glue and glue brush
silver glitter
tray

Try This: Celebrate Trung Thu

- Study the moon.
- Share stories that are connected to the moon in some way.
- Have children wear masks and take part in a procession.
- Find traditional moon cakes to share or share a substitute "moon cake."

Spooky Secret Messages

Materials
- white bond paper
- sheet of waxed paper to cover bond paper
- pencil
- colored pencils

Let's Make It
1. Place waxed paper over bond paper.
2. The writer will write a message on the waxed paper, pressing very firmly with a pencil.
3. The waxed paper is then discarded and the blank page is given to a partner.
4. The recipient of the secret message must rub a colored pencil back and forth across the paper to reveal the message. The wax on the page resists the color and makes the message visible!

Create a Costume

Bring elements of planning and design to this simple Halloween activity.

Materials
- solid-colored shirt or sweatshirt
- various colors of adhesive-backed craft felt (found in craft stores)
- fine-tipped markers

Let's Make It
1. Have each student bring a solid-colored shirt to school.
2. Using this shirt as the base for a costume, have children create a design that makes use of the felt to turn their shirt into a costume. Black shirts with white felt will create skeletons, ghosts, or robots; orange shirts with black felt can create tigers or jack-o'-lanterns; and so on. Encourage children to use their imagination.
3. Once children have developed designs, they can draw and cut out the felt pieces they need to decorate their shirts.
4. Apply the pieces to the shirts to create instant costumes. Children can wear their costume shirts over their clothes as Halloween attire.

Haunted House

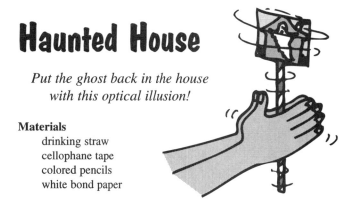

Put the ghost back in the house with this optical illusion!

Materials
- drinking straw
- cellophane tape
- colored pencils
- white bond paper

Let's Make It
1. Children cut two 3" x 3" (7.5 x 7.5 cm) squares from the bond paper.
2. Children draw the outline of a haunted house on one piece of paper.
3. Next, children place the black paper on top of the outline of the house and draw a ghost that will fit in this outline of the house.
4. Children place the squares back-to-back and tape all of the edges together except for a straw-sized opening in the center of the bottom.
5. The straw is inserted through the opening and taped securely in place.
6. Now the fun begins! Children hold the bottom of the straw between their palms and rub their palms back and forth. As the straws turns, the pictures rotate and the ghost appears to be inside the house.

Name _____

A Mysterious Message

To find the hidden message in the pumpkin patch, begin at the top of Column 1 and read to the bottom. Read only the pumpkins that have spiders. Continue down each column until the mysterious message is revealed.

Code: Hidden in the pumpkin patch is my friend Jack. Can you find him?

by Monica A. Harris

TLC10299 Copyright © Teaching & Learning Company, Carthage, IL 62321-001

Holiday newsletter

Getting used to the back-to-school routine also includes fitting homework into your schedule. Take a shot at success with these tips from teachers who are also parents. Choose an area of the house where your child can be comfortable and will be able to concentrate. Make necessary supplies readily available. Choose a time of day to do homework and make it part of your regular routine. Help your child keep track of assignments and due dates to avoid last-minute frustration. If certain subject areas are more difficult for your child, help out when necessary, but remember to let your child do the work. Sometimes asking questions about the difficulty allows the child to find solutions independently. And finally, encourage your child to complete assignments he or she will be proud to hand in. It's a great self-esteem booster and will demonstrate to the teacher that the child made the effort.

Simple Science

Fingerprint Day in October is a time when many local law enforcement agencies offer to help parents record each child's permanent identification. Each person's fingerprints are different, and the pattern of these prints remains the same throughout our lives. With white glue and a paintbrush, you can help your child make glue prints of both hands. First, spread a thin layer of white glue over the inside of one hand. Extend this film of glue from the wrist to the fingertips. Allow the glue to dry completely (it will be clear); then carefully peel it off. Proceed in the same manner to print the opposite hand. Compare the glue prints to each hand and to each other.

On the Move

Invite the entire family to join you in creating and playing this outdoor game to commemorate Family Fitness Day in September. Retrieve the shuttlecock from your summer badminton game. Add autumn color to it by using masking tape to add craft store feathers around the outside. Cut several bleach (or similar) bottles into paddle shapes. Tape the handles for a better grip, and to cover any rough edges. Outside you can bat the shuttlecock between players or teams, or count the number of times individuals can tap the shuttlecock up before there is a miss and it falls to the ground. **Variation:** Let individuals tap the shuttlecock up with their hands until it falls to the ground.

Cut or rip the cheese slices to resemble bat wings and set these on a plate. Peel the banana half and set it on top of the wings for a body. Gently push two raisins into the top of the banana for ears. Cut one raisin in half and press the pieces into the front of the banana for eyes. Set a carrot curl under the eyes for a mouth. Cut two triangular shapes from the apple slice and set these below the mouth for fangs.

Creative Kitchen

Hands-on snack creation can help your child achieve a sense of independence and experience the feelings of accomplishment and success that follow a job well done. Although bats are nocturnal by nature, your child can enjoy the following recipe any time of day.

Banana Bat

banana half	carrot curl
apple slice	raisins
2 cheese slices	

Reading Room

Celebrate Literacy Day this September by taking a trip to your local library for books about autumn events.

Apples and Pumpkins by Anne F. Rockwell, Macmillan.

Grandpa's Teeth by Rod Clement, HarperCollins.

Little Nino's Pizzeria by Karen Barbour, Harcourt Brace Jovanovich.

More Spaghetti, I Say! by Rita Gelman, Scholastic.

My Best Friend by Pat Hutchins, Greenwillow.

Squirrel Watching by Miriam Schlein, HarperCollins.

2 x 2 = Boo! A Set of Spooky Multiplication Stories by Loreen Leedy, Holiday House.

by Marie E. Cecchini

From the Art Cart

Tissue paper jack-o'-lanterns are easy, fun decorations children can make themselves. First, crumple a piece of newspaper into a ball. Tape the paper to hold this shape and set the ball into the center of a square of orange tissue paper. Now lift the ends of the tissue paper and gather them tightly around the top of the ball. Use a green pipe cleaner as a twist tie to hold the tissue paper closed. Curl the ends of the pipe cleaner to resemble a pumpkin vine. Finally, cut and glue yellow construction paper facial features to these pumpkins to make jack-o'-lanterns. **Variation:** Replace the newspaper with a popcorn-filled plastic sandwich bag to make Halloween party treats.

Mathworks

Practice math skills every day as you challenge your child to observe how many times we use measurement in our daily activities. Have your child estimate, then help to measure the following. How much cereal was poured into the breakfast bowl? How much milk will it take to fill the lunch box thermos? How far is the walk to the bus stop? How far is the ride to school? How much time will homework take? How much does the backpack weigh? How many inches of water make the bedtime bath? Work with your child to discover what additional daily activities make use of some form of measurement. For another challenge, try to observe how many times in the day we need to count things.

Communication Station

Playing games with old newspapers in honor of Newspaper Week in September can help your child develop language and observational skills. For the first game, prepare a scavenger hunt list of items for your child to find and cut from the newspaper. Examples might include the weather forecast, a picture of a sports player, specific words, a telephone number, and so on. Help your child to read the list as necessary. Make the game more fun by including friends or family members and turning it into a contest. For the second game, copy a favorite picture book story of your child's, omitting some of the verbs and nouns. Help your child search for and cut out newspaper words that name actions (verbs) or people, places, or things (nouns). Use a glue stick to insert these words in the story in appropriate places. Read your humorous story together.

Poetry in Motion

The excitement of returning to school in the fall includes at least a little apprehension about making new friends, getting on the right bus, remembering a new teacher's name and finding the correct classroom. You can help ease these apprehensive feelings by working with your child to create a short poem, song, or chant to help remember room and bus numbers, and the teacher's name. An example might be, "Bus 310, bus 310, takes me to school, then home again." Encourage your child to draw and color a picture; then write the song, rhyme, or chant below. Sometimes visual images help us to remember better.

Cooking with Kids

Simple food preparation projects encourage children to make use of their sequencing, reading, and measuring skills. Seasonal recipes can be used to introduce or culminate various units of study. Here are a few you may want to include this fall.

Clown Muffins
August—Clown Week

Ingredients
English muffins, halved
cream cheese
sunflower seeds
maraschino cherries
raisins
carrot shavings

Toast the English muffin halves. Have the students spread cream cheese over one toasted half. Let them add sunflower seed eyes and a cherry nose; then shape a smiling mouth with raisins. Top with carrot shavings hair.

Johnny Squares
September—Johnny Appleseed's Birthday

Ingredients
apples   cream cheese   lemon juice
cinnamon   graham crackers   sugar
applesauce

Have the students help to peel and core several apples. Cut these apples into bite-size chunks. Place the apple chunks into a bowl, sprinkle with lemon juice, then toss. This will prevent them from turning brown. Set these aside. Have the students combine applesauce with the cream cheese to make a spreadable mixture. Break whole graham crackers in half, creating squares. Let the students spread the cream cheese mixture over their squares, set apple chunks onto this mixture; then sprinkle their snack squares with cinnamon and sugar.

Chocolate Oatmeal Cookies
October—School Lunch Week

Ingredients
margarine
sugar
milk
cocoa powder
vanilla
oatmeal (not instant)

Melt ½ c. margarine in a large saucepan. Add 2 c. sugar, ½ c. milk, and ¼ c. cocoa powder, and stir to combine. Boil the mixture for 3-5 minutes. Remove the pan from the heat, stir in 1 tsp. vanilla, then stir in 3 c. oatmeal. Use teaspoons to drop bite-size cookies onto waxed paper to cool.

by Marie E. Cecchini

Spicy Pumpkin Seeds

September—Hispanic Heritage Month

Ingredients

dried pumpkin seeds
cooking oil
paprika
cumin
red pepper
Parmesan cheese, grated

Place the dried pumpkin seeds in a bowl and set aside. Into a small jar or lidded plastic container, measure ¼ c. cooking oil, 1 tsp. paprika, ½ tsp. cumin, and ½ tsp. red pepper. Cover the container; then shake to combine the ingredients. Dribble this oil mixture over the pumpkin seeds; then stir to coat the seeds. Cook the seeds over medium heat in an electric frying pan or wok, stirring constantly until they are lightly browned.

Variation: Spread the seeds on a cookie sheet and bake at 325°F until lightly browned. After cooking, return the seeds to the bowl, sprinkle with Parmesan cheese, toss, and enjoy.

Sailing Ships

October—Columbus Day

Ingredients

cottage cheese
shredded lettuce
pear halves
cheese slices
raisins
fish-shaped crackers
blue food coloring
toothpicks

Use the food coloring to tint the cottage cheese blue for water. Have the students spoon some of this "water" onto a plate, then sprinkle it with shredded lettuce for seaweed. Set a pear half boat into the water and place raisin people in the hollow of the pear. Tear a cheese slice into a sail shape. Insert a toothpick through the sail; then mount the sail to the boat. Sprinkle fish-shaped crackers into the cottage cheese water around the fruit boat.

Popcorn-Peanut Butter Clusters

October—Popcorn Month

Ingredients

popped corn (about 8 cups)
light corn syrup
peanut butter
sugar
margarine

Place about 8 cups of popped corn in a large bowl. Set aside. Measure ½ c. corn syrup and ¼ c. sugar in a saucepan. Cook over medium heat until the mixture comes to a boil and the sugar is dissolved. Remove the pan from the heat, add ½ c. peanut butter, and stir until smooth. Pour the warm mixture over the popped corn in the bowl and stir until the corn puffs are coated. Have the students coat their hands with a small amount of margarine before creating cluster shapes with the popcorn mixture.

Seasonal Science

In the process of carrying out their science work, children should be encouraged to discuss their ideas, make observations, and draw conclusions. Reinforcing these science explorations with projects allows children to mentally record their newly acquired understanding with pictorial representation. Creative project work makes it real. Celebrate National Chemistry Week in November (second full week) with the following science ideas.

Crystals

Activity

Crystals are formed when molecules arrange themselves in a definite pattern. Snowflakes are examples of crystals. Different substances form various crystal shapes. Demonstrate the formation of crystals on a piece of glass or a mirror using Epsom salts, water, and a measuring cup. Dissolve some Epsom salts in water. Pour a few large drops of this solution onto the glass. Allow the water to evaporate. What remains are salt formed crystals.

Project

Have the students work with adult helpers to make colorful crystal ornaments. You will need wide-mouthed jars, such as those from pickles or mayonnaise; water; borax (from the supermarket laundry section); food coloring; pipe cleaners; string; and a pencil. Have an adult fill the jar with boiling water. Mix borax into the water until powder begins to settle on the bottom of the jar. Stir in several drops of food coloring to achieve a dark tint. Let the students bend a pipe cleaner into a shape. Tie one end of a length of string to their pipe cleaner shapes, the opposite end of the string to a pencil. Suspend the pipe cleaner shape into the solution and rest the pencil over the mouth of the jar. Allow the project to stand overnight. As the water cools, the tinted borax molecules will stick together around the pipe cleaner shape. Allow the ornaments to drip dry.

Molecules

Activity

The density of a substance refers to how closely packed the molecules of that substance are. The higher the density, the heavier the substance. Experiment with water, ice, and cooking oil for a visual demonstration of this concept. Experiment 1: Pour a little water into a clear jar. Tint the water with food coloring. Add a little cooking oil, seal the jar, and shake. Observe the action as you allow the liquid to settle. Note that the water has the higher density and will sink to the bottom, while the less dense oil will rise to the top. Experiment 2: Tint water with food coloring, then freeze into cubes. Fill a clear container about half full of cooking oil. Drop in a tinted ice cube. Which has the greater density, the oil or the ice? Observe what takes place as the ice cube melts. Water drops form and slowly fall through the oil to the bottom of the container. Help the students summarize their conclusions comparing the density of water in its liquid and solid forms, and oil.

Project

Celebrate a job well done with cranberry ice drinks. Pour cranberry juice (or a cranberry juice combination) into ice cube trays. Drop one cranberry into each section and freeze. When frozen, add the cranberry cubes to glasses of orange juice. What happens to the orange juice when the ice melts?

by Marie E. Cecchini

Germs

Activity

Because of the relatively short shelf life of food items, many have added preservatives, natural or chemical. Preservatives are substances added to food so it will remain edible for a longer period of time. Food that sits for too long becomes a host for germs. Eating this germ-laden food will make us sick. Explore germs with a simple experiment using three clear glasses, water, a cooked hot dog, salt, and vinegar. You will also need a knife (adult use) and measuring spoons. Cut three small slices from the hot dog, each about the same size. Place one hot dog piece into a glass filled with water, the second hot dog slice into a glass of water with an added teaspoon of salt, and the third slice into a glass of vinegar. Use the same amount of liquid in each glass. Let the glasses sit for a week. What happens? The glasses in which cloudy liquids form are full of germs. Which liquid was best at preserving the hot dog slice? Ask the students to contribute ideas on ways their parents and grandparents preserve foods (like freezing or canning). Have them research methods used by the Pilgrims.

Project

Prepare a fun snack while you check for preservatives. You will need hot dogs (one for each child), two large containers of cottage cheese, one package of fish-shaped crackers, blue food coloring, a knife (adult use), saucepan, water, spoon, heat source, paper plates, and disposable spoons or forks for eating. Tint the cottage cheese blue with a few drops of food coloring. Boil the hot dogs, then slice the bottom half of each to create several legs. Let the students spread a cottage cheese sea over a plate, then open the legs of their sea creatures and sit them in the cottage cheese. Sprinkle fish crackers around the creature. Have the students check the food labels to name the preservatives used in each of their snack ingredients.

Solutions

Activity

Some substances, when added to a liquid such as water, break apart or dissolve and seem to disappear. Have your students perform a tasting experiment to discover whether or not the original substance still exists. You will need water, clear plastic drinking glasses, drinking straws, spoons, and sugar. Have the students add a spoonful of sugar to their glasses of water. Stir to dissolve the sugar. Let the students use the straws to taste the water at the top, middle, and bottom of their glasses. Does the water taste sweet? Has the sugar really disappeared? Although we cannot see the sugar, it still exists. Now use a medicine dropper to place several drops of the sugar water in an aluminum pie pan. Place the pan in a sunny area to help evaporate the liquid portion (water) of the solution. What remains is sugar.

Project

Make salt color pictures. Pour a little table salt into two containers. Add 1-3 drops of red food coloring to one and 1-3 drops of blue to the other. Place the lids on the containers and shake to tint the salt. Have the students place a sheet of white paper on newspaper. Sprinkle the white paper with a little salt of both colors. Let the students carefully mist their papers with a spray bottle of water. Use the water carefully, as too much will pool and spoil the design. The students will observe the salt dissolving and the colors blending to make purple. Allow the water to evaporate and the salt crystals will reappear while the colors remain.

A Dandy Drum

Did you know November is Drum Month? Drums are instruments that belong to the percussion family–those that are shaken or struck to make sound. Look carefully to find and highlight with a crayon these drum-related words look up, down, across, and diagonally.

| snare | conga | music | rhythm | bass |
| mallets | shell | bongo | sticks | timpani |

```
t  i  m  p  a  n  i  e  k  f
c  b  t  g  y  s  s  a  b  g
c  j  n  a  d  n  z  j  o  q
d  o  s  n  a  r  e  g  n  r
c  p  t  a  i  h  f  p  g  d
h  b  i  w  x  y  m  m  o  g
c  l  c  h  s  t  e  x  u  k
i  v  k  e  s  h  y  s  r  y
s  i  s  u  i  m  e  y  t  z
u  r  q  f  x  n  z  l  s  j
m  a  l  l  e  t  s  w  l  m
```

by Becky Radtke

Name _____

Playground Votes

The village of Newtown has to vote soon on this question:

Should our town build a new playground?

Below are comments that some people have made. How do you think each person will vote on the questions? Put a Y in the blank if you think the person will vote *yes*. Put an N in the blank if you think the person will vote *no*.

1. "Children need more places to play." _____

2. "It will cost too much money to build the playground and keep it clean." _____

3. "The land would be more useful as a parking lot." _____

4. "More people will visit our town and bring business to our shops." _____

5. "It isn't safe to have children playing on a city playground." _____

6. "School classes could have the job of picking up litter." _____

Think of one more good reason for people to vote *yes* and one more reason why people might vote *no* for the playground. Write your reasons on the back.

by Ann Richmond Fisher

Growing Through Reading

Celebrate the month of November with books.
Start with National Author's Day on November 1 and continue with
National Children's Book Week (the week before Thanksgiving).

National Author's Day
November 1

Emphasize the appreciation of the men and women who have made our literature possible. Explain that authors are real, everyday people with interests and talents much like the children in your class. Obtain biographical tidbits about authors and share this information with your students before reading a new book. Perhaps invite a local author to your classroom.

Encourage your students to become authors today by writing a story; something that is important to them. Artistically create colorful binders and display your new authors' publications on a table for all to enjoy.

National Children's Book Week

This week is dedicated to spreading the word about children's literature and the joys of reading. Book Week has been celebrated since 1919. Last year's theme, "Plant a Seed—Read," is one that can be used anytime. Start young children with books and they will grow up to be readers. For further information on Book Week, contact:

Children's Book Council
568 Broadway, Suite 404
New York, NY 10012

web site—www.cbcbooks.org
e-mail—staff@cbcbooks.org

by Tania K. Cowling

"A Bloomin' Room—We Grow with Books"

Bulletin Board

Have each child create a large colorful flower using construction paper and crayons. You will need a close-up photograph of each child (brought from home or use a Polaroid™). Glue the child's photo (cut into an oval or circle) in the center of the paper flower. Arrange these "flower children" on the board. Add paper stems and leaves. Also include a few paper book shapes placed randomly on the background.

Secret Garden

Create a cozy corner for silent reading in your classroom. Since the theme is planting, decorate your corner with such items as garden tools (use plastic—no sharp tools), silk flowers, watering can, garden gloves, birdbath, green plants, and stuffed animals to adorn the garden (like rabbits, birds, and squirrels). Stock a shelf or table with a variety of books including *The Secret Garden* by Frances Hodgson Burnett.

Dress Up as Children's Book Characters

Gather a collection of Mother Goose books. There are many books with rhymes arranged and illustrated by various authors. Fill a large box with props (plastic spider, horn, clock, candlestick, toy mouse, crown, fiddle, and so on). Have the children participate in the following activities:

- Guess the nursery rhyme by looking at one of the props.

- Re-create a nursery rhyme with actions and use of the props.

- Use the props and create a new original rhyme.

72

Tree of Reading

Prepare a large paper tree trunk on the wall. Cut out numerous paper leaves from construction paper. After a child reads a book, he can write the name of the book along with his name on the leaf. The kids can tape their leaves on the tree. This is a fun motivator for reading. Who can add the most leaves to the "Book Tree"?

This tree could be a year-round celebration of reading. As the seasons change, vary the leaves.

Fall—red, yellow, brown, and orange leaves. Place some on the ground as "fallen" leaves.

Winter—the leaves can be replaced by snowflakes covering the bare tree.

Spring—the tree sprouts new green leaves.

Summer—green leaves

Growing Chains

Provide the children with strips of colored construction paper. As they finish reading a book, the title is printed on a strip. Start the chain with a seeded strip, taping a flower seed onto the paper. Make a circle and staple it closed. Continue adding book strips to form the chain. At the end of the week, make a paper flower to glue onto the last strip. Compare the length of the kids' chains. Who has read the most books?

Have a Poetry Festival

Read a favorite poem aloud or create a new one.

Haiku
17 syllables that suggest an aspect of nature.
Blue, red, yellow birds (5 syllables)
Singing softly in a tree (7 syllables)
Makes me so happy (5 syllables)

Five Senses
November is a fall month.
It tastes like pumpkins and apples.
It smells like hot cinnamon cider.
It sounds like crackling logs in the fireplace.
It feels as soft as a fleece blanket.
It looks so colorful.

Make and Take Home

Headbands

Send the kids home with headline headbands; a perfect sharing activity with parents. Use sentence strips or cardboard to make headbands. On the band, print,

"Today we read _____

by _____.

Ask me about it!"

Fill in the blanks and have the child decorate the strip with drawings from the story. This should spark some literature talk at home!

Bookmarks

Set up a center with short strips of poster board and art materials. Give each child a time to visit the center and create an original bookmark to make and take home. Supply the center with crayons, markers, and stickers. Laminate each bookmark with clear adhesive paper.

Flower Awards

At the end of the week, give your students incentive awards that they can take home and enjoy. Attach a special note of recognition to a long stem silk flower. Punch a hole in one corner of your note and tie it to the flower with yarn or ribbon. "The more I read, the more I know. Reading books helps me grow."

TLC10299 Copyright © Teaching & Learning Company, Carthage, IL 62321-0010

A Book Week

Book Worm

A worm is an insect larva.
A larva could become a frog.
Or it could become a tadpole
Sitting on a log.

A book worm is a name for tiny insect larva.
It begins to grow and change how it looks.
Each day it gets bigger and bigger
As it feeds on the pages of good books.

You can be a book worm
In your favorite nook,
By "devouring" many pages
Of any good book.

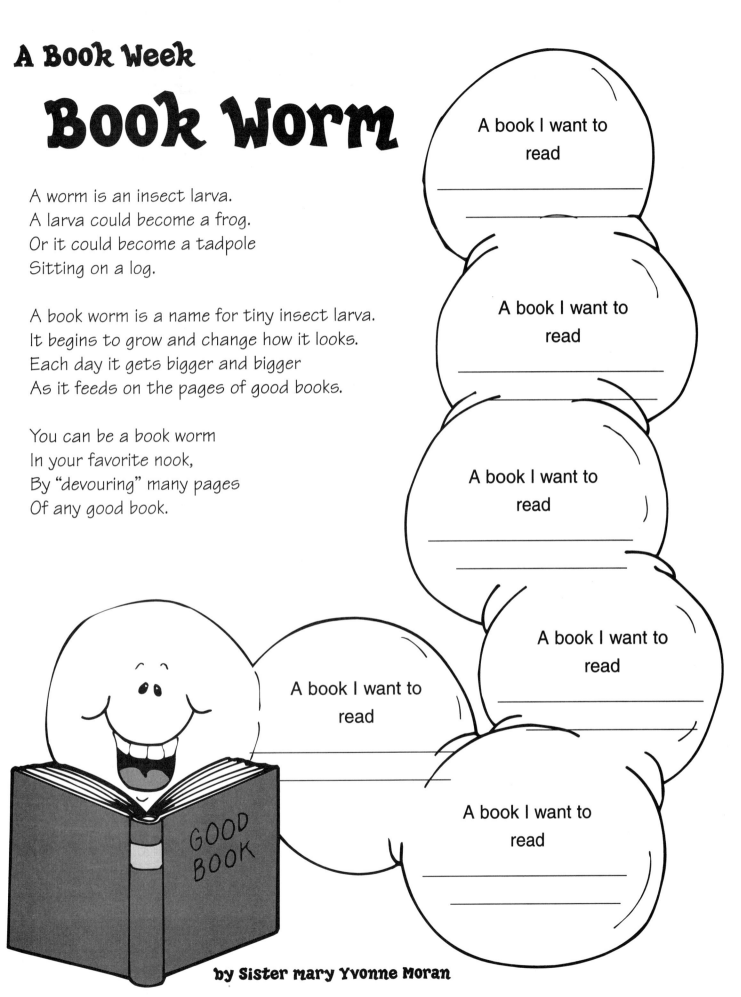

A book I want to read

A book I want to read

A book I want to read

A book I want to read

A book I want to read

A book I want to read

GOOD BOOK

by Sister Mary Yvonne Moran

New Tradition

You just can't blame the Pilgrims, there wasn't much to eat.
When someone caught a turkey, it must have been a treat!
The Indians smelled the cooking, and came to share the meal.
Best to make them welcome, and show your welcome's real!
You just can't blame the Pilgrims for all the food and fuss.
If grown-ups could stop talking, they might consult with us.
Now, Bridget can't stand turkey, and Pat won't touch a yam,
Myself, I don't like stuffing, and Shaun refuses ham.
Yet here comes ol' Thanksgiving with relatives galore
Who never do stop talking, from the time they hit the door!
They eat and eat; and Mom says, "A little more won't hurt."
We nibble corn and pickles while waiting for dessert.
When I grow up I'll tell them all, "Consider my position.
Why should some hungry Pilgrims start our family's tradition?"
You all can come to my place; it's bound to be a winner.
Enjoy and help me celebrate *Thanksgiving Pizza Dinner!*

by M.D. Howitt

TURKEY, TARGETS, AND BALL

Francis Billington and Giles Hopkins raced across the shore of Plymouth Bay early on an October morning in 1621. Their bare feet slapped against the wet sand. John, Francis' younger brother, ran after them.

The three boys dug clams and chucked them into wooden buckets. Other Pilgrim boys checked eel traps in the bay or gathered nuts in the woods.

Ellen Billington, Francis and John's mother, and the other three Pilgrim women who'd survived last winter's sickness, had risen at dawn to bake bread. Now they were pulling fragrant loaves of corn bread and "Injun and rye" bread, a coarse dark bread, from the outdoor oven.

Pilgrim girls, dressed like their mothers in long-skirted dresses of dark green, blue, and russet, pulled leeks from the gardens and plucked watercress from the brook. They cleaned carrots and cut up pumpkins to be boiled.

Everyone worked, preparing a feast to celebrate the harvest.

Several days earlier, four Pilgrim hunters brought home, enough wild fowl to feed everybody for a week. Willing hands plucked and prepared the wild turkeys, ducks, and geese for roasting.

But that was before Governor Bradford had invited the Indian Chief Massasoit and his braves to share the Pilgrims' three-day harvest celebration. No one had known how many Indians would come.

Early that morning, 90 Wampanoag braves followed Chief Massasoit into the tiny Plymouth settlement. They'd brought five deer with them to share. Even so, the Pilgrim women had looked at one another and sent the boys and girls to gather more food.

Later that day, Francis and John stuffed themselves with venison, eel, corn bread, and beans. They'd

rather have feasted on English wheat bread and beef, but they were thankful for these strange American foods.

They'd never have had such a good harvest if Squanto hadn't helped them. Squanto was an Indian who had once been a Spanish slave. He'd escaped from Spain to England, and learned English there. Squanto was their friend.

Last spring, he'd shown the Pilgrims how to build a fish trap to catch herring. They'd eaten many herring, and dried more for winter. But most importantly, Squanto had shown them how to place three fish in a circle, heads together, to fertilize each hill of Indian corn.

by Jeanne Field Olson

Francis and Giles had piled brush for bonfires to frighten wolves, attracted by the smell of rotting fish, away from the corn-fields. Later, they'd dug cut-worms, and scared crows away from the precious young plants. Corn, beans, and pumpkins had all been planted together, as the Indians grew them. And how they had grown!

Francis nibbled some dried blue-berries for dessert. He couldn't remember when he'd been so full. He'd never forget the hun-gry days of last winter and spring.

Francis was full, but not too full for a game of stool-ball. Stool-ball was his favorite game, but there'd been no time to play games in America, until today.

Francis and Giles carried two tall stools from their houses. They placed the stools well apart. Francis scratched a bowling line in the dirt halfway between the two stools. He and Giles chose children to be on their teams.

From the bowling line, Giles threw a soft leather ball at one stool. Francis knocked the ball away with his hand and ran. He scored for his team, but Giles hit the stool with his next throw, and Francis was out.

Francis played stool-ball until he saw Captain Standish carry-ing two muskets. Francis ran to watch. The men poured black powder down the musket muz-zles, then aimed and fired at tar-gets in a cloud of smoke and flames. The Pilgrim men enjoyed shooting to see who was the best marksman. They also hoped to impress the Indians with the power of English muskets.

The Indians watched, then took out their bows and arrows. THWACK, THWACK, THWACK, the Indian arrows hit their tar-gets. They were also expert marksmen. Francis Billington smiled and yawned. It had been a wonderful day. Of course, he didn't know that he had been part of America's first Thanksgiving, but we do.

First Thanksgiving Bibliography

Bradford, William. *Of Plymouth Plantation 1620-1647.* Edited by Samuel Eliot Morison. New York, Knopf, 1975.
Duryea, Walton. "Stool-Ball: A Holiday Game" *Cobblestone*, Nov. 1989.
Karter, Diane. *Thanksgiving.* NY, Applebaum, Facts on File, 1984.
Morison, Samuel Eliot. *The Story of the "Old Colony" of New Plymouth.* New York, Knopf, 1956.
Rutman, Darrett B. *Husbandmen of Plymouth; Farms and Villages in the Old Colony 1620-1692.* Boston, Beacon, 1967.
Willison, George F. *The Pilgrim Reader.* Garden City, Doubleday, 1953.

Turkey Cup

Materials

- paper cup
- tinfoil
- scissors
- tape
- glue
- ruler
- brown, yellow, red construction paper
- construction paper in various colors
- white paper
- blue and black markers
- pencil

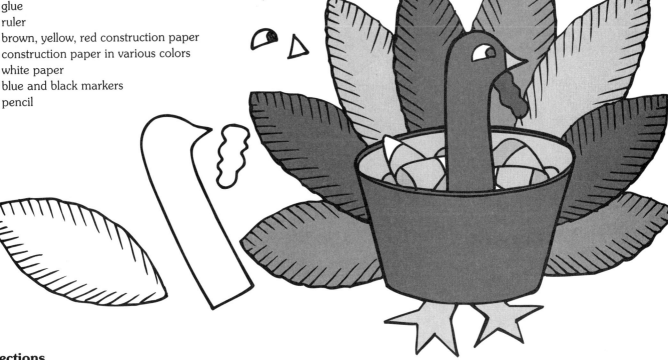

Directions

1. Measure 2½ inches from the bottom of your paper cup and mark it with a pencil. Using the mark as your guide, cut around the cup.

2. Cut out a piece of brown construction paper 9" long and 2½" high.

3. Wrap the piece of brown construction paper around the paper cup and tape the ends together. This will be the back side of your turkey cup.

4. Using a pencil, draw a turkey's head with a beak and a long neck about 4" in length. Tape the bottom of the turkey's neck on the inside of the cup at the front.

5. Cut out a small circle from white paper for the turkey's eye. Using a blue marker, color in the corner of the eye and glue it on the turkey's head. Using yellow construction paper, cut out a tiny triangle and glue it on the turkey's beak. Using a pencil, draw a small turkey wattle on red construction paper and cut it out. Tape the wattle to the back side of the turkey's head, underneath the yellow beak.

6. Using different colored construction paper, cut out 8 feathers, each 5" in length, 1½" wide. On each feather cut small slits along both sides to give the feathers definition.

7. Tape the feathers, one by one, on the back side of the turkey cup.

8. Cut two medium-sized turkey feet from yellow construction paper. Using a black marker, outline the feet, then tape them to the bottom of the paper cup.

9. Cover the inside of the cup with tinfoil.

Note: When you finish making your turkey cup, fill it with candy corn, or grapes and walnuts. For your Thanksgiving Day dinner, write the name of a guest on each turkey cup and place them on your dinner table so the guests know where to sit.

by Holly Barry

Paper Plate Turkey

Materials

- white paper plate
- brown, yellow, red, black construction paper
- construction paper in various colors
- white paper
- black and blue markers
- glue
- tape
- scissors
- pencil
- hole punch
- brown yarn
- ruler

Directions

1. Cut off the outside rim of a paper plate.

2. Place the circle on a piece of brown construction paper. Using a pencil, trace around the circle, then cut it out.

3. Glue the brown circle on top of the white circle. This will be the turkey's body.

4. Using a pencil, draw a large turkey's head with a beak and a long neck, about 4" long, and cut it out. Tape the bottom of the turkey's neck to the back side of the turkey's body.

5. Cut a small circle from white paper for the turkey's eye. Using a blue marker, color in the corner of the eye and glue it on the turkey's head. Using yellow construction paper, cut out a tiny triangle and glue it on the turkey's beak. On a piece of black construction paper, draw a medium-sized Pilgrim hat and glue it on top of the turkey's head. Cut out a small square from yellow construction paper. Using a black marker, draw a square in the center of the yellow square and color it in. Glue the yellow square in the middle of the black Pilgrim hat for the buckle.

6. Using different colored construction paper, cut out six feathers, each 5" long and 2" wide. On each feather cut small slits along both sides to give the feathers definition.

7. On the left side, tape the feathers, one by one, on the back side of the turkey's body.

8. Cut two strips from yellow construction paper, measuring 4" long and 1" wide. Accordion fold each strip. Cut two medium-sized turkey feet from yellow construction paper. Using a black marker, outline each foot. Tape one foot on the bottom of each yellow strip. These are the turkey's legs. Tape the two legs on the back side of the turkey's body.

9. Punch two holes, side by side, on the top of the turkey's body. Thread a 12" piece of brown yarn through the two holes. Tie the ends together and hang your Thanksgiving Day turkey to decorate your doorway.

Harvest Basket

Materials

white paper plate
brown, black, green markers
scissors
glue
yellow, green, purple, red, brown,
    orange construction paper
pencil

Directions

1. On the inside of the paper plate, beneath the rim, draw a half circle with a pencil. Cut out the half circle.

2. Turn the plate over. Using a brown marker, draw crisscross lines all around the rim of the plate, making it look like a basket.

3. To make a pumpkin, cut a medium-sized circle from orange construction paper. Using brown construction paper, cut out a small stem and glue it on top of the orange circle. Cut two small leaves from green construction paper and glue them on either side of the brown stem. Using a green marker, draw the veins on each leaf.

4. To make an apple, cut a medium-sized circle from red construction paper. Cut a small stem from green construction paper and glue it on top of the apple.

5. Cut a medium-sized squash from yellow construction paper. Using brown construction paper, cut out a small stem and glue it on top of the squash.

6. Using purple construction paper, cut out eight small circles for grapes.

7. Using yellow construction paper, cut out two medium-sized ears of corn. Cut four long, thin leaves from green construction paper. Glue two green leaves on each ear of corn. Using a black marker, draw small squares on both ears of corn for the kernels.

8. Glue all the fruits and vegetables in the middle of the basket. Hang the colorful Thanksgiving Day basket in your kitchen or on any doorknob to decorate your home.

Name _____

Gobble Up a Code

Hidden in the turkey's feathers is a special holiday message! In order to find the message, you need to identify the letters in the striped feathers. Begin with the first row of turkeys and then continue with the next row. There is extra space at the bottom of the page if you need to keep track of the letters.

by Monica A. Harris

Dinner Mix-Up

Can you unscramble these mixed-up words to make Thanksgiving Dinner?
Use the pictures below to help you.

EPI   __ __ __

NROC   __ __ __ __

ATTOSEOP   __ __ __ __ __ __ __ __

YERTKU   __ __ __ __ __ __

RGVYA   __ __ __ __ __

PEAPSL   __ __ __ __ __ __

SLROL   __ __ __ __ __

PKNUPIM   __ __ __ __ __ __ __

by Veronica Terrill   83

Turkey Math

How fast can you "gobble up" these math problems?

$$\begin{array}{r} 6 \\ \times\ 2 \\ \hline \end{array}$$

$$\begin{array}{r} 12 \\ -\ 4 \\ \hline \end{array}$$

$$\begin{array}{r} 9 \\ +\ 5 \\ \hline \end{array}$$

$$\begin{array}{r} 3 \\ \times\ 2 \\ \hline \end{array}$$

$$\begin{array}{r} 10 \\ +\ 5 \\ \hline \end{array}$$

$$\begin{array}{r} 19 \\ -\ 7 \\ \hline \end{array}$$

$$\begin{array}{r} 3 \\ \times\ 3 \\ \hline \end{array}$$

$$\begin{array}{r} 10 \\ -\ 8 \\ \hline \end{array}$$

$$\begin{array}{r} 15 \\ +\ 4 \\ \hline \end{array}$$

$$\begin{array}{r} 4 \\ \times\ 4 \\ \hline \end{array}$$

$$\begin{array}{r} 13 \\ +\ 5 \\ \hline \end{array}$$

$$\begin{array}{r} 11 \\ -\ 3 \\ \hline \end{array}$$

$$\begin{array}{r} 4 \\ \times\ 2 \\ \hline \end{array}$$

$$\begin{array}{r} 9 \\ -\ 3 \\ \hline \end{array}$$

by Veronica Terrill

84

Holiday newsletter

The multilayered holiday season offers opportunities for us to explore diversity with our children. Understanding and accepting cultural differences can be a confusing and challenging experience for them. However, by observing the similarities and differences among the people they know and their various holiday traditions, children can begin to appreciate the wonders of living in a diverse world.

Simple Science

Our physical world is made up of solids, liquids, and gases. The air around us is a gaseous substance. The molecules in a gas are very far apart and they have no color, which is why we cannot see or feel air. Experiment with your child during National Chemistry Week in November to demonstrate how temperature affects the behavior of gas molecules. You will need a party balloon, a piece of string, and a black marker. Blow up the balloon, tie it closed, then tie a string to the knot to use as a handle. Let your child write a name or short slogan on the balloon. Place the balloon in the refrigerator. Check it after an hour and note what has happened to the balloon and the words. The balloon will be smaller because cooler temperatures cause gas molecules to contract or come closer together. Now, set the balloon in a sunny spot. As heat from the sun warms the air inside the balloon, it will again expand so you can read the words. Heat causes gas molecules to expand or spread out.

November
Book Week

Reading Room

Choose a few seasonal books from your local library to share during Children's Book Week in November. Keep in mind that books also make great holiday gifts.

Auntie Clause by Elise Primavera. Harcourt Brace.

Celebrating Kwanzaa by Diane Hoyt-Goldsmith, Holiday House.

Navajo ABC: A Dine Alphabet by Lucy Tapahonso, Simon & Schuster.

On the Mayflower by Kate Waters, Scholastic.

Pippi Longstocking's After Christmas Party by Astrid Lindgren, Penguin.

Thanksgiving at the Tappletons' by Miriam Cohen, Bantam.

When Mindy Saved Hanukkah by Eric A. Kimmel, Scholastic.

Mathworks

The Pilgrims learned about popcorn from the Native Americans. Invite your child to add corn puffs while creating a popcorn tree. Make extra popcorn for snacking later. Begin by gluing one popped puff in the center at the top of a piece of construction paper. Below this, glue on a row of two, then a row of three, and so on continuously adding one puff to each new row down the length of the paper. Leave room at the bottom for your child to draw a tree trunk. Flash Card Snack: For this game you will need a set of math equation cards and the extra popcorn you made for snacking. To play, show your child a flash card, such as $6 + 2 =$ or $8 - 5 =$. Have your child separate the number of corn puffs that answers the equation. Your child then snacks on the popcorn.

by Marie E. Cecchini

Cooking with Kids

Spice up the holidays with colorful cooking experiences.

White Cats
November—National Cat Month

Ingredients
English muffins
cream cheese
banana slices

triangle-shaped crackers
pretzel sticks
raisins

Toast English muffin halves, one for each child. Let each child spread cream cheese over one muffin round for the cat's head and two triangle crackers for ears. Set these on a plate, crackers above the muffin. Have the children add banana slice eyes with raisin pupils, a raisin nose with pretzel stick whiskers, and half a banana slice for a mouth.

Turkey Plate
November—Thanksgiving

Ingredients
lettuce leaves
cottage cheese
green, red, and yellow peppers

black olives
cheese slices

Place a lettuce leaf on a plate. Scoop a mound of cottage cheese onto the lettuce leaf and press it into a circular shape for the turkey body. Cut pepper strips of red, yellow, and green. Arrange these pepper strip feathers in a colorful pattern across the top of the turkey body. Below the pepper feathers, add two black olive eyes and a cheese triangle beak. At the bottom of the plate, add two cheese strip turkey legs.

Pumpkin Nut Pudding
November—Thanksgiving, Harvest

Ingredients
2 c. canned pumpkin
2 tsp. pumpkin pie spice
2 T. honey
3 c. milk

2 (3¾ oz.) packages instant vanilla pudding
¾ c. chopped walnuts
whipped cream (optional)

In a large bowl, combine the pumpkin, spice, honey, and nuts. Stir in the milk. Mix thoroughly. Add the pudding and beat until the mixture begins to thicken (about 1-2 minutes). Chill before serving. Top individual servings with whipped cream, if desired.

by Marie E. Cecchini

CRAFT CORNER

Thanksgiving Pinch Pot

Commemorate native people and early settlers at your Thanksgiving table with this simple, functional work of art.

Materials
> one handful of self-hardening clay per student
> tray or board for drying pots
> acrylic paint and paintbrushes

Discuss
- What did the land offer native people and early settlers to help them survive? Consider shelter, food, clothing, furniture, and accessories.
- How might a pot have been used in early times? Consider food storage, preparation, and serving. Pottery was made in many forms for many purposes. Create a functional pot that represents your thanks to the Earth.

Let's Make It
1. Knead a handful of clay in your hands until it is soft and pliable.
2. Shape the clay into a round ball. Throw the ball onto a flat surface.
3. Wet your hands and press your thumbs into the top center of the ball.
4. Use your thumbs and fingers to pinch the area around the center hole to form the walls of your pot.
5. Pinch and shape as you slide your thumb and fingers around the walls, pinching and shaping to form a dish shape you desire.
6. When you have the shape you desire, wet your fingers and smooth the surface to a finished texture. A clay tool can be used to add markings.
7. Let the pot dry in a warm place for at least 24 hours or as directed by the clay product. Thick walls will require more time to dry.
8. When the pot is dry, remove it from the flat surface using a wire pulled along the surface where the clay meets the table. Leave the pot upside down until the bottom is dry.
9. The dry pot may be painted with acrylic paints. Paint the bottom first, allow it dry, and then paint the pot.

Stick It On

A little paste and creativity will turn a box into a wonder.

Materials
> paper-covered box
> craft glue and glue stick or brush
> jewels, sequins, glitter, buttons, pasta shapes, rice, dried beans, seeds, shells, colored sand, craft sticks, yarn, foil, tiny pom-poms, trinkets, and so on

Let's Decorate
1. Children will choose decorating materials and plan their designs. Remind children to keep decorations below the base of the box top.
2. Children will apply glue and position decorations.

by Robynne Eagan

Clip Art for Fall

Clip Art for Fall

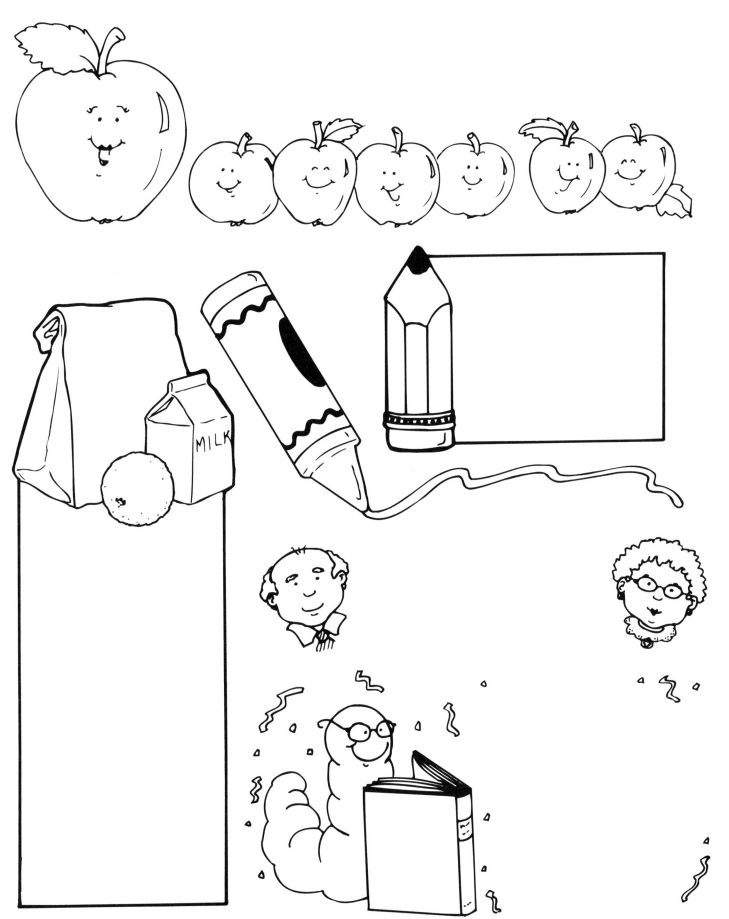

Clip Art for Fall

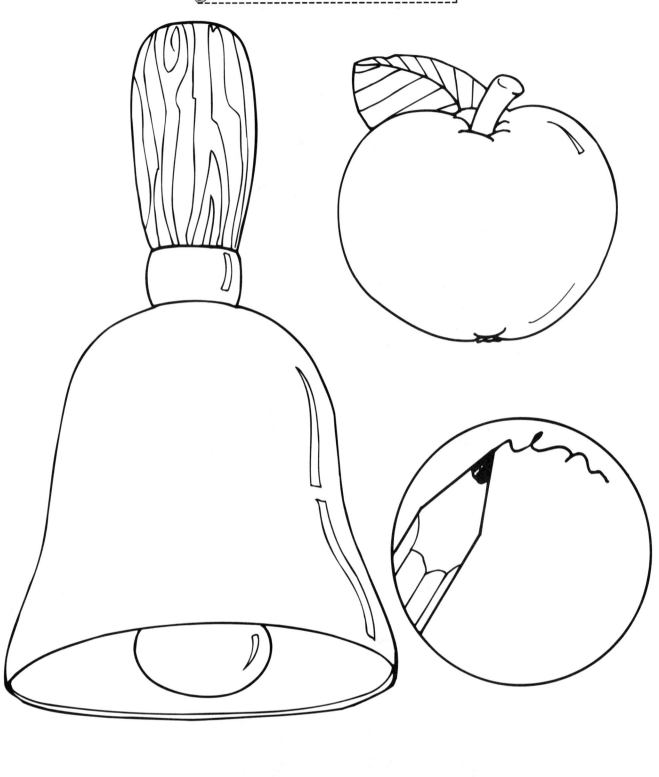

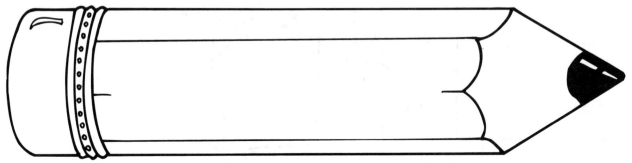

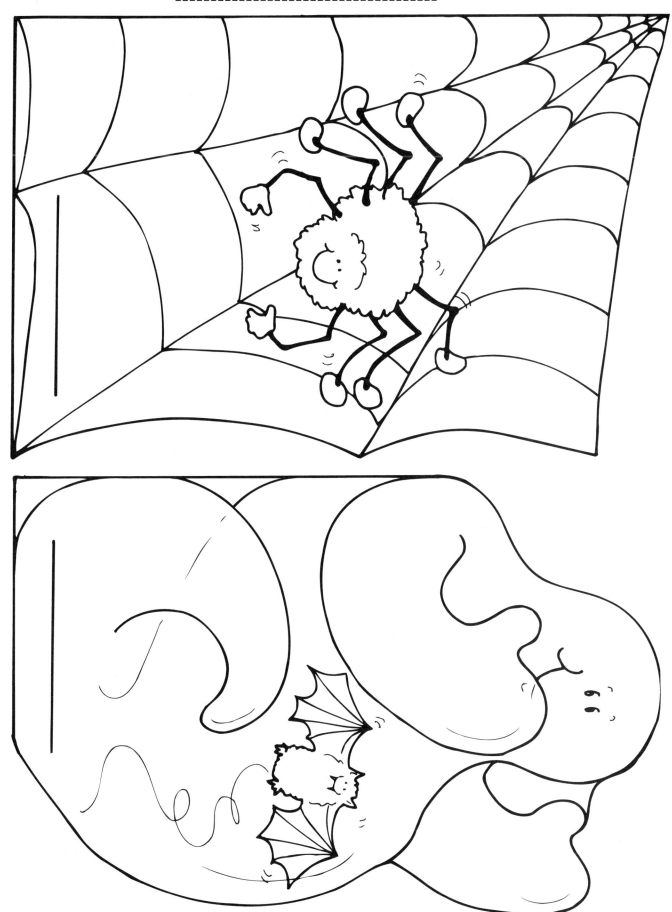

Clip Art for **Fall**

Be Safe!
Be Smart!
Don't Play
with Fire!

93

Happy Thanksgiving

Happy Turkey Day!

Gobble, Gobble, Gobble!

MY SNOW DAY

I wake up in the morning and get up
to go to school;
Then I look out my window and
exclaim, "How cool!"
Snow's coming down like crazy; must
be six inches deep!
"No school today," says Mom, so I go
back to sleep.
Later on I wake up and eat a piece of
toast.
Then I dress up warmly, so hot I think
I'll roast.
I go outside, tongue sticking out, to
taste the snow that falls
Then I make tracks around the yard
and throw a few snowballs.

This day needs only one thing to
be the very best,
And so I roll a huge snowball
(then take a little rest).
I roll a second, smaller ball and
stack the two together;
Then add a top hat and a scarf
and gloves of worn out
leather.
Some rocks for eyes and nose
and mouth, and Mr.
Snowman's done!
His cheerful company will make
my snow day lots more fun.

BY MARY TUCKER

95

Winter Discoveries

Greet winter with a smile and some winter wear when you engage in school yard learning adventures created for the snowy season.

A Winter Wonderland

Take a hike outside after a snowfall and marvel at the wonders of winter. Encourage students to use all of their senses to describe the experience. Take the observations and feelings inside to the classroom where children can follow up by writing or drawing their impressions with a vigor that can only come from real-life experiences.

Winter Stories

After experiencing the outdoors in winter firsthand, ask children to use winter as a setting for a story. Suggest the following topics as ideas for students to base their stories:

❋ Jack Frost is a mythical character whose cold breath is said to freeze anything in an instant. Legends about this character report that he can cover the Earth with frost and his thunderous roar can shatter icebergs.

❋ Long ago, early settlers had to burn wood to keep warm in winter. They had to travel by foot, skis, or horsedrawn sled.

❋ A severe snowstorm is called a blizzard. High winds and blowing snow can make it impossible to see.

❋ Precipitation in the form of balls or lumps of clear ice and compact snow is called hail. A hailstorm can be devastating and dangerous.

❋ A swift movement of snow, ice, mud, or rock down a steep slope or a mountainside is called an avalanche.

96   by Robynne Eagan

How's Your Arm?

There is something irresistible about tossing a snowball. As innocent as that little white ball appears, it can harm anyone who ends up in its way. That's why most schools ban the tossing of snowballs. Why not take advantage of the fact that kids love snowballs and use the little white balls to develop ball-handling skills and hand-eye coordination?

1. On a good snow-packing day, set up a series of targets in a row. For targets, consider a windowless school brick wall that can be marked with chalk or tape. Other possibilities include buckets, sleds, hats, and mittens placed along the ground or hung from a fence row, pylons or other markers.
2. Have students stand behind a specified area, make snowballs, and fire away. No student may cross the line, and there is no need to retrieve balls.

Make Tracks

Don't let a winter go by without making the first tracks at least once! Use the opportunity to make marks on the snow as a springboard for a variety of activities. The following activity will encourage creativity, verbal skill development, and group cooperation.

Directions
1. Divide your class into groups of 4-5 students.
2. Have students develop a game using tracks or other markings made on the snow. Facilitate as needed. Encourage children to keep their games simple and fun.
3. Have each group teach their game to the other groups and have everyone join in the fun.

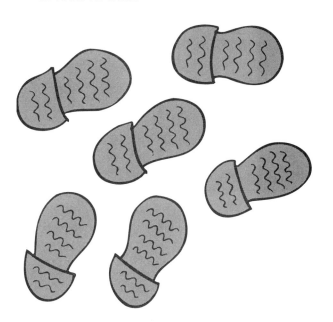

Tales in a Winter Forest

Winter is the perfect time for students to become forest sleuths.
What tales can a winter forest tell?
Look for the stories in the markings on the snow.

❋ Who lives in the forest? When did they last come out of their homes?
❋ What were they doing? What did they eat?
❋ Where does the creature who made the tracks live?
❋ Who ate the bark off the tree?
❋ Can you find a bird's home that was hidden in the summer?

Kid Space

School Yard Learning Adventures

Feeding Station Creation

You Need
- birdseed, sunflower seeds, or unsalted peanuts
- dried and fresh fruit

Directions
Some birds fly south for the winter while others stay on to await the cold weather. Their territories become covered in a blanket of snow. These feathered friends embark on a winter-long search for the food sources they need to help them survive the season. Birds such as chickadees, woodpeckers, and nuthatches who survive on insects in the other seasons need high-energy foods to keep them going through the long, cold months of winter. Suet and seeds such as the black oil sunflower seeds have high energy and are favorites of these birds. Blue jays and cardinals will welcome fruit and berries.

What to Do
1. Supply students with seeds and other materials or request these from home. Collect (but don't encourage) discarded fruit from student lunches.
2. Have students design a simple message or picture on a piece of paper before venturing outside.
3. Have students replicate their design, only much larger, on the snow by spreading the seeds. This message will make a welcome winter treat for the feathered friends of flight or the squirrels and other land creatures.

Follow-Up
- Have children observe their feeding station creation and keep notes about their observations.
- How many birds discovered the feast? What types? Describe the birds.
- Did the bird come alone or with a group of birds? What might this tell you?
- What times of day did the birds tend to feed? Did any birds return?
- Which foods did particular birds favor?
- How did the birds crack open the seeds or peanuts?
- Did some types of birds scare others away?
- Did any other creatures find the feast?

Take a Look at Snow

Take a close look at the snow that fills the sky and covers the ground. A close-up look will reveal nature's tiny artistic masterpieces—snowflakes.

Discussion
How do snowflakes form? The temperature must be below the freezing point (32°F or 0°C) for snow to fall. When water vapor in the air condenses (turns from vapor to water), drops of water form and freeze to become crystals. Several small crystals attach to one another to form a snowflake.

You Need
- snowy day with large flakes falling
- magnifying glass
- sheets of dark construction paper

What to Do
1. Catch snowflakes on your dark construction paper.
2. Use your magnifying glass to help you take a close-up look at individual flakes.

Discuss
- What do you see?
- Each individual snowflake is a thing of wonder and beauty. These intricate icy creations are hexagonal, which means six-sided. Each is perfectly formed and each is different from every other flake.

Follow-Up
Inside the classroom, draw pictures of snowflakes in a sketchbook, create a descriptive word chart together and have children write poems about the snowflakes.

Have your local library locate a copy of Wilson "Snowflake" Bentley's fabulous book *Snow Crystals*. Bentley was a farmer and scientist with a great interest in snowflakes. He spent his spare time studying and taking photographs of snowflakes. He took over 5800 photographs of snow throughout his life. His studies led to much of what we now know about these icy wonders.

98

School Yard Learning Adventures

The Magic of Melting

Make use of a warm winter day, melting snow and the scientific method to make some interesting discoveries.

Have children help to come up with scientific questions that such a day brings into focus.

Discussion

- Where will the snow melt the fastest? Choose areas of study such as the grassy field, the dark pavement, light concrete, a shaded area, and a sunny area.
- Find the temperature outside. How long will it take for a snowball to melt at this temperature? Take estimates. Who was the closest?
- What will happen to snow in a cup? How much water will be left? What is at the bottom of the cup? What conclusions can you draw from this experiment?
- Why does snow pack better when it is warm?
- Where will the water go when the snow melts?

Wintry Experiment

Let the cold outdoors assist you with this simple experiment. Take this opportunity to follow the scientific method in writing this experiment. Did you know that lakes and ponds freeze in the winter but oceans do not? What is different between lakes and ponds? (Salt water vs. fresh, large vs. small, moving vs. still.) Let's investigate one of these factors: salt water vs. fresh water.

You Need
- two paper cups
- salt
- water
- temperature below the freezing point

Question
Will salt water freeze faster than fresh water?

Hypothesis
I think that fresh water freezes at a higher temperature than salt water.

Procedure
Fill two paper cups with exactly the same amount of water. Add salt to one of the cups. Place both cups outside in the same location when the temperature falls below the freezing point.

Results
Record what happened. How long did it take for each cup to freeze?

Conclusion
What do you think these results showed you? What did you learn?

Follow-Up
Repeat the same experiment using cups with varying amounts of salt. Pour salt on ice and watch what happens.

Think About This
In what ways do people use the properties of salt to help them in the winter?

LC10299 Copyright © Teaching & Learning Company, Carthage, IL 62321-0010

99

Frozen Trees?

Did you know that most trees consist of 80 to 90% water? What do you think happens to trees in freezing temperatures? Well, since water freezes solid, you would assume that trees freeze solid in the cold winter temperatures.

Take a Look

Check out some trees on a freezing cold day. Do you think that they are frozen? Trees do freeze and it doesn't hurt them. Nature has a way of preparing trees for the cold temperatures. When cold weather sets in, the sugar content in a tree's cells increases. The sugar acts like antifreeze. It keeps the tree from freezing solid on all but the coldest of days.

The Running of the Sap

As spring nears, the nights are cold but the days start warming up. In North America, when the night temperatures drop below 0°C (32°F) but rise above freezing in the day, the watery sugar-fluid called sap begins to flow through the inside of maple trees. It is this sap which we use to make maple syrup from maple trees.

The first white settlers to areas now known as eastern Canada and northeastern United States were taught by the native people to tap and use the sweet sap of the maple tree. The natives called the weeks of the sap run, the Maple Moon. The sap flows for about three weeks, usually in late February, March and sometimes early April depending upon when the climate is just right for the sap to run. The sweet sap run lasts until the first buds begin to appear on the trees.

Early Syrup Production

Using the materials and tools found in nature, native people used an effective but time-consuming process to remove water from the sap. Watery sap was left outside in clay or wooden containers for a week or two. On cold nights the water would separate from the syrup and rise to the top of the container and freeze. The ice was scraped off of the surface, leaving a thick, syrupy liquid. Large, red-hot stones were then added to this concentrated liquid until the liquid boiled down enough to form the sweet maple syrup. It takes 30 to 40 gallons of watery sap to produce one gallon of maple syrup.

by Robynne Eagan

100

Pioneer Syrup Production

The process of making syrup became easier with the arrival of iron pots. For many early settlers, maple syrup and maple sugar were the only substances available to sweeten foods throughout the year. When the sap began to run, the settlers got busy! The entire settler family camped in the sugar shack in the bush to take advantage of the sap run.

Family members involved in the production of maple syrup had to hand drill the trees, make wooden spikes or taps and tap these into the trees. Buckets were hung from the spikes until they filled with sap. Full buckets were carried by hand and foot or sometimes horse and wagon to the sugar shack. In the sugar shack a fire was kept burning as the sap was boiled down in iron pots. Empty buckets were returned to trees and the process continued for many days and nights. There was a lot of work involved in making syrup. In eastern Canada, most schools have a March break that falls during "sugaring off" season. In the early days this was probably a working holiday.

From the early 1600s until the 1940s very little changed in the process of maple syrup production. By the 1940s piping, evaporators and vehicles were incorporated, making the syrup production business much less laborious for the farm family.

Turn Sap to Syrup

Try the early maple syrup-making process for yourself: a little work, a lot of patience and a dedicated group of hardy volunteers will make this project a success. It is worth the effort to see excited young faces peering into pails.

You Need
- hand drill with a $\frac{7}{16}$" (11 mm) drill bit
- stand of mature sugar maple trees
- spikes (available at hardware and farm cooperative stores)
- large pails with handles and lids
- large pot, outdoor cook stove (wood or propane) and volunteer to monitor
- sterilized glass bottles or jars with lids
- small sticks with one whittled sharp end
- small hammer

What to Do
1. Decide how much syrup you want to produce. An average tree will produce about 12 gallons (55 l) of sap over a three-week run. You'll need about 40 gallons (180 l) of sap to make 1 gallon (5 l) of syrup.
2. Drill one or two holes in each tree about 3 feet above the ground. If you drill two holes they should be on opposite sides of the tree.
3. Tap the spikes into the holes and hang the pails from the spikes.
4. Cover the bucket with a commercial pail cover, a plastic cover or a plastic bag held in place by an elastic band.
5. Have students check the buckets every day. Sap should be collected into a large container and kept cool until added to the heating pot.
6. Pour the sap into a large pot kept at a simmer on the outdoor stove. Indoor cooking will leave a sticky residue throughout the cooking area.
7. Watch the pot carefully. Rising steam indicates the evaporation of water, which means the sap is thickening. Add sap as the level drops in the pan. As the sap thickens, it will change from a clear fluid to a thick amber-colored syrup.
8. When the syrup reaches the desired consistency and taste, have a volunteer run jars through a sterilizing process—either in a dishwasher or in a stovetop canning device. Pour the hot syrup into the sterilized jars and seal. Allow the syrup to settle and cool before enjoying!
9. When you have collected the desired amount of sap or the sap stops running, remove the spikes from the trees and plug the holes with the whittled sticks by hammering the pointed end into the hole.

Freezing Experiment

Conduct a simple experiment while waiting to collect the sap.

You Need
- 2 clear plastic cups
- water
- sugar—2 tsp. (4 ml) per cup
- spoon
- outdoor freezing temperatures or a freezer

What to Do
1. Fill each cup half full of water.
2. Add 2 teaspoons (4 ml) of sugar to one cup. Stir the water until all of the sugar has dissolved.
3. Place the cups outside or in a freezer for one hour.
4. Examine the contents of the cups after one hour. Record your observations. Do you notice any differences between the contents of the two cups? If the pure water has not frozen solid, replace the cups for one half hour and observe again.

Results
Your experiment will demonstrate that pure water will freeze solid before sugar-water. If you leave the cups in the freezer long enough, both liquids will eventually freeze.

What's Going On?
Ask students why they think that one cup of water freezes more slowly than the other. Students who realize that the sugar is the cause have found the answer. The sugar acts as a kind of antifreeze in the water. The pure water will freeze solid more quickly and at a higher temperature than the sugar-water mixture. If your freezer temperature is set at 0°C (32°F), the freezing point of water, the pure water will freeze solid but the sugar-water will not. At a cooler temperature, both will eventually freeze.

Discuss
What will freeze more quickly, pure water or the watery sap that runs through maple trees?

Host a "Sugaring Off" Celebration

Sugaring off is a term used to refer to the process of boiling the sap to leave the sticky, sweet syrup. The term also refers to the time at the end of the syrup harvest when everyone celebrates and enjoys the bounty of sweetness.

Pioneer children were rewarded for hard work in the bush with a sugaring off party. Eastern townships of Quebec, Canada, are famous for gatherings called Festival de la Cabane a Sucre (Festival of the Sugar Shack).

Native people of North America have long celebrated the end of winter by gathering at stands of maple trees at the time of the "maple moon." The first running of the sap brought a springtime feast to celebrate the passing of winter, and the end of the season brought celebrations of the sweet harvest. The Iroquois people held two religious ceremonies related to this gift of nature: the Bush Ceremony in which the Creator was asked to bring forth the sap, and the Maple Ceremony, which gave thanks for the flow.

Pancake Breakfast

Host a pancake breakfast for your class. Round up picnic tables, outdoor cook stoves or skillets, and volunteers. You will need plates and utensils, juice, coffee and, of course, some maple syrup. Celebrate sug-

aring off season and Shrove Tuesday (pancake Tuesday) on the same day!

Taffy Pull

Share a pioneer tradition with your students. Find a clean patch of snow and pour hot syrup patches on the snow. The syrup will cool to form a sticky taffy which children can wrap around a craft stick and enjoy.

Tales of the Discovery of Maple Sap

There are many stories about the discovery of maple syrup. Recurring themes include the tale of a native woman who accidentally threw sweet water into her cooking pot and the native man who watched a squirrel drink the dripping sap from a maple tree. Have your group make up stories about the discovery of maple syrup and share these at the pancake breakfast.

Take a Trip

The running of the sap is one of the first signs of spring. Experience the transition of the seasons firsthand with a trip to the Sugar Bush. This outing will offer great opportunities to explore the seasons, native life, pioneers, trees and states of matter.

Seasonal Science

Science activities invite children to investigate why and how things happen. Nature offers us many opportunities to observe how things change, while collecting and interpreting data can help us hypothesize why these changes take place. Help your students learn to piece together clues and use their reasoning skills to find answers for themselves.

Slip and Slide

Activity

Use two ice cubes to discover what makes it possible for ice skates to glide over ice. Squeeze two ice cubes together. Notice that some of the ice will melt under the pressure. When this happens, the surface of the ice becomes slick and the ice cubes slide. When the pressure is released, the melted ice should refreeze, sticking the ice cubes together. Ice skates work in the same way. The pressure created by the blades causes the ice to melt, providing a slick layer of water on which the skaters glide.

Project

Collect a variety of rough and smooth flat surfaces to be used as racetracks for ice cubes. Ideas might include a piece of wood, a piece of cardboard, a cookie sheet, a plastic tray, a piece of fabric or sandpaper placed over a sturdy backing. Prop each surface to create a racing ramp and let the students take turns setting ice cubes at the top of the ramps and observing the speed with which they slide downward. Which surfaces allow faster travel? Why?

by Marie E. Cecchini

104

Sink and Float

Activity

Experiment to discover why icebergs float, and what makes them so dangerous. Use soft, wet snow to make three snowballs. Pack one hard, one fairly hard and one loosely. Float these mini icebergs in a sink or plastic tub and compare how they float.

The children will observe that the loosely packe snow floats very low, while the firmly packed snowball floats somewhat higher. Help the students to understand that the hard-packed snow has air bubbles trapped inside, and since air is lighter than water, it floats higher. The more loosely packed snowball absorbs some of the water, becomes heavier and sinks down. Icebergs are dangerous because what we see above the water level is only about one tenth of the actual mass. Variation: If you live in an area where no snow is available, float an ice cube in a clear plastic glass and discuss.

Project

Use ice and dry tempera paint or fabric dye to create color blend art. Place dry paint or fabric dye in old salt and pepper shakers. Choose two colors that will blend together to create a third, such as red and blue. Let the students sprinkle both dry colors onto a sheet of white paper; then lightly sprinkle crushed ice pieces over the colors. Observe what happens as the ice melts and the dry powder dissolves in the water.

Room and Board

Activity

February is National Bird Feeding Month. Can your students tell why? Invite the students to help make a special treat for the birds and observe how higher and lower temperatures affect the molecules of various substances, changing their consistency. You will need 1 c. cornmeal, 1 c. peanut butter, 1 c. sugar, 1 c. flour, 1 c. water and 1 c. birdseed. Combine the first five ingredients in a saucepan. Heat and stir over low to medium heat until the ingredients are melted and blended. Stir in the birdseed, then cool before handling. Press the mixture into a ball and refrigerate until firm. Place the ball into a mesh produce bag. Secure the top with string and suspend outdoors to help feed winter's feathered friends. Talk about how heating certain substances, such as the peanut butter and sugar, allowed the molecules to move faster and farther away from each other creating a looser substance. The cooler temperature of the refrigerator causes molecule movement to slow down, creating a firmer substance. How did the water affect the flour and cornmeal?

Project

Divide the students into small groups and let them use milk cartons and self-adhesive plastic paper to create homes for small winter birds, such as chickadees. Have the students cut and peel the backing from the paper and use it to cover the milk carton. Help to cut a 1" entrance hole on one side of each carton near the top. Poke drainage holes in the bottoms and ventilation holes in the sides. Poke a hole at the top, thread with wire and hang outside.

Name _____

Mr. Silly Snowman

Numbers on a snowman!
Silly as can be!
Numbers on a snowman,
Which ones do you see?

Numbers on a snowman!
See them everywhere!
On his hat, on his shoes,
Even in his hair!

Read and Match

1. How many fingers do you have?

2. How many ears do you have?

3. How many eggs in a dozen?

4. How many minutes in an hour?

5. How many hours in a day?

6. How many days in a week?

7. How many days in a year?

8. How many weeks in a year?

9. How many years in a century?

10. How many states in the USA?

11. How many nickels in a dollar?

12. How many 0s in a thousand?

by Estelle Feldman

106

TLC10299 Copyright © Teaching & Learning Company, Carthage, IL 62321-0010

Snowman Goes Shopping

In this draw and design activity, children will review coin combinations.

Snowman went shopping
On a winter day.
What will he buy?
How will he pay?

What set of coins
Will Snowman use to pay
When he is shopping
On a winter day?

Draw what he will buy.
Things that are so nice,
(Sure to keep him warm)
When there's snow and ice!

Snowman's shopping list:

hat ☐
earmuffs ☐
scarf ☐
mittens ☐
sunglasses ☐

A.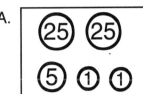

B.

C.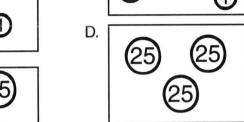

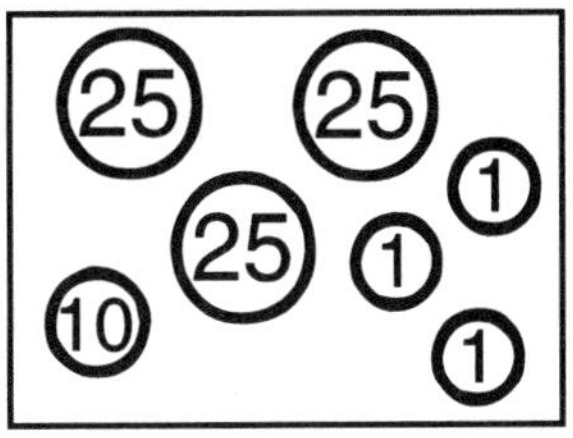

D.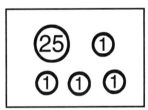

E.

Directions

Add the coins in each box and write the total amount.
What can Snowman buy for each amount?
Write the correct letter next to each thing Snowman wants to buy.

"I'll buy a tall hat.
See me near or far.
Be able to find me
Wherever you are."

Hat
$1.00
_____

(Draw the hat on the snowman's head.)

"I'll buy earmuffs.
I know they'll look fine.
I'll buy a pair
With a lovely design."

Earmuffs
$.75
_____

(Draw earmuffs on the snowman's ears. Make your own design.)

"I'll buy a scarf,
One that will keep me warm.
Who knows? There might be
Another snowstorm!"

Scarf
$.57
_____

(Draw a scarf around the snowman's neck. Make your own design.)

"Mittens! I need mittens,
One for each hand,
To keep fingers warm
No matter where I stand!"

Mittens
$.88
_____

(Draw mittens on the snowman's hands. Make your own design.)

"I'll buy sunglasses,
That's what I'll wear
When I'm standing outside
In the sunshine's glare."

Sunglasses
$.29
_____

(Draw sunglasses on the snowman's nose. Design the frame of the glasses.)

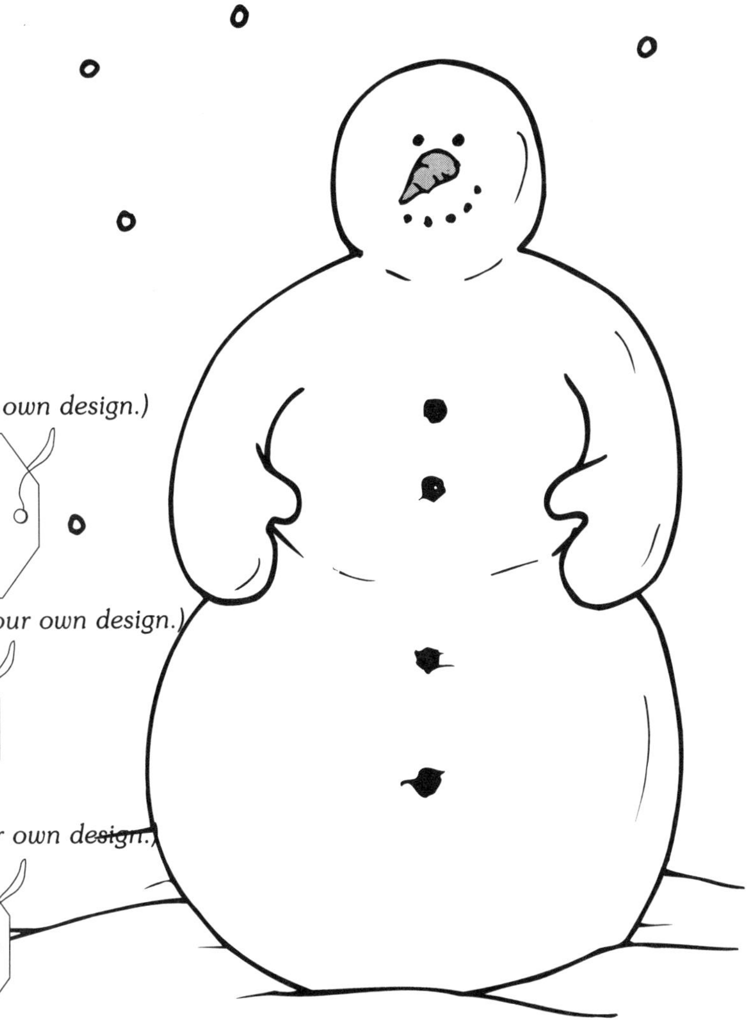

by Estelle Feldman

107

Name _____

Snowman Dress-Up

Here is a plain snowman.   Here is a snowman I have drawn.

Hat
Santa hat

cowboy

baseball cap

derby hat

I have made my snowman come alive by giving him a face. His eyes are made of buttons. His nose is a carrot. And his mouth is made of a smile of raisins. I gave him a long Santa hat and branches for arms. He has three stones in a line down his belly.

Eyes

marbles

olives

buttons

acorns

Nose

banana

pinecone

apple

carrot

Can you draw a plain snowman?

Mouth

twig

straw

raisins

red licorice

Arms

branches

brooms

Buttons Down His Middle

Can you make him come to life by choosing one thing from each list and drawing them on your plain snowman? Let's see what your snowman will look like!

stones

cherries

108   by Dawn Avery Furey

Snowflakes

Snowflakes at the window—
I run and take a peek.
They say every flake is different;
Every flake unique.

How can they all be different
When they look so all alike?
I catch them on my mittens—
Round, and wet and white.

But snowflakes are like people:
From far away it's hard to tell
That each person's quite special
When you get to know them well.

This simple project makes a great refrigerator magnet, or create a snowstorm of all your school friends for your locker. They could also be pieces for a mobile of all your friends, or punch a hole in the top and thread the snowflake onto a key chain and hang it on your book bag. You can never have too many friends around!

What You Need

> craft foam: white and royal blue
> sequins (tiny royal blue and larger ice blue)
> class pictures of your friends
> optional: magnetic tape, thread or key chain
> white glue

Let's Make It

1. Trace snowflake onto white foam and cut out carefully. Cut out center of snowflake with small sharp scissors.
2. Position class photo behind photo window; trim any part that shows outside of white snowflake.
3. Glue class photo in place at back of photo window.
4. Glue white snowflake to blue foam. Cut around blue foam, leaving about ⅛-inch showing around white.
5. Glue ice blue sequin, cupped side up, to end of each snowflake point. Then glue royal blue sequin inside each of the larger sequins.

Optional: Stick magnetic tape to the back of the snowflake. Or glue thread to the top of the snowflake to hang. If the snowflake is for a backpack, punch a hole through the top of the snowflake and thread the key chain through the hole to make a hanger.

by Jan Fields

109

Snowflake Bentley

written by Jacqueline Briggs Martin
illustrated by Mary Azarian

Introduction

Wilson Bentley marveled at what he saw around him. He was fascinated by the natural wonders that were right outside his window. He was captivated by the beauty of a single snowflake. He wondered at the different designs. He was the first to discover no two were exactly the same. His neighbors thought he was wasting his time studying snow. In Vermont, they said, "Snow is as common as dirt." But, because of Bentley's dedication, he left behind a record of his life's work, his photographs of beautiful snowflakes.

Mary Azarian won the 1999 Caldecott Medal for her hand-painted woodcuts. The medal is awarded to the illustrator of the most distinguished picture book published in the United States during the previous year.

The purpose of this unit is to acquaint students with the accomplishments of Wilson Bentley and to help them discover more about all forms of precipitation, but especially snow. Opportunities are presented to identify different types of snowflakes, kinds of moisture and a variety of clouds. You will find activities that require conducting investigations, making predictions and drawing conclusions. There are questions to answer, writing ideas to pursue and art projects to complete.

Story Summary

Jacqueline Briggs Martin traces the life of Wilson Bentley from his early childhood until his death. She tells about his love of snowflakes and how he found a way to share their beauty with others.

After you read the book, use the questions to guide thinking about the life and accomplishments of Wilson Bentley. Choose the ones that best suit the interests of your students.

Questions

1. What is snow?
2. Where does it come from?
3. What do you know about snowflakes?
4. What else would you like to find out about them?
5. What would you like to learn about someone named Snowflake Bentley?

Questions for Discussion

1. Wilson Bentley loved snow more than anything else in the world. Is there anything you feel that strongly about?
2. Why is it so difficult to collect snowflakes?
3. What words would you use to describe Willie? Explain your choices.
4. What was Willie's goal in life? What traits helped Bentley reach his goal?
5. What contributions did he make to science?
6. What questions would you like to have asked Willie?
7. In what ways are you like Wilson Bentley? In what ways are you different?

by Patricia O'Brien

110

TLC10299 Copyright © Teaching & Learning Company, Carthage, IL 62321-0010

Story-Related Activities

1. Place the information about Wilson on a time line to show his achievements.
2. Sum up Bentley's life in one sentence.
3. What would each of the following people say when they view Bentley's photographs of snowflakes?
   a. farmers from Jericho, Vermont
   b. a college professor of meteorology
   c. an artist interested in design
4. While Mary Azarian created woodcuts to illustrate the biography, you can make a monoprint using a foam plate or tray. Draw directly on the foam with a ballpoint pen or thick pencil. Cover the surface with a colored felt-tipped marking pen. Avoid getting ink in the etched lines. While the ink is still wet, cover the surface with a clean sheet of paper. Rub the back of the paper carefully with your hand to transfer the color to the paper. The lines will show white against a colored background.
5. Make a Venn diagram to show how you compare to Snowflake Bentley.

Related Literature

Read and enjoy *Snow*, a 1999 Caldecott Honor Book, written by Uri Shulevitz.

When a small boy announced the arrival of snow, skeptical adults depending on radio and television reports, said there would be no snowstorm. But the snowflakes continued falling. They twirled and whirled, turning the city into a magical fantasy land.

Suppose Wilson Bentley was in this city where the story took place when the "boy with dog" announced it was snowing. What do you think he would have said? (Note: Additional snow-related fiction is listed at the end of this unit.)

Weather

Wilson Bentley studied all types of weather and kept a record of it. He was fascinated by all forms of moisture, but he especially loved snow.

Words to Know

moisture	frost	dew	snow	sleet	evaporation
hail	drizzle	fog	rain	shower	blizzard

Did you ever wonder where rain comes from? On a sunny day water evaporates from rivers, lakes, oceans and puddles. It turns into a vapor and rises into the air. As it rises, it cools and tiny droplets form clouds. When the droplets bump together, they join to other drops. When these drops grow heavier, they fall to the ground as rain. Then on a sunny day, water evaporates and eventually clouds form and under the right conditions, rain falls again.

Clouds

Clouds come in different shapes and sizes. Some are white and fluffy, while others are dark and menacing. You can learn to "read" clouds. Meteorologists, who forecast the weather, can study the clouds and have a good idea of upcoming weather conditions. They also have other tools that help them make predictions.

Precipitation

Precipitation is any water that falls from the sky. Rain, hail, sleet and snow are different types of precipitation. There may be drizzle, showers, thunderstorms or blizzards depending on how much precipitation there is, how fast it falls and how cold the temperature is.

Warm air holds more moisture than cold air. At night, when the air cools down, moisture forms on the ground. It's called dew. If it's very cold, the dew freezes and becomes frost.

Activities

1. Fold a sheet of paper into four rectangles. Illustrate one type of precipitation in each space. Label the boxes.
2. Use the weather words listed on page 16 to complete one or more of the following activities.
   a. List the words in ABC order.
   b. Compile a glossary of weather words. Write a definition and draw a picture to describe each type of weather.
   c. Use each word in a sentence.
   d. Write a story using some of the words.
3. Learn about the different kinds of clouds.
4. Observe cloud formations in the sky. Can you tell which ones bring rain or snow?
5. For one week keep a daily record of the weather. What is the temperature at different times during the day? How much precipitation was there? Was it rain, snow or fog? Observe the sky and predict what kind of weather to expect.
6. Select a weather-related poem you like. Copy all or part of it and draw a picture to illustrate the scene.

Special Study: Snow and Snowflakes

When it is cold enough, the water droplets in the clouds become ice crystals. Like the water droplets, crystals bump against each other. They become snowflakes, beautiful six-sided works of art that fall to the ground when they are too heavy to stay aloft. Scientists have learned that how snowflakes are formed depends on the amount of moisture in the air and the temperature. Just as no two people are exactly the same, no two snowflakes are alike. They come in different shapes, depending on how they are formed. Some have star-like points. Others are like six-sided plates with a pattern within.

Activities

1. Share experiences you have had in the snow. If you live someplace where it doesn't snow, what do you think you would like to do in the snow?
2. As snow is falling, catch flakes on a dark surface. Quickly use a magnifying glass to observe the designs.
3. How would the following people define *snow*? Write a definition as you think each would describe it: scientist, farmer, Wilson Bentley, you.
4. How many different ways can you finish the following phrases? *Snow is ____. Snowflakes are ____.* Make an accordion book to display your responses.
5. Write a haiku about snow.
6. Gather pictures of winter scenes from calendars, cards and magazines. Select a picture and choose one of the following activities to complete:
   a. Put yourself in the scene and write a story about what is happening.
   b. Write a poem about something you are reminded of by the picture.
   c. Write a weather report based on what you can observe in the photo.
   d. Write a caption to identify the plants and animals.
7. If possible, take a snowy day walk or watch falling snow from a window. Later brainstorm with other members of the class to list words that describe the flakes as they flutter down. Use the words to write a cinquain, a five-line descriptive poem.
8. Follow the directions to make a snowflake. For a basic snowflake, begin with a five-inch square.
   a. Fold the paper in half diagonally in both directions.
   b. Fold the triangular shape in thirds, turning one side to the front and the other to the back.
   c. Clip across the top. Now you are ready to design a six-sided snowflake.
   d. Cut designs along each side. Open the folded paper to see what you have created. You may use copy paper, colored tissue, waxed paper or coffee filters.
9. Make a list of words using the letters in the word S N O W F L A K E.

References
Nonfiction

Branley, Franklyn. *Snow Is Falling.* New York: Thomas Y. Crowell, 1986.

Elsom, Derek. *Weather Explained: A Beginner's Guide to the Elements.* New York: Henry Holt and Company, 1997.

Farndon, John. *Weather.* New York: Dorling Kindersley, Inc., 1992.

Gibbons, Gail. *Weather Words and What They Mean.* New York: Holiday House, 1990.

Simon, Seymour. *Weather.* New York: Morrow Junior Books, 1993.

Fiction

Chapman, Cheryl. *Snow on Snow on Snow.* New York: Dial Books for Young Readers, 1994.

Honda, Tetsuya. *Wild Horse Winter.* San Francisco: Chronicle Books, 1992.

Khalsa, Dayal Kaur. *The Snow Cat.* New York: Clarkson Potter, 1992.

Martin, Jacqueline Briggs, illus. by Mary Azarian. *Snowflake Bentley.* Boston: Houghton Mifflin, 1998.

Prelutsky, Jack. *It's Snowing! It's Snowing.* New York: Greenwillow Books, 1984.

Shulevitz, Uri. *Snow.* New York: Farrar Straus Giroux, 1998.

Steig, William. *Brave Irene.* New York: Farrar Straus Giroux, 1986.

Stevenson, James. *Brrr!* New York: Greenwillow Books, 1991.

Tresselt, Alvin. *White Snow, Bright Snow.* New York: Lothrop, Lee & Shepard, 1947.

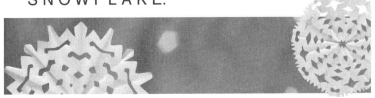

Newspaper Holiday Fun

by Marcia Jeffries

Newspapers are a source of reading material available to everyone. They are inexpensive and readily available. It really makes no difference what grade a child is in—there is a wealth of reading opportunities within the pages of the newspaper. With a little imagination, you and your students may discover dozens of projects and activities that can make learning to read an exciting part of your sharing time together. As a teacher, you can help your students feel comfortable with the newspaper. Try these activities in your classroom today!

Provide each student with a folder to keep all their holiday activities in. Let the students decorate them according to the holiday.

Activity One

Ask your students to cut out four or five headlines from the newspaper. Direct students to glue them on pages that can be placed in their holiday folders. Allow students to create their own holiday stories from the headlines and write them in their folders. You may wish to have students read or tell their stories to the class.

Activity Two

Ask students to cut out letters from newspaper headlines that spell the name of the holiday. Glue these on a page to be placed in the holiday folder. Beside each letter they write a holiday sentence that starts with that letter. Example:

Christmas comes in December.
Holly is a Christmas decoration.
Rudolph has a red nose.
I love Christmas surprises!
Santa lives at the North Pole.
Trees are decorated with colored lights.
Merry Christmas, everyone.
Angels told of the Christ child's birth.
Special gifts are wrapped in colored paper.

114

Activity Three

Have students cut out of construction paper a design to represent the holiday (like a tree for Christmas, a bunny for Easter, and so on). Students glue the construction paper cut-out to a page that can be placed in their holiday folders. Direct students to cut out things from the newspaper that are associated with the holiday and glue them onto the cut-out piece of construction paper. For instance, on the Christmas tree they could glue things like presents, reindeer, Santa, lights, candy canes, and so on.

Activity Four

Cut out several holiday words from the newspaper and ask students to place them in alphabetical order on a piece of paper that can go in their holiday folders.

Activity Five

Cut out comic strips from the newspaper. Use white-out to cover all captions. Have students glue their comic strips to pieces of paper to be put in their holiday folders. Direct students to make up holiday captions to go with their comic strips. These can be shared with the class.

Activity Six

Pick out ads from the sports page or fashion section of the newspaper and ask students to choose 10 to 20 words they know from the ad. Have them write the words on pieces of paper to be placed in the holiday folders. Then direct each student to write a holiday paragraph using the words he or she chose.

Activity Seven

Point to selected words in headlines and ask students to write a holiday rhyming word for each. Keep these lists in the holiday folder.

Holiday Creation of the Month

Work with your students to create an advertisement for a recently read holiday book. Look at several examples in old magazines or newspapers and have each student create an original advertisement for his or her favorite holiday story.

Note to the Teacher

Check to see if a local or nearby newspaper has a Newspaper in Education (NIE) program. If so, ask for a free guide to their programs.

The Magic Mittens

In a faraway land, quite a long time ago,
   Lived the poor widow Pinch with her little son, Joe.

The widow wove clothes for the rich to admire,
   While Joe gathered sticks to be sold for the fire.

When the widow fell ill, and the fields turned to
   snow,
   Then their garden was gone and their fortunes
were low.

"Dear Mother," said Joe, "Now our cupboard is bare,
And there's hardly a stick to be found anywhere!"

"I must go in the woods with my eyes on the ground,
For that's where the twigs and
   the sticks will be found."

There are beasts in the woods
   that may eat me alive,

   But I must go and try if
   we wish to survive."

   In the woods Joe found
   sticks, but he said, "This
   is dumb!
   I've just gathered a few
   and my fingers are numb!"

"If wolves come around, my
   poor toes will be chewed.
I'll just have to hope they don't
   like frozen food!"

He sniffed and he said, "Say! I think I smell smoke!
Someone close has a fire—I'll go find the bloke!"

He followed his nose to a cabin so cozy,
Where lived an old lady, all jolly and rosy.

"Come in by the fire," she said with a smile.
   "Come in and thaw out; stay and visit a while."

   "I'd give you some soup, but I can't lift the pot
   Or haul water for tea; young and strong I am not!"

   Joe lifted the pot, and fetched water outside,
   And told the old lady how hard he had tried.

   "My dear!" said the lady, "Your story is tragic.
   You're smart and you're brave . . . What you need
is some magic."

   "These mittens are magic—you'll never be cold,
   You'll gather much kindling and soon have much
gold!"

"But I do need some help in return for the mitts,
We can help one another if we just use our wits."

The mittens were soft and incredibly warm,
So that Joe wasn't chilled by the very worst storm.

He found sticks to burn and as many to sell.
He bought food and clothing; his mother got well.

At the old lady's cottage, he helped her with chores.
He hauled all the water and scrubbed all the floors.

Pretty soon, Joe was rich; he had plenty of gold,
But the springtime had come; it was no longer cold!

He gave back the mittens, all tattered and worn.

   "What is wrong?" asked the
   lady. "You look so forlorn!"

   "I'm grateful," said Joe,
   "and I know it is wrong,
   But I hate to return what
   has made me so strong."

   "Once again I'll be poor; I'll be
   weak and afraid.
   Oh, I'll still do the chores; you
   can never be paid."

   "Why, Joe!" laughed the
   lady. "You surely must
   know,
     It wasn't the mittens
     that made your wealth
     grow!"

"The work made you strong and you always were smart;
The warmth that you felt was the warmth in your
   heart!"

"Since you've brought me a pail and a pot that is
   small,
I can do my own chores; I can handle it all."

"But don't stay away; come and visit with me,
And share all the news while I make you some tea."

"I've made you more mittens. They're pretty and new.
You really don't need them—the magic's in you!"

So Joe did just fine in that faraway place,
And he always wore mittens, you know, just in case!

by M.D. Howitt

Santa, Santa!

Santa, Santa, I've been good,
Doing everything I should.
Never was I mean or bad,
Always shared the things I had.

Never pulled my sister's hair,
Gave my pets the best of care,
Made sure they were always fed,
Never ran to play instead.

At the table sat up straight,
Finished what was on my plate.
Made my bed neat every day,
Always put my toys away.

Wiped the dishes, swept the floor,
Took the garbage out the door.
Never would I push or shove.
What I gave to all was love.

Santa, Santa, can't you see?
I've been good, as good can be.
When you're down my chimney,
Santa, PLEASE remember me.

by Estelle Feldman

The Littlest Star
A Christmas Story

Once there was a tiny star
Whose twinkle was so bright.
He twinkled when the sun set low
And twinkled through the night.

Then one cold, clear Christmas Eve,
The strangest thing occurred.
Bouts of laughter in the sky
Was all that could be heard.
"Little Star, oh, Little Star,
You're making such a fuss!"
Cried the biggest of the stars,
"Your laugh's disturbing us!"

But the Little Star kept laughing
And a teardrop filled his eye,
And the sounds of giggles echoed
In the darkening Christmas sky.

"Oh really, now," one star said,
"We've got to make him cease!
A Christmas sky, as we all know,
Should be filled with love and peace!"

"He's just so loud," cried a cloud.
"Quiet please," sang the trees.
"He's bothering me," yawned the sea.
"What's wrong with that one?" asked the sun.
"He wants to be heard!" yelled a bird.
"It's been hours!" complained the flowers.

by Katie Lynn Newell

118

But the Little Star kept laughing,
And it was none too soon
That someone new offered hope.
It was the Great Big Moon.
"Sorry, stars, I think the laughter
Could possibly be my fault."

He shifted around a little bit
Then the giggling came to a halt.

"Ahhhhhh," hummed the stars above,
"Our thanks we'd like to send.
Great Big Moon, what did you do
To make that giggling end?"

The moon took a deep breath in
And let out one big sigh.
"Because it's Christmas Eve tonight,
I wanted a special sky!

I thought I'd put an extra kick
Into my moonbeams.
But I tickled your littlest star.
At least that's what it seems."

So the moon took it down a notch,
But still glowed strong and bright.
And the tiniest star just twinkled
On that peaceful, Christmas Eve night.

Santa's

Calling all teachers! Peter Rabbit is hopping by with some special Christmas activities and crafts for your youngsters in *Peter Rabbit's Christmas Activity Book* (from the original and authorized stories by Beatrix Potter, F. Warne & Co., 1999). Your class will love making "Through-the-Window" cards, mini stockings, and popcorn and cranberry strings. They will also enjoy going on Benjamin Bunny's Treasure Hunt and playing Mr. Jeremy's Fishing Game. If the children are hungry after all those activities, treat them to Cecily Parsley's Fruity Punch and Tabitha Twitchit's Toasties. Bon appetit!

Delight your class with even more appealing holiday crafts from *Rainy Days Christmas* by Denny Robson (Gloucester Press, 1992). This handy book is brimming with exciting holiday decorations and crafts that are simple to make with easy-to-find materials. If you aren't expecting snow where you live, your children can create a snowstorm in a jar or a pretty snowflake mobile. Other crafts in the book include "stained-glass" pictures, tree decorations, Christmas crackers, garlands, and gift boxes. Some other books in the Rainy Days series include: *Having a Party; Puppets; Masks and Funny Faces;* and *Kites* and *Flying Objects.*

The Mouse Before Christmas
by Michael Garland
Dutton Children's Books, 1997

A little mouse gets more than he bargains for when he stays up late on Christmas Eve to see Santa. The lucky mouse gets a thrilling worldwide ride in Santa's sleigh, zooming over such sights as the Eiffel Tower, the Leaning Tower of Pisa, the Sphinx, and the Statue of Liberty. To top if off, the little mouse gets the perfect present from Santa—a tiny hat just like Santa's!

• Be a geography whiz! Learn more about the following fascinating landmarks featured in Santa's worldwide sleigh ride. Use an encyclopedia, reference book, or the internet to help in your research. Make a picture book with information and pictures of each landmark. Locate each of the landmarks on a map or globe.

Eiffel Tower
Leaning Tower of Pisa
Sphinx
Statue of Liberty

• Grab your suitcase! If you could take a winter vacation anywhere in the world, where would you go? Draw a picture of what you would pack in your suitcase.

by Mary Ellen Switzer

Book Nook

Merry Christmas, Space Case
by James Marshall
Dial Books for Young Readers, 1986

When Buddy McGee's father announced the family would be spending Christmas at Grannie's, the boy was upset. His friend from outer space, the Thing, was planning a Christmas visit. Would his space friend be able to find him at Grannie's house? Luckily, the Thing manages to arrive at Grannie's just in time to rescue Buddy from the mischievous Goober twins. What a wonderful Christmas surprise for Buddy!

• Make a list of clues that Buddy could have left to help his space friend find Grannie's house.

• Create stick puppets for the main characters in *Merry Christmas, Space Case*. Write a script of the story and ask friends to help you give a puppet show.

• 5, 4, 3, 2, 1 . . . Blast off! Pretend you could travel in space. What places would you like to visit?

An Elf for Christmas
by Michael Garland
Dutton Children's Books, 1999

Oops! Santa's hard-working elf named Tingle accidentally gets wrapped up with a toy airplane and ends up being delivered to a little boy on Christmas Day. The clever elf has the perfect plan—he'll fly back to the North Pole in the toy plane. Will the brave elf's plan succeed?

• Put on your "thinking caps" and come up with another plan to get Tingle back to the North Pole.

• Draw a picture of your favorite part of the story.

• Make a list of all the words you can think of using the letters in *North Pole*.

Santa Mouse & the Ratdeer
by Thacher Hurd
HarperCollins, 1998

'Twas the night before Christmas and poor Santa Mouse seems to have one mishap after another. To top it off, his ratdeer—Blunder, Basher, Lousy, Loopy, Bugsy, and Twizzlebum—are in a grumpy mood. When Santa Mouse's sleigh malfunctions, he and his ratdeer crash-land into a snowbank. A little mouse named Rosie comes to their rescue with some steaming hot chocolate and warm cookies. Santa Mouse and his ratdeer are soon in better spirits and off to deliver their Christmas presents.

• You're an inventor! Design a new state-of-the-art sleigh for Santa Mouse. Draw a picture of your design and label the parts.

• Design a thank-you card that Santa could have made for Rosie to thank her for the refreshments.

• Be an author! Write a story about how you save Christmas when Santa's sleigh crash-lands.

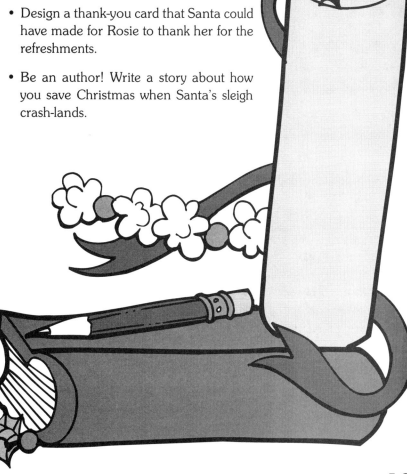

Lyle at Christmas
by Bernard Waber
Houghton Mifflin Company, 1998

That lovable crocodile Lyle is back—just in time for a hilarious Christmas adventure! While Lyle is enjoying the holiday season, his neighbor, Mr. Grumps, has the "blahs," especially when his special cat disappears. Lyle soon decides the Christmas present he wants the most is to find Mr. Grumps' missing cat. Can he find the cat in time for Christmas?

• Design a "missing" poster that Lyle might have made about Mr. Grumps' cat. Draw a picture of the cat and write a description at the bottom of the poster.

• Calling all detectives! Write a crime report about "The Case of the Missing Cat."

• Be a crocodile expert! Research the amazing crocodile. Create a trivia quiz with questions and answers about this reptile.

Sugar Snow
adapted from the Little House Books
by Laura Ingalls Wilder
illustrated by Doris Ettlinger
HarperCollins Publishers, 1998

Travel back in time to get a firsthand look at pioneer life in the winter. Meet a little girl named Laura and her loving family in the Big Woods of Wisconsin. Hear her Pa explain how "sugar snow" enables the family to enjoy rich maple syrup and tasty maple sugar cakes during the year.

• Time yourself for five minutes. See how many adjectives you can think of to describe maple syrup.

• Design a billboard to advertise Aunt Martha's Maple Syrup. Use some of the adjectives from your list in the ad.

• Draw a picture of a snowman that Laura might have made in the Big Woods of Wisconsin.

There's Music in the Air . . .
Have an old-fashioned songfest with your class, singing some of the selections in *My Little House Songbook, Adapted from the Little House Books* (HarperCollins, 1995). To add to the excitement, you may want to treat your hungry little singers to a delicious snack of pancakes topped with maple syrup after the songfest!

122

Christmas Critter Crafts

Lunch Bag Reindeer

Materials
- brown paper lunch bag
- reindeer pattern (page 41)
- glue
- 2 craft eyes
- 1 red pom-pom
- cotton
- narrow ribbon

Directions
1. Use the pattern to cut two reindeer shapes from the paper bag.
2. Place cotton between the two shapes; then glue them together around the edges.
3. Glue craft eyes on both sides of the head and a red pom-pom nose on the edge.
4. Glue a small ribbon bow to the neck of the figure on both sides.
5. Glue ribbon to the top for hanging.

Spoon Reindeer Pin or Ornament

Material
- wooden ice cream spoon
- brown paint
- tan or brown felt
- glue
- 2 craft eyes
- 1 small red pom-pom
- narrow ribbon
- pin backing (optional)

Directions
1. Paint the spoon brown and let it dry.
2. Cut two ears and two antlers from felt and glue them to the top of the spoon.
3. Glue craft eyes and a red pom-pom nose to the top of the spoon.
4. Glue a small ribbon bow to the neck of the spoon.
5. Glue the pin to the back of the spoon or glue ribbon to the top for hanging.

Spoon Snowman

Materials
- wooden ice cream spoon
- white paint
- purple felt
- glue
- 2 craft eyes
- 3 small pom-poms (1 pink, 2 purple)
- narrow ribbon
- pin backing (optional)

Directions
1. Paint the spoon white and let it dry.
2. Cut a top hat from felt and glue it on the top of the spoon.
3. Glue craft eyes and a pink pom-pom nose to the top of the spoon.
4. Glue a small ribbon bow to the neck of the spoon and two purple pom-poms for buttons underneath.
5. Glue the pin to the back of the spoon or glue ribbon to the top for hanging.

Gingerbread Boy Ornament

Materials
- brown cardboard or poster board
- gingerbread boy pattern (page 41)
- glue
- 2 craft eyes
- small pom-poms (2 blue, 1 pink)
- ribbon

Directions
1. Use the pattern to cut a gingerbread boy from cardboard or poster board.
2. Laminate the figure.
3. Glue craft eyes and a pink pom-pom nose on the face.
4. Glue on blue pom-poms for buttons.
5. Glue a small ribbon bow to the figure's neck.
6. Glue ribbon to the top for hanging.

by Christine Fischer 123

Critter Crafts
Patterns

The Christmas Wish

Julina had one wish for Christmas.
She wanted just a sled.
She wished it would be made of wood
And painted bold, bright red!

With runners made of shiny steel,
And handles on the sides
To help her stay inside her sled
On daring downhill rides.

Julina knew that hers would be
The sleekest sled around.
She'd push off high atop a hill
And glide to level ground.

This special wish for Christmas
Came true two weeks ago,
So now Julina spends her time
Wishing it would snow!

by Genevieve Petrillo

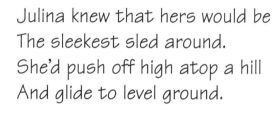

Celebrate Math

Cheer up your math sessions with some holiday shape and pattern activities.

Your students can make lovely poinsettia pictures and learn the properties of triangles by making this traditional Christmas flower. Give them the reproducible sheet and have them fill in the flower shape with triangles cut of red paper (using the triangle pattern given) or instruct them to make the flower with just the shapes (a less structured but perhaps more difficult task). Use glue to hold the shapes in place. Small yellow triangles can be added later to the center of the flower, and stem and leaves drawn with green crayon or marker.

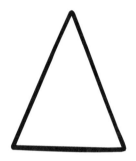

by Sheila M. Hausbeck

Photo Puzzle Wreath

Check rummage sales to find old used puzzles with pieces approximately one inch in size to use for this project.

Trace the four-inch circle below twice on sturdy cardboard and cut them both out. Set one circle aside. Cut a two-inch hole from the center of one circle, leaving a one-inch circular frame.

Using this circular frame, have your students glue puzzles pieces to the top, overlapping some of the pieces. Let the glue dry completely. Paint your frames with bright green tempera paint. Set aside to dry.

Meanwhile, take photos with an instant camera or ask students for a photo of themselves and glue it to the solid circle so the face is centered. Using a glue stick, apply glue to the back of the puzzle frame and place on top of the photo like a sandwich. Add small red sequins for colored berries and a red ribbon on top.

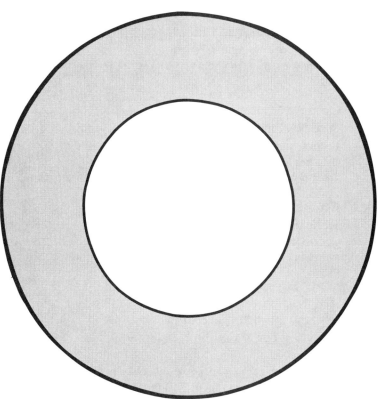

by Ann E. Scheiblin

127

The 12 Nations of Christmas

To the tune of "The Twelve Days of Christmas"

Lines from the skit may be sung or recited. Each child is dressed in a traditional costume of his or her country. The 12 countries represented are Germany, Belgium, France, Holland, England, Sweden, China, Russia, Italy, Brazil, Switzerland, and the United States of America.

A children's chorus waits backstage until the last player exits. Children in the chorus are dressed in Christmas robes. As players take center stage, they each carry a sack and place it on the floor beside them. After singing or reciting their last line, the players reach into the sacks and pull out the actual object or a picture or symbol of the object they received from the legendary gift-giver of their land.

Props (these items or pictures of them): wienerschnitzel, Belgian waffles, bottle of perfume, pair of wooden shoes, fish and chips, several plums in a dish, bottle of massage oil, Chinese restaurant menu, soup bowl and sour cream container, package of frozen lasagna, Brazil nuts, Swiss chocolate, skis, pair of in-line skates.

Child 1: On the first day of Christmas,
 Kriss Kringle gave to me
 Breaded schnitzel from Germany.
 (Reaches into sack and holds up wienerschnitzel. Player 1 exits.)

Child 2: On the second day of Christmas,
 St. Nicholas gave to me
 Waffles from Belgium to eat.
 (Reaches into sack and holds up package of waffles. Player 2 exits.)

Child 3: On the third day of Christmas,
 Pere Noel gave to me
 French perfume that's made in Paree.
 (Reaches into sack and holds up perfume bottle. Player 3 exits.)

Child 4: On the fourth day of Christmas,
 Sinter Klaas gave gifts to me—
 Shoes from Holland to wear on my feet.
 (Reaches into sack and holds up pair of wooden shoes. Player 4 exits.)

Child 5: On the fifth day of Christmas,
 Father Christmas gave to me
 Fish and chips and plum pudding rich and sweet.
 (Reaches into sack and holds up a package of fish and chips and plums in a dish. Player 5 exits.)

128   **by Jacqueline Schiff**

TLC10299 Copyright © Teaching & Learning Company, Carthage, IL 62321-00

Child 6: On the sixth day of Christmas,
Jultomten gave to me
A Swedish massage, head to feet.
(Reaches into sack and holds up a bottle of massage oil. Player 6 exits.)

Child 7: On the seventh day of Christmas,
Lan Khoong-Khoong gave to me—
Shrimp chow mein, fortune cookies, and tea.
(Reaches into sack and holds up Chinese restaurant menu or pictures of items. Player 7 exits.)

Child 8: On the eighth day of Christmas,
Babouschka gave to me
Russian beet soup with sour cream.
(Reaches into sack and holds up soup bowl and sour cream container. Player 8 exits.)

Child 9: On the ninth day of Christmas,
Befana gave to me
Lasagna from Italy.
(Reaches into sack and holds up package of lasagna. Player 9 exits.)

Child 10: On the tenth day of Christmas,
Pape Noel gave to me
Brazil nuts he plucked from a tree.
(Reaches into sack and holds up plate filled with Brazil nuts. Player 10 exits.)

Child 11: On the eleventh day of Christmas,
Christkindli gave to me
Swiss chocolate and an Alps trip to ski.
(Reaches into sack and holds up chocolate and a picture of skis. Player 11 exits.)

Child 12: On the twelfth day of Christmas,
Old Santa gave to me
In-line skates, helmet, and pads for knees.
(Reaches into sack and holds up picture of skates. Player 12 exits.)

Children's Chorus
Twelfth—U.S. skating
Eleventh—Swiss candy plus skiing
Tenth—Brazil nuts eating
Ninth—Italian pasta
Eighth—Borscht from Russia
Seventh—Chinese chow stuff
Sixth—Swedish body rub
Fifth—English things
Fourth—Dutch wood shoes
Third—French scents
Day two—Belgian food
And veal cutlet from Germany!
(Chorus exits.)

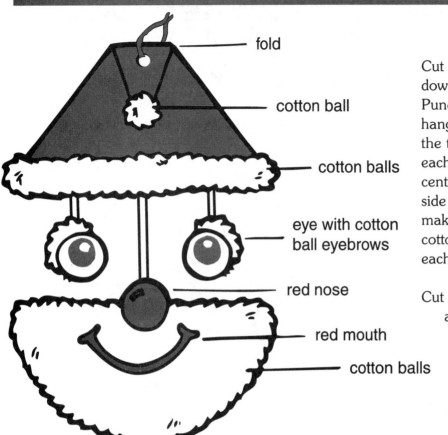

- fold
- cotton ball
- cotton balls
- eye with cotton ball eyebrows
- red nose
- red mouth
- cotton balls

Tiny Angel

Materials

white poster board
1–6" round paper doily
1 cotton ball
1 white chenille stem, cut into thirds
1–½" wood bead
1 permanent marker
glue
tape

Cut a 6" circle from poster board. Cut it in half. Form a cone and glue. Use tape to hold until glue dries. Drape the doily over the cone for the gown. Glue bead onto cone tip for head. Draw features with marker. Glue on cotton ball for hair. Glue two chenille stems for arms.

Bend the third chenille piece into a stem with a ¾"–1" loop at the top for the halo. Glue the stem up the back of the angel. Fold the second half of poster board in half. Glue the fold to the back for wings, cut side up. Add ribbon if desired.

Santa Mobile

Cut an 11" triangle from red poster board. Fold down 2" at the top point. Glue on a cotton ball. Punch a hole in the top center and attach a yarn hanger. Punch three holes along the bottom of the triangle, one in the center and one 1 ½" on each side. Attach a 5" piece of white yarn to the center hole. Attach a 3" piece of yarn in each side hole. Glue cotton balls along base of hat to make brim. Cut two 2" blue paper eyes. Glue on cotton ball eyebrows. Punch a hole in the top of each and tie on the 2" to 3" string.

Cut an 11" half-circle from poster board. Punch a hole in the center top of the straight edge. Tie to 5" string. Cut a red nose and glue it on center hole. Cut a red mouth and glue it in place. Cover rest of circle with cotton balls.

glue doily on top of poster board

glue on wooden bead

draw wings

by Sherry Timberman

Make-Your-Own Christmas Decorations

Gingerbread Border

Provide students with gingerbread men stencils (using the pattern below) to trace onto brown construction paper. Let them add eyes, buttons, and other icing details with white crayon, paint, or chalk. Staple these around the edge of a bulletin board with their arms joining to form a unique border.

by VaReane Heese

Tabletop Elves

Materials

1 frozen juice can per elf
construction paper
red, green, and white felt
glue and glue sticks
decorative objects (buttons, glitter, garland, cotton, fabric, bells,
  tiny trinkets, wiggly eyes)

Get Ready

1. Prepare construction paper strips in the appropriate sizes to cover the juice cans.
2. Display materials and at least one sample elf.
3. Encourage students to use their imaginations!

Directions

1. Children will cover the juice can by gluing construction paper around the can.
2. The open end of the can will be the bottom of the elf. This part will sit on a tabletop, mantle, or bookshelf edge.
3. Children will cut arms from felt and glue these on either side in the middle of the can.
4. Children will design, cut out, and paste felt legs to the front bottom edge of the can. Shoes may be added by gluing fabric, felt, cotton, glitter, or other decorative touches.
5. For the finishing touch, children will cut out a round face, add eyes, nose and mouth using fabrics, tagboard, and other decorations.
6. Top it all off with a hat or hair glued to the top of the can.

by Robynne Eagan

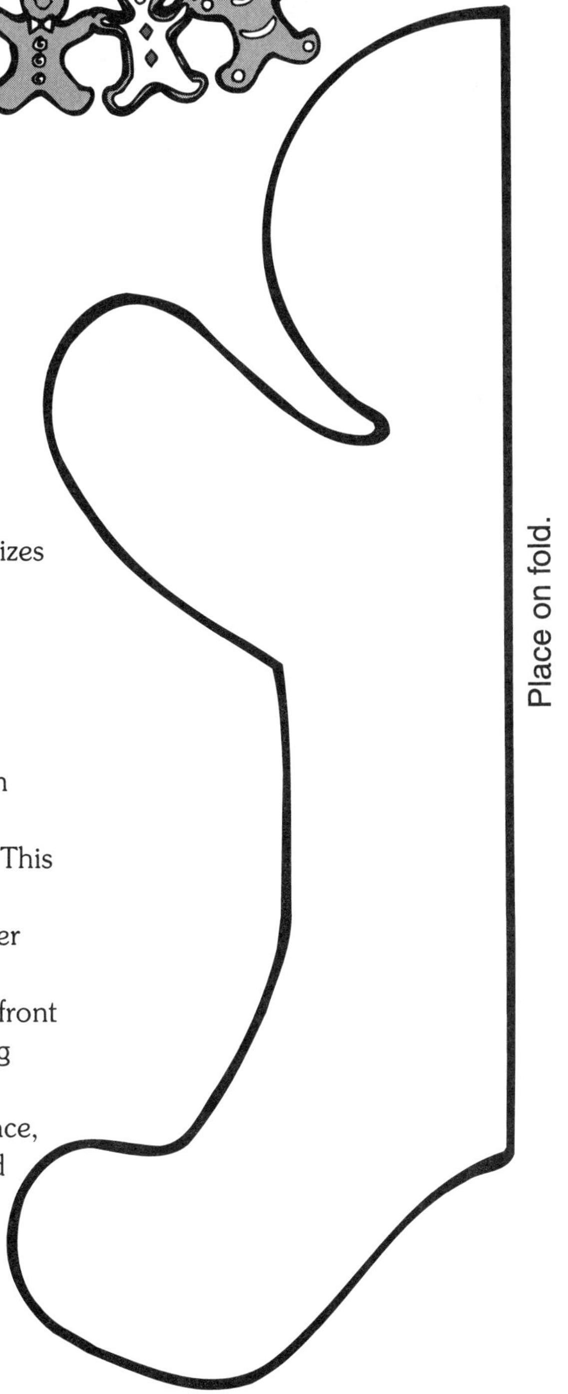

Place on fold.

Name _____

Helping Santa with Addition

Help Santa get to his sleigh. Start where Santa is and go through the boxes until you reach his sleigh.

Find the path that equals 9.
Find the path that equals 12.
Find the path that equals 15.
Find the path that equals 16.

by Carolyn R. Tomlin

TLC10299 Copyright © Teaching & Learning Company, Carthage, IL 62321-00

Christmas Greeting Puzzle

Copy the puzzle below on heavy stock. Add a message and color it with crayons or markers.
Cut out the pieces on the heavy lines and place in an envelope.
Send it to a friend or relative to put back together for a holiday message!

by Veronica Terrill

133

Name _____

Santa's Christmas Jumble

Use the picture clues below to unscramble Santa's Christmas words.

FTIG

ENEIRRED

AASNT

TRSA

LFE

WSON

OCISTGKN

KOCOEI

RCDA

by Veronica Terrill

Holiday newsletter

The multilayered holiday season offers opportunities for us to explore diversity with our children. Understanding and accepting cultural differences can be a confusing and challenging experience for them. However, by observing the similarities and differences among the people they know and their various holiday traditions, children can begin to appreciate the wonders of living in a diverse world.

Communication Station

As the holidays draw near, encourage the members of your household to think about the important part each individual plays in making the group a family. Have everyone write a list of at least five ways in which each family member contributes value to the unit. Share your thoughts with others after a holiday dinner or at another special time. This is also the perfect time of year to show your child how to properly address an envelope, and where to place the return address and postage stamp. Let your child help address family holiday greeting cards.

On the Move

Decorate the tree, a paper tree that is, with a colorful beanbag toss game. Cut a large paper bag open to lie flat. Let your child draw and color a large tree shape on the paper. Draw various shapes on the tree to represent ornaments and write a different number in each ornament. Use felt or scraps of fabric with fabric glue to make several colorful beanbags. Fill the beanbag ornaments with dried beans or rice and seal the openings with fabric glue. Allow the glue to dry, then toss the beanbags to decorate the paper tree. Let each player take turns tossing all of the beanbags and record the ornament numbers hit. Total the scores at the end of several tosses to determine the winner.

Creative Kitchen

Wassil is a traditional holiday beverage used to toast good health. Let your child help combine fruit juices with spice to create a Holiday Party Wassil to share with friends and family. Combine 1 gal. apple juice, 1 qt. orange juice, 2 c. lemon juice, 1 (16 oz.) can frozen pineapple juice (thawed), 1 c. sugar, 3 cinnamon sticks, and 2 tsp. whole cloves in a large soup pot. Stir to combine, bring to a boil, then reduce the heat to low and allow to simmer for an hour. Strain the heated beverage, removing the cinnamon sticks and cloves. Ladle the wassil into cups. Serve hot.

From the Art Cart

Add a little scented sparkle to your window decor for the holiday season. You will need citrus fruit (lemons, limes, oranges), a knife, paper towels, glitter pipe cleaners, shiny holiday curling ribbon, scissors, and string. Cut the fruit into slices about ⅜" - ½" thick and pat them dry with paper towels. Cut pipe cleaner lengths and shape into hooks. Place a hook through each fruit slice. Suspend a length of string across a sunny window and hang your fruit along the string to dry for about three days. When the fruit circles have dried, tie a shiny ribbon bow to each hook. Hang the decorations in windows, on your tree or wreath, or use them as small gifts.

by Marie E. Cecchini   135

Latkes for Santa

"Ouch!" Santa muttered, rubbing his shin. He flicked on his flashlight and saw several unpacked boxes in the middle of the room.

"Looks like somebody's moving," he said. "They don't even have a Christmas tree."

Santa picked up a green blanket from the sofa and draped it over a high-backed chair. Then he reached into his sack and pulled out a handful of colorful ribbons which he hung on the cloth. "This will make a nice tree," he said, as he put on a red and green striped ribbon.

"Who's there?" a soft voice called out.

Santa looked up and saw a young boy creeping down the steps. The boy stopped and peeked through the slats of the banister. "Santa Claus? Is that really you?"

Santa laughed. "You caught me in the act. You must be Edward Johnson."

"No, I'm Benjamin Cohen. Edward moved away and now I live here," Ben said.

Santa looked at his list. "Edward Johnson. Johnson. Hmmm. I don't have a change of address for him. And I don't have your name on this year's list."

"I didn't write to you," Ben said.

Surprised, Santa raised his eyebrows. "Why, I thought all children wrote to let me know what they want for Christmas."

"But I'm Jewish," Ben said. "We celebrate Hanukkah."

Just then, Mr. Cohen came down the stairs. "Who are you talking to, Ben?"

"It's Santa Claus."

Mrs. Cohen, walking behind her husband, pulled her blue robe around her. "Oh my," she said. "Why is Santa here?"

Santa explained that he thought the Johnson family still lived here, until Ben told him he was too late.

"Since I'm here, may I give you some gifts?" Santa asked. "I always carry a few extras— just in case I miss someone."

"No, thank you," Mrs. Cohen said. "Hanukkah is our holiday. But would you like some latkes before you go?"

"What are latkes?" Santa asked.

by Judy Wolfman

 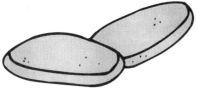 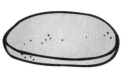 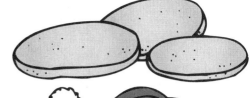

"They're potato pancakes fried in oil," Mrs. Cohen said. "And they're delicious."

Santa's eyes twinkled. "I'd be foolish not to taste at least one."

While Mrs. Cohen prepared the latkes, Santa sat in an overstuffed chair and put his feet on the footstool. "Ben, tell me about Hanukkah."

Ben sat on the floor, and told the story that happened over 2000 years ago. How the Syrians destroyed the Jewish temple in Jerusalem and ordered the Jews to worship the Greek gods. Ben told how a brave Jew named Mattathius and his five sons formed a small army to fight back.

"His oldest son, Judah, was the leader," Ben said, "and the army got bigger. They fought bravely for three years, making surprise attacks on the Syrians until the Syrian ruler, Antiochus, finally gave up." Ben smiled at the thought of the Jews beating the Syrians.

"The Jews got their temple back, but it was a mess, so they had to clean it up." Ben frowned as he pictured the overgrown weeds, altars with idols of Greek gods, and pieces of broken glass strewn about.

"When they were ready to rededicate the temple, they only had enough oil to burn for one night, so they sent a messenger to get more. The lamp was lit, and . . ." Ben paused and looked at Santa. "That's when the miracle happened."

"What miracle?" Santa asked.

"The lamp burned for eight days and nights until the new oil came. That's why we celebrate Hanukkah for eight days—so we don't forget that miracle."

"The latkes are ready," Mrs. Cohen called.

Ben led Santa into the kitchen, where he sat at the table and tasted a latke.

"Delicious!" he said. "I've never tasted anything so good."

As Santa finished one batch, Mrs. Cohen heaped another on his plate. Finally, after eating several latkes, Santa patted his stomach and said he was full.

"I usually get cookies and milk on my route," Santa said, "but I get tired of eating too many sweets. This was a welcome snack. Now, I must get back to work—there are still a lot of homes to visit before the sun comes up."

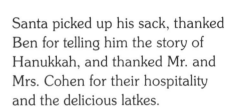

Santa picked up his sack, thanked Ben for telling him the story of Hanukkah, and thanked Mr. and Mrs. Cohen for their hospitality and the delicious latkes.

Then laying his finger at the side of his nose, Santa flew up the chimney and climbed into his sleigh.

"What a nice man," Ben said.

Mr. and Mrs. Cohen agreed. "And he certainly liked my latkes," Mrs. Cohen said. "He ate 38 of them—but who's counting?"

They went to the window and watched as Santa's sleigh lifted into the air and slowly disappeared into the starry sky. And, as he rode out of sight, they heard Santa call, "Merry Christmas and Happy Hanukkah to all, and to all a good night."

Indoor Maccabiah

If it weren't for Judah Maccabee, Jews throughout the world might not be celebrating Hanukkah. Over 2000 years ago, Judah led a small army of Jews to fight Antiochus, the Syrian king. The king ruined the Jewish temple and tried to force the Jews to worship Greek gods. After a three-year fight, the Jews beat the Syrians and were able to rebuild their temple. Judah was a strong and well-loved leader, who became known as *Judah the Maccabee,* which means "Judah the Hammer."

Show your strength, as individuals or team members, in these Olympic Games.

Follow Judah, the Leader

"It" is Judah, the leader. Everyone gets in line behind Judah, following him and doing whatever he does. Change leaders to let others have a turn.

Matzoh Ball Toss

See who can toss the matzoh ball (cotton ball) the farthest.

Burning Candles

Each child stands tall, gradually "melting." See who takes the longest time to "melt."

Latke Fling

Using paper plates, see who can fling one the farthest.

Spin the Dreidel

Find some dreidels (from Jewish members in the school or community). Spin the dreidels and see whose dreidel spins the longest.

Dreidel Spin Relay

Divide the class into two teams. Each player runs to a dreidel, spins it until they spin a gimel, then returns to his team. The first team to have all players spin a gimel wins. NOTE: All of the letters on the dreidel stand for the phrase, "a great miracle happened there."

Tug of War

Divide the class into two teams—The Maccabees and the Syrians—with each team holding on to its designated side of the rope. Each team tugs on the rope, trying to pull the other team over a center line.

Hot and Cold

One player is "it" (the messenger who goes to find the oil). "It" leaves the room, while a small jar (the oil) is hidden. "It" returns and looks for the jar. When "it" gets close, the players clap loudly. When "it" is not close, the players clap softly. When "it" finds the jar, he names someone to replace him.

Going to Jerusalem

Place chairs in two rows, back to back (one chair per child, less one). The players march around the chairs while music plays (tape or piano). When the music stops suddenly, everyone tries to sit in a chair. Whoever does not get a chair is "out," and a chair is removed. The music begins again, and the game continues until there is only one chair left. The player who sits in that chair is the winner. He or she has reached Jerusalem!

by Judy Wolfman

A Song for Kwanzaa

To the tune of "The Twelve Days of Christmas"

On the first day of Kwanzaa we sing and celebrate
Family unity.
On the second day of Kwanzaa we sing and celebrate
Learning all we can,
And family unity.
On the third day of Kwanzaa we sing and celebrate
Helping one another,
Learning all we can,
And family unity.
On the fourth day of Kwanzaa we sing and celebrate
Sharing what we have,
Helping one another,
Learning all we can,
And family unity.
On the fifth day of Kwanzaa we sing and celebrate
Purpose in our lives,
Sharing what we have,
Helping one another,
Learning what we can,
And family unity.
On the sixth day of Kwanzaa we sing and celebrate
Creativity,
Purpose in our lives,
Sharing what we have,
Helping one another,
Learning what we can,
And family unity.
On the seventh day of Kwanzaa we sing and celebrate
Faith in each other,
Creativity,
Purpose in our lives,
Sharing what we have,
Helping one another,
Learning what we can,
And family unity.

by Mary Tucker

Name _____

Kwanzaa Logic

Follow the logic clues to color some of the items on the Kwanzaa table the correct colors.

The Candles (Mishumaa Sabu)

1. The black candle is between a red one and a green one.
2. There are an equal number of red and green candles
3. The first candle on the left is red.
4. The last candle on the right is green.
5. All three red candles are lined up next to one another.

The Gifts (Zawadi)

1. The gift wrapped in green paper with a red bow is in the middle.
2. The gift wrapped in blue paper and bow is between the green wrapped gift and the one wrapped in white with a red bow.
3. The gift wrapped in yellow paper with a green bow is next to the gift wrapped in green paper.
4. The last gift is wrapped with red paper with a red bow.

by Mary Tucker

140

New Year Extravaganza!

Plan the best New Year party ever with these fun ideas for your class.

Resolution Snowstorm

Have a snowflake-making station in one area of your room where students cut out snowflakes. On a separate, smaller piece of paper record resolutions for the New Year. Give examples such as: read a new book every week, watch less TV, start a journal, make my bed, etc. Be sure to make one for yourself and talk about how, though we are all good people, we can all be better and the beginning of a new year is a good time to begin. Glue the resolutions to the snowflakes and hang them from your ceiling with thread to make a blizzard.

Time Capsule

Everyone in class should bring in some sort of box or container, perhaps a coffee can or shoe box, for a time capsule. Make a list on the chalkboard of all the types of things that could be included. Here are some examples:

- Favorite book title
- Best friends' names
- Favorite song titles (perhaps a tape)
- Current picture
- A letter to oneself about dreams for the future
- A picture of the class

Some of these things can be gathered in class with a bit of planning. For instance, you could make an instant camera available for taking pictures of students and friends. Blank cassette tapes could be brought from home to record renditions of favorite songs. As a class, decide when the capsules are to be opened. In one year? Five years?

Food

Make this as simple or as extravagant as you want. If this is a party on the first day back after break, microwave some popcorn and buy some soda. If you want better fare, include your students in the planning. Perhaps you'd like to choose a theme that goes along with a popular movie, like: **Star Wars**. Serve Luke's favorite chip dip along with Leah's favorite fruit snacks. Maybe you'd like to choose a book written the previous year and plan your food around that.

As an end to the party and the school day, read a book that is new to your students and notice when it was published. As soon as possible, bring in a new book published in the new year.

by Sheila M. Hausbeck

Time Capsule Craft

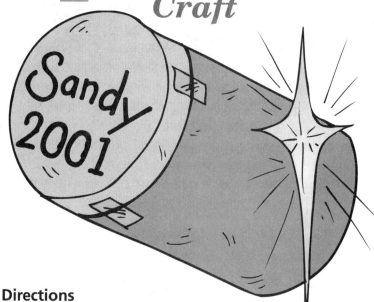

Have too many special things saved up to remember the year by? Here's how you can make a "time capsule" storage container and memory holder in one.

Materials

large empty oatmeal container (cylindrical)
aluminum foil
clear tape
marking pen
artwork, schoolwork, photos, and so on
paper and pen

Directions

1. Cut and measure a sheet of aluminum foil to cover the outside of the oatmeal container and tape in place.
2. Fill the oatmeal box with anything special you want to save.
   a. a photo of yourself (and your friends)
   b. drawings, poems, stories
   c. an audiocassette of yourself singing or speaking
   d. a videocassette of yourself showing off a talent, your room, a pet, and so on
   e. a list describing the three most important things that happened in your life that year, and predictions of three things that you would like to see happen in the future
   f. a list of your favorite music group, television show, movie, sport, and book
   g. pictures from magazines of your favorite actor, singer, and sports star
   h. a list of three popular fads, and a picture of current clothing and hairstyles
   i. anything else you want to add that tells about "you" and your life
3. Write your name, age, and the date on the lid with a marker and cover the canister. Tape lid shut.
4. Hide your "time capsule" in the back of a closet or seldom used drawer and don't open until the same date next year. Then see how you (and your life) have changed! Make a time capsule every year to have a time line of your life!

by Kelly Musselman

Holiday Sing-Alongs

by Mabel Duch

New Year Bells

To the tune of "Jingle Bells"

New Year bells,
New Year bells,
Listen, you can hear
New Year bells,
The New Year bells,
They're welcoming the year.
Now's the time,
Now's the time
For promises to keep.
Let's make our New Year promises
Before we go to sleep.

Background

Hundreds of years ago, many people believed that evil spirits could cause bad luck when a new year began, so they made lots of noise to frighten away the spirits.

This is thought to be the beginning of the custom of making noise as the new year begins with bells, horns and other instruments and noisemakers.

Another New Year custom is the making of resolutions. People like to forget the mistakes of the old year and make the new year better, so they make "resolutions" or promises to themselves to improve in some way. (For example, someone who is often late may resolve to always be on time.)

Discussion

1. What resolutions (or promises) have you made that you were able to keep? Tell us about one.

2. Is it easy to keep a resolution? What might help you keep it? (Work at keeping it one day at a time. Tell your resolution to someone who cares. You won't want to disappoint them.)

3. Your promises to yourself can also be promises to someone else. What promise or promises can you make that would make someone else happy?

New Year Promise Scrolls

Have (or help) children write promises on the following page. Let them illustrate their promises and color. Roll it up and tie with a bright ribbon.

Some promises might be "I promise to pick up my toys without being asked" or "I promise to come to dinner the first time I am called."

Older children's promises might read: "I promise to set the table every night" or "I promise to take out the trash every day" or "I promise to do my homework before watching TV."

My New Year's Promise

signature

CRAFT CORNER

Weather Words

How's the weather today? Help your students create some winter weather words that can be used throughout the season to describe conditions outside.

Let's Make It!

1. Brainstorm and make a chart listing as many winter weather words as your group can think of.
2. Allow each child to choose a word or two. Cross the words off the list once they have been selected.
3. Provide children with the materials they need to print and decorate their weather words. Black construction paper and chalk can be used for snowy pictures, cotton and white paper for clouds and so on.

New Year Numerals

Help young readers bring art and print together in this simple activity. Invite children to give print visual punch by decorating numerals with meaning-rich words and illustrations.

Materials

rectangular sheets of white paper (size optional)
black marker
coloring tools (crayons, paint, markers)

Let's Make It!

1. Have each child neatly print the numerals of the new year in the center of their page.
2. Discuss some symbols for the New Year: happy faces, bells, clocks, sand timers, calendars, Father Time, New Year's party decorations and cultural symbols specific to your group.
3. Have children decorate in, around, and on the numerals with pictures and colors that represent the New Year and their hopes, resolutions and wishes for the year to come.

by Robynne Eagan

Snow Festival Castles

Sapparo, Japan, and Quebec City, Canada, are among many cities that celebrate winter festivals. Ice castles and sculptures command attention at most winter festivals. Give students the opportunity to create their own ice sculptures to enhance a relevant winter celebration for your group.

Materials
- royal icing (see instructions on the right)
- sugar cubes
- candy glitter
- white foam plates

Royal Icing

Prepare the frosting ahead of time. This recipe will make 4 cups (1000 ml) of frosting, which should be enough for about 16 children.

Materials
- 4 egg whites
- 1 tsp. (2 ml) cream of tartar
- 7 cups (1750 ml) sifted powdered sugar
- large bowl
- electric mixer or whisk
- damp cloth

Let's Make It!

1. Beat the egg whites in a large bowl until thick and frothy.
2. Add the cream of tartar and continue beating until firm.
3. Add the powdered sugar gradually. Beat well between each addition.
4. Cover the bowl with a damp cloth so the frosting will not dry out before you are ready to use it.

Let's Makes the Castles!

1. Supply each child with a smock, a bowl of icing, a stack of sugar cubes, a white foam plate, a spoon and a blunt knife or craft stick.
2. Demonstrate how children can build with cubes and icing "mortar" on the snowy surface (the plate). Encourage children to use only as much mortar as necessary.
3. Have children plan their design before they begin creating.
4. When the basic structure has been completed, children can decorate using a variety of exciting craft materials.

146

Fiesta Lanterns

Many winter celebrations make use of light. In the Philippines each village takes part in a celebration to honor a patron saint appointed by the Catholic Church. Mass, folk dances, music, performances and feasts are part of the celebrations. Lanterns are made and hung from porches during this time. Grades 2 and 3 students can make their own lanterns with adult supervision. These lanterns will make wonderful holiday decorations or gifts.

Materials

- tin can for each student
- paper, pencil and scissors
- tape
- hammer and nails of different sizes
- wire (for the handle)
- small flashlight (optional)
- pad of folded cloth

Let's Make It!

1. Fill the can with water and let it freeze overnight.
2. Cut a piece of paper to a size that will fit nicely around the can.
3. Lay the paper flat and draw a simple design or pattern on the paper.
4. Wrap the paper around the can again and tape it in place.
5. Place the can on its side on the pad of folded fabric. Hammer the nail a little ways into the ice and remove, leaving small holes along the pattern lines.
6. When the design is compete, make two larger holes on either side of the top of the can for attaching the hanging wire.
7. Remove the paper and place the can upside down outside or in a sink until the ice melts and falls out.
8. Attach the wire handle to the lantern and place a light source inside. Wait for darkness to fall so you can appreciate the full effect.

Try This

- Winter scenes or symbols of holidays can be depicted on the can to make this craft suit particular holidays or celebrations.

Winter Scene Craft Decorations

- clear crystal marbles
- silver sequins
- white craft glue (dries to clear)
- winter scenes and figures from magazines
- glitter
- candy snowmen, mint leaves, white jelly beans, cake decorations

Try This

- Bring all of the creations together on a table covered with a white tablecloth or roll of felt snow.
- Hang white twinkle lights around the display.
- Close the classroom blinds, turn off the lights and admire the wintry spectacle.
- Invite others to your classroom to view your magnificent creations.

Christmas Cookie Center

These delicious-looking decorations will look good enough to eat!

Materials
- lightweight cardboard
- cookie trays
- cookie cutters in holiday shapes
- pencils
- scissors
- hole punch
- wool
- craft glue and thin glue brush
- cookie decorations (candy glitter, candy stars, silver balls, candy holly leaves, mini M&M's ™, colored icing)
- small spoons

Get Ready

- Set up a cookie-making center that includes cardboard, cookie trays, cookie cutter shapes, pencils, scissors, and a hole punch.
- Set up a cookie-decorating center that includes glue pots and brushes and trays or bowls of decorations with a spoon in each.
- Before you begin, make it clear to young "bakers" that these cookies and decorations are for decoration . . . not eating.

Let's Make It

1. Help children trace cookie cutters onto the cardboard.
2. Help children cut out the shapes.
3. Children should write names or initials on the back of their cookies.
4. Children will carry cookies on a cookie tray to the decorating center.
5. Have children apply glue to their cookies and then add decorations of their choice.
6. When cookies are decorated, have children carry their tray to the "oven" area where cookies will "cook" (dry).
7. When the cookies are "done" and the glue has hardened, children can attach a string that will allow them to hang their decorations.

Boxing Day Boxes

This December 26 holiday originated in Britain with the custom of giving boxes of necessary items (including food) to those who helped in the community. Today people of British origin often make Boxing Day an extension of their Christmas festivities. Some people box up their decorations and clutter from Christmas celebrations on this day. Make these crafty boxes to commemorate Boxing Day. The box can hold a gift or be a gift in itself to store special treasures, photos, jewelry, or collections.

Materials
- box with a lid
- large bowl or plastic bucket
- 1 cup flour
- 1 cup water
- 2 Tbsp. salt
- newspaper

Let's Make It!

1. Have each student bring in a box with a fitted lid. With the lid in place, children will draw a line around the box just beneath the rim of the lid.
2. Children can help to mix the flour, water, and salt in the large bowl to form a smooth paste.
3. Children will tear newspaper into thin strips.
4. Children will dip a strip in the paste, wipe the excess paste from the strip, and then carefully wrap the strip around the box below the pencil line. Strips should be smoothed to remove any bubbles of air or paste.
5. Continue in this manner until the entire box has been covered.
6. Repeat the process until the box has been covered with two or three layers.
7. A final layer of white tissue paper strips should cover the box. These strips should be applied to the wet newspaper and then smoothed with a paste-covered paintbrush.
8. Cover the outside of the lid in the same manner. Ends will be wrapped around to the inside of the box when necessary. Take care to keep the layer that wraps around as thin as possible.

148

Holiday Concentration Game

Have your class create a learning game with a group project designed to fit any holiday you choose.

Get Ready
- Purchase a deck of blank cards from an educators' store or create your own by cutting out two cards from tagboard for each child in your group.

Let's Make It!
1. Provide each child with two cards on which to draw identical holiday pictures. These pictures can be of any object related to the child's celebrations at this time of year: a menorah, a Christmas tree, a gift, a bell, a lantern, and so on.
2. Laminate the cards. You will end up with a pair of matching cards from each child in the class.
3. Store the cards in a labeled sealed plastic bag, small box or plastic container.

How to play the game of Concentration (1-4 players)
Get Ready
1. Players will turn all cards facedown on a flat surface. Cards will be shuffled around and then placed in a grid pattern without being turned over.
2. The first player will turn over two cards. If the cards are a matching pair, this player keeps the pair. If the cards do not match they are turned facedown in their original positions on the grid.
3. Each player will take his or her turn in this manner.
4. When all pairs have been discovered, each player will count their pairs. The player who collects the most matched pairs wins the game.

Try This
- Use the game as an aid to developing concentration and memory.
- Let the game act as a springboard for discussions about multicultural celebrations.
- Encourage friendships by setting up groups to play the game.
- Play this game at the class holiday party.

Decorating Gift Boxes

Materials
> dry papier-mâché covered box or plain unmarked box
> white craft glue and water
> mixing bowl and spoon
> paste or paintbrushes
> gift wrap, tissue, rice or homemade papers, stamps, magazine pictures

Get Ready
1. Collect materials for decorating boxes.
2. Have students assist in setting up decorating centers. They can help you prepare collage paste by mixing one part water to two parts craft glue. Prepare small paper pieces in a variety or uniform sizes.

Let's Decorate!
1. Children will paint a section of the box using the paintbrush and prepared collage paste.
2. Next, children will apply the decorating paper carefully, layering one piece over another. Edges should be carefully wrapped. The paper can be smoothed gently with fingers or a paintbrush.
3. When the entire box is covered, paint a thin coat of the glue mixture over it to seal the paper. This will dry to a shiny, clear coat.

Cooking with Kids

Teaching children how to balance a variety of foods for proper nutrition should be an ongoing priority, both at home and at school. Incorporating inventive snack ideas for the holidays can help. Here are some recipes you might want to try.

Crunchy Soup
January—Soup Month

Ingredients

variety of fresh vegetables (carrots, celery, onions, green beans, peppers, spinach leaves and so on)

chicken or beef broth (one cup for each child)

Have the children wash and cut the vegetables into bite-size pieces. Measure and heat the broth. Have the students place the vegetables of choice into their bowls. Pour broth over the vegetables to complete this soup.

Snowball Sweets
January—Winter

Ingredients
2 cups powdered sugar
1 cup flaked coconut
1 ¼ cup sweetened condensed milk

Measure and sift powdered sugar into a bowl. Stir in the milk; then stir in the coconut. Dust a tabletop surface with powdered sugar. Turn the coconut dough out onto the lightly powdered surface and knead. Shape portions of the mixture into small "snowballs." Place the finished sweet treats on a cookie sheet or tray and allow them to sit until firm.

Spicy Pink Drink
February—Valentine's Day

Ingredients
8 cups tomato juice
2 cups plain yogurt
½ tsp. celery seed
dash soy sauce

Place all of the above ingredients into a blender container. Cover and blend. Chill before serving.

Cherry Parfait
February—National Cherry Month

Ingredients
2 cups whipping cream
2 cans cherry pie filling
4 tsp. sugar

Beat the cream with the sugar until peaks form. Fold in the cherry pie filling until blended. Spoon the mixture into single serving cups, one for each student. Freeze until firm.

by Marie E. Cecchini

TLC10299 Copyright © Teaching & Learning Company, Carthage, IL 62321-001

Santa Salad

December—Christmas

Ingredients
tomato slices
cottage cheese
black olives, halved

carrot slices
peas

Place a tomato slice on a plate for the head. Spoon on cottage cheese for hair, a beard, and a mustache. Add olive half eyes, a carrot slice nose, and a mouth shaped of peas.

Peanut Butter Treats

December—Seasonal Holidays

Ingredients
flour
baking soda
salt
red cinnamon candies
1 (14 oz.) can sweetened condensed milk (not evaporated)

creamy peanut butter
1 egg
vanilla

Measure 1 c. peanut butter and 1 tsp. vanilla into a mixing bowl. Add the condensed milk and egg. Blend together until smooth. To this mixture, add 2 c. flour, 2 tsp. baking soda, and ½ tsp. salt. Mix well. Let the students mold a little of this dough into their favorite holiday shapes or gingerbread-like people. Press red cinnamon candy trim into the shapes and bake at 350°F for about 6-8 minutes.

Peppermint Puff Squares

December—Seasonal Holidays

Ingredients
vanilla wafers
peppermint candy
whipping cream (1 pint)

mini marshmallows
kitchen scale
self-seal plastic bags

Invite your students to experience cooking with weights and measures. Have the students place vanilla wafers and peppermint candies into two different self-seal plastic bags. Seal the bags. Use a kitchen mallet to crush both ingredients. Crush enough to make ½ lb. vanilla wafers and 1 c. peppermint candy. Combine the crushed vanilla wafers and peppermint candy; then divide the mixture into two equal portions. Spread one portion of the mixture on the bottom of a 9" x 13" baking dish. Pour the whipping cream into a bowl and beat until peaks form. Fold ½ lb. mini marshmallows into the whipped cream. Spread the marshmallow mixture over the crumb mixture in the baking dish. Sprinkle the remaining portion of the crumb mixture on top of the cream and refrigerate until firm. Cut into squares to serve on individual plates.

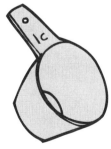

Name _____

Alphabet Soup

January is Soup Month. Here are the names of 18 different kinds of soup. Number them from 1 to 18 in alphabetical order. On the back, write the first names of everyone in your family in alphabetical order.

_____ lentil

_____ turkey

_____ fish chowder

_____ broccoli

_____ minestrone

_____ egg drop

_____ rice and chicken

_____ ham and cheese

_____ corn chowder

_____ zucchini

_____ okra

_____ noodle

_____ alphabet

_____ vegetable

_____ gumbo

_____ split pea

_____ potato

_____ duck

by Ann Richmond Fisher

POPCORN MACHINE MANIA

Calling all popcorn fans! The Popcorn Machine is piping hot with tasty ideas to celebrate Popcorn Month.

Set the stage for Popcorn Month by sharing *The Popcorn Shop* by Alice Low (Scholastic, 1993). This humorous story is about a gal named Popcorn Nell who buys a new popcorn machine. This remarkable machine works day and night until all the streets are piled high with tasty popcorn. After reading the story to your class, ask students to share ideas on what could be done with all the popcorn that filled the streets.

Captivating Commercial

Ask your budding young writers to write and give an oral presentation of a commercial for popcorn. Explain to them that their commercial should convince people to eat more popcorn because it is a tasty and healthy snack. Have a brainstorming session to discuss how to make their script appealing to the audience and what television commercials they like best and why. Encourage your youngsters to make props and visual aids for their presentation.

Corny Trivia Challenge

Create a popcorn trivia game in your classroom. Decorate a light-colored lunch bag with a popcorn theme to hold the trivia cards and label it *Corny Trivia Challenge*. Ask your students to write trivia questions (and answers) about popcorn on small cards and deposit them in the decorated bag. The children can use encyclopedias, books on the subject, or the internet to help in their research.

Here are two trivia questions to get you started:
What country grows most of the world's popcorn? (United States)
True or false? Popcorn is one of the oldest types of corn. (True)

Web Site

For some positively perfect popcorn activities and background information, click on over to www.popcorn.org. This handy web site is brimming with popcorn "surprises," such as coloring pages, worksheets, art activities, recipes, a book list, and the history of popcorn. The Popcorn Trade Association sponsors this superb web site.

BY MARY ELLEN SWITZER

POPCORN WRITING CORNER

Put your budding young writers to work creating their own special stories for Popcorn Month. Here are some poppin' good starters to get everyone in the mood:

Surprise! It's your birthday and you get a new popcorn popper. Much to your amazement, it's magic! Tell what happens next.

Is it a dream? You look out your window one day and discover a gigantic pile of rainbow-colored popcorn in your yard. Write a diary entry about your exciting day.

Congratulations! You have just finished making the biggest popcorn ball in history. Write a news story about this remarkable accomplishment.

Write a mystery called "The Case of the Missing Popcorn." Use these words in your story: *missing, window,* and *animal tracks.*

BY MARY ELLEN SWITZER

154

Name _____

POPPING IDEAS

January is popcorn month. Popcorn is a tasty treat, and it's good for you! You can eat it plain, with butter and salt, in a popcorn ball or as caramel corn. What is your favorite way to eat popcorn?

What else can you do with popcorn? Write new ways to use popcorn on the popcorn pieces.

BY ANN RICHMOND FISHER

Hatbox Hoopla

1. Try this captivating cap challenge! How many words can you make using the letters in *baseball cap*?

2. Be an inventor! Design a new hat that will keep your ears warm in winter. Draw a picture of your hat and think of a catchy name for it.

3. Write a tall tale about the tallest cowboy hat in history.

4. Congratulations! You have just won a prize in your school's Funniest Hat Contest. Draw a picture of your award-winning hat.

5. Rhyme Time! Write a list of five words that rhyme with *hat*. Now write a silly poem using the words on your list.

6. If hats could talk! Write the conversation between two cowboy hats on a hat rack.

7. Construction workers wear hard hats at construction sites. Tell why you think this is a good idea.

8. Be a detective! Write a mystery called "The Case of the Missing Hat." Use these clues in your story: *key, torn note, and flower*.

by Mary Ellen Switzer

Name _____

Hidden Picture Fun

Help! Some flowers are missing from the hats at Aunt Violet's Hat Shop.
Color all the hidden flowers you can find in the picture.

by Mary Ellen Switzer

157

Hats! Hats!

The third Friday in January is Hat Day. Read the rhyming directions and stories. Complete the rhymes with the job that is described. Cut out the hats from the bottom of the page and paste them on the correct snowmen to show the right jobs.

Snowman, snowman, tall and fat,
Carrot nose, but where's his hat?
On his head, which will he wear?
Read each rhyme; then paste it there.

Snowman 1
Crooks and robbers
Had better beware!
I am a _____.
Which hat will I wear?

Snowman 2
When I make pastries
I cover my hair.
I am a _____.
Which hat will I wear?

Snowman 3
I make you laugh
Whenever I appear.
I am a _____.
Which hat will I wear?

Snowman 4
I'm part of a team;
We always play fair.
I am a _____.
Which hat will I wear?

Snowman 5
I sit on a throne;
I rule far and near.
I am a _____.
Which hat will I wear?

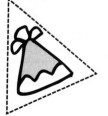

Hooray for Hobby Month!

's Hobby Month, so let's celebrate! Spark enthusiasm in your classroom for this special month with the ollowing Happy Hobby activity cards. Reproduce the cards and laminate for durability, if you wish. Have our students work on the activities during the month.

Hooray for Hobby Month! Create a picture of a billboard sign to advertise this special month.

Create a design that could be used for a special coin to commemorate your state.

Design a sports card for your favorite athlete. Include a picture and facts about the person.

A boy named Carlos is collecting rocks, when all of a sudden he spots a shiny rock. Much to his surprise . . . (Finish the story.)

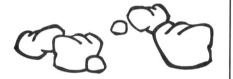

Create a word search with words pertaining to hobbies.

Conduct a mini interview with three friends or relatives. Ask them: What is your favorite hobby and why?

Make a list of six items that children might like to collect for a hobby. Put the list in alphabetical order.

Be a detective! A valuable doll has disappeared from Roxanne's collection. Write a mystery about "The Case of the Missing Doll." Draw a "missing poster" showing a picture of the doll.

Help! Jose is starting a new insect collection. Make a list of at least five insects he might like to have in his collection. Draw a picture of one of the insects.

hare a Hobby

dd pizzazz to Hobby Month by inviting guest speakers to visit your classroom to share their hobbies. uring Hobby Month, have a Happy Hobby Day and ask your students to bring in their special collections, ch as rock, shell, doll, insect, or stamp, to share with the class. Choose classroom reporters to interview e students about their collections. You may wish to submit the interviews to your school newspaper, if ou have one.

Orderly Coins

Bryce's hobby is collecting old pennies. He has set out these 10 pennies and wants to put them in order, starting with the oldest. Number them from 1 to 10 to show how he should arrange them.

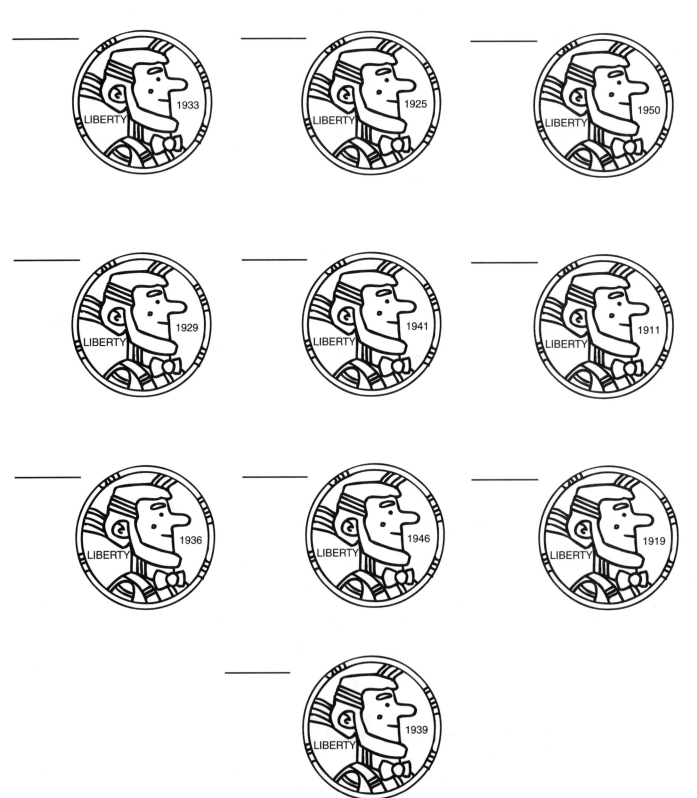

by Ann Richmond Fisher

WINTER FAMILY

Color the bear and her cubs.

Snug in her den,
Cozy and warm,
Mother bear sleeps
With two cubs, just born.

Safe from the cold,
The bears hibernate.
Until spring arrives,
They rest and they wait.

BY MARIE E. CECCHINI

Celebrating Tet

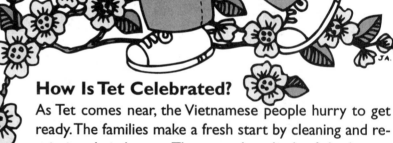

What Is Tet?

Chuc Mung Nam Moi (CHOOK MOUNG num MOOEE) means "Happy New Year" and is heard for three days as the Vietnamese celebrate their new year. This important holiday is called Tet and falls between January 21 and February 20. The Vietnamese follow the Chinese calendar, which is based on the moon. A new moon symbolizes the beginning of a new month. Tet begins on the first day of the new lunar year.

Each day of the Tet celebration has a purpose. On the first day, families gather together to await the coming of spring on the eve of their new year. They invite a favorite friend or family member to come over and be their first visitor in the morning. It is an honor to be the first Tet visitor. The second day celebrates friendship, and the third day is devoted to business. Tet is a time to pay homage to ancestors, pay off debts, and turn over a "new leaf." It is believed that what happens on Tet will be repeated during the coming year.

How Is Tet Celebrated?

As Tet comes near, the Vietnamese people hurry to get ready. The families make a fresh start by cleaning and re-painting their homes. The new, clean look of the homes matches the newness of nature and the rebirth of spring.

The color red is placed all around the home. Red is a symbol of good fortune and happiness.

Plum blossoms are another symbol of Tet. The fragrance is sweet. Vases hold branches of blossoms and are placed all over the home. The blossoms promise a new beginning as spring approaches.

Vietnamese businesses are booming this time of year. People love to give gifts on Tet. Children are given new clothes from parents and grandparents. The children also receive gifts of money presented inside small red envelopes. This is called "li xi" (leesee).

BY TANIA K. COWLING

162

New Year's cards are sent out. These cards have pictures of plum and peach blossoms, birds, firecrackers and rice cakes. The cards wish good luck and happiness for the new year.

Dragons are important to the Vietnamese people, who are called the "children of the dragon" according to legends. Children imitate dragons with dragon puppets, dances and costumes.

There are many gatherings where the community comes together. Good food such as square, filled rice cakes *banh chung* (bang-chung), egg rolls and *thit nuong* (tit-NUNG), barbecued meat on a stick are served. Firecrackers explode in very loud displays. There is festive music, dancing and poetry recited. Poetry is very important to the Vietnamese people. The poems are called *cau doi*. They are written about the people's yearning for home (the mother land of Vietnam) and family.

Activities for the Classroom

Plum Blossom Art
Take the children on a nature walk and gather twigs. Glue a twig onto construction paper. Plum blossoms can be made in one of the following ways: pink tissue paper wads, pink cotton balls, pink fingerpaints or popped popcorn coated with red or pink gelatin. Affix the blossoms alongside the twig with glue. Display these pictures in the classroom as you study this holiday.

Da-Cau
A favorite game of the Vietnamese children is called *da-cau* (dah-COW). It is traditionally played with a decorated coin; however, you can use a beanbag. Place a red beanbag on top of your foot. Kick the beanbag in the air and then try catching it again on your foot before it reaches the ground.

Vietnamese Dragon Puppet

Draw two dragons on white paper. Have the children color and decorate this traditional creature. Cut out the dragons and glue them together, placing a straw halfway inside as a handle. Attach crepe paper streamers as a tail. Red and yellow are the festive colors of Tet.

Poetry

The Vietnamese people are proud of their poetry. Compose a class poem about the mother land and Tet. You might want to use the Haiku method. The first line contains 5 syllables, the second line has 7 syllables and the third line contains 5 again. Here is one example:

Vietnam, my home
Family and friends are there
Memories to share.

Fireworks Art

Using white glue, draw lines to look like a fireworks display in the sky on black paper. Sprinkle colorful glitter over the glue. Shake off the excess.

Instead of glitter with very young children, make colorful glue by mixing drops of food coloring in the glue bottles. You can now squirt out lines of colorful glue that will dry shiny and with texture.

164

Chinese New Year
Fortune Cookie Math

Can you solve the math problem in each cookie below and find the "fortunate" answer?
Draw a line to connect the cookie to the right answer.

by Veronica Terrill

Dr. Martin Luther King, Jr. worked hard to bring people together. He wanted African Americans to have the same rights and treatment as everybody else in America. Many people disliked him for his work, and he was killed while still a young man.

How can we honor him today? Let's sing a song about treating one another the way Dr. King wanted us to.

Have children begin the song standing in a circle. As they sing, they should walk around the circle touching hands, every other child going a different direction around the circle. On the second stanza, let children clap hands with another child as in "Patty Cake." On the third stanza, have children join hands in the circle and swing hands up and down.

After children have sung the song, talk about what *tolerance* and *acceptance* are. Ask them to come up with specific things that may cause us to be prejudiced against someone else. Then discuss the importance of respecting one another and treating others the way we would like to be treated.

HAPPY BIRTHDAY, Dr. King!

How to Treat Each Other
To the tune of "Did You Ever See a Lassie?"

We should always treat each other with kindness, with kindness.
We should always treat each other with kindness and love
By helping and sharing and smiling and caring.
We should always treat each other with kindness and love.

We should always treat each other with patience, with patience.
We should always treat each other with patience and love
For we are all people and we should be equal.
We should always treat each other with patience and love.

Let's appreciate each other, each other, each other.
Let's appreciate each other the way that we are.
Each color and size should look good to our eyes.
Let's appreciate each other the way that we are.

BY MARY TUCKER

166

Splatter a Shadow on
Groundhog Day!

Join the shadow fun on February 2.

Materials
groundhog stencils (tagboard)
scissors
black paint
toothbrushes
paint smocks
heavy white paper
brown and black markers, crayons or pencil crayons

Get Ready
1. Prepare the groundhog stencils ahead of time. Photocopy the pattern on page 168 and then place the paper over heavy tagboard. Cut up the bottom of the picture and cut out the shape.
2. Set up the paint tray, brushes, stencils and other materials.
3. Prepare a sample copy to be used as a guide.

Lets Make It!
1. Part 1: Have children fold an 11" x 17" (28 x 43 cm) piece of paper in half. Have children tape the template on the top half of their page and trace the groundhog. Details can be added, including a face and color.
2. Part 2: Students will match the base of the groundhog with the painting template to make the groundhog's shadow. Children should fold the top portion of the paper and place it facedown while they create the shadow of the groundhog on the lower portion. The painting template should be taped in position. Students should dip the toothbrush into the black paint and then gently rub down the bristles with their finger or with a craft stick to splatter the paint over the template. When the space is filled with shadowy drops, the template can be carefully removed and the shadow can be left to dry.

by Robynne Eagan

168

Exercise Some Logic

Five friends each have their own favorite way of getting exercise. Use the clues to match each person to the correct activity.

Arlene	jogging
Jose	swimming
Paula	tennis
Julia	cycling
Nick	soccer

1. Paula can do her activity without a pool or any special equipment.

2. Someone whose name begins with a J likes to play soccer.

3. Nick and Julia use balls.

4. Jose doesn't know how to swim.

What is your favorite way to exercise? How can your family exercise together?

by Ann Richmond Fisher

169

Valentine

Fluffy's Valentine's Day
by Kate McMullan
illustrated by Mavis Smith
Scholastic, 1998

That cuddly, lovable guinea pig named Fluffy is back—just in time for another humorous valentine adventure! Ms. Day's class is getting ready for their Valentine's Day party and decides that Fluffy needs a bath and shampoo for the occasion. Fluffy manages to survive the ordeal, only to find there's another Valentine's Day problem. The class decides that Fluffy needs a new "friend" for the big day— a pesky guinea pig named Kiss. Will Fluffy be able to enjoy the Valentine's Day party with his new obnoxious friend?

• Home Sweet Home! Pretend that Fluffy visits your classroom for a month. Design the perfect pet home for your cuddly visitor.

• Make a list of tips for Ms. Day's class on taking good care of their pet guinea pig.

• Conduct a mini interview with five friends or relatives. Ask them: What animal is your favorite pet and why?

Put some sparkle in the valentine season with the exciting ideas in Kids' Holiday Fun by Penny Warner (Meadowbrook Press, 1994). This handy book features an array of fantastic crafts, activities, party ideas, decorations and recipes. Some of the Valentine's Day activities include Heart Bingo, Puzzle Card, Treasure Hunt and Heart Mobile.

Treat your class to more holiday projects from Valentine Fun Activity Book by Judith Stamper (Troll, 1997). Your students will love making a variety of valentine crafts using easy-to-follow directions and are sure to enjoy concocting the special valentine sundae recipe.

Need the perfect card for holidays and special occasions? Paper Tags and Cards by Florence Tempo (Millbrook Press, 1995) provides directions for some unique greeting cards, including pop-ups and 3-D. There's also a section on how to make your own paper.

by Mary Ellen Switzer

FRIEND SWEETIE WOW! MY HERO BE MINE BE HAPPY YOU R CUTE

Book Nook

A Valentine for Ms. Vanilla

by Fred Ehrlich
illustrated by Martha Gradisher
Viking, 1991

You're cordially invited to a Valentine's Day party in Ms. Vanilla's class! Join the children as they share the humorous valentine rhymes they have written and find out what giant holiday surprise the class made for their special teacher.

- Let's go on a Happy Heart Alphabet Hunt! Choose any letter from the alphabet. Go through the pages of *A Valentine for Ms. Vanilla* or any other picture book and make a list of items that begin with the letter. Happy hunting!

- Be a holiday game designer! Create a picture scavenger hunt that another child would enjoy. First select a valentine or seasonal picture book. On a blank sheet of paper, draw eight small pictures of items that are shown somewhere in the story. Challenge a classmate to find all the items on your scavenger hunt sheet in the selected book.

- Pretend that you found a magic valentine that could grant your wishes. Write a story telling what you wished for and how the wishes changed your life.

Winnie the Pooh and Valentines, Too

by Liza Alexander
illustrated by Carol C. Haantz
Scholastic, 2000

Calling all Winnie the Pooh fans! Here's a delightful new holiday story you won't want to miss! Winnie and his friends at the Hundred-Acre-Wood are worried that Christopher Robin has a new girl friend and won't have time for them anymore. When Owl suggests that Christopher Robin has been bitten by a lovebug, Winnie and friends decide to search in the forest for another lovebug to "unbite" the boy. Can the friends find a lovebug in time?

- Design a special valentine for your favorite Winnie the Pooh book character.

- Write a list of the names of the characters in *Winnie the Pooh and Valentines, Too.* Make a word game by scrambling the letters of each name on another sheet of paper. Give to a friend to unscramble.

- "V" is for *valentine*. List as many words as you can that start with the letter "V."

Pink Snow and Other Weird Weather

by Jennifer Dussling
illustrated by Heidi Petach
Grosset & Dunlap, 1998

Think pink this winter valentine season as you learn some wacky, weird weather facts. Find out why snow can sometimes look dark pink, and how frogs and fish can fall from the sky during a waterspout. Don't miss this amazing, wacky weather book!

- Create a Wacky Weather Poster to show some of the incredible weather facts that were featured in this book.

- Be a weather reporter! Write a pretend television news report about a pink snowstorm that occurred on Valentine's Day.

- Draw a picture of a snowman that you would enjoy making in the pink snow.

I Love You with All My Heart

by Noris Kern
Chronicle Books, 1998

When a friend tells a young polar bear named Polo that his mother loves him "with all her heart," the bear is puzzled. Polo decides that the best way to find out the true meaning of this perplexing phrase is to ask his Arctic friends. Each of the animals gives his own special version of how much he is loved by his mother. Finally, Polo asks his mother about her love and finds out all the many ways that she loves him.

- Write a list of the Arctic animals that are featured in this book. Put the list in alphabetical order.

- Choose your favorite Arctic animal in the story. Create a picture book about the animal with facts and pictures. Use an encyclopedia, a reference book or the internet to help in your research.

- Wish you were here! Pretend that you are a scientist on a fact-finding expedition in one of the Arctic regions. Create a picture postcard on a 4" x 6" index card. Draw an Arctic picture on one side of the card and a message telling about your latest adventure on the other.

Curious George in the Snow

based on Margret & H.A. Rey's Books
Houghton Mifflin Co., 1998

Curious George and the man with the yellow hat are off to a winter vacation on the ski slopes. You can imagine what happens when the mischievous monkey decides to "borrow" a sled during a sports competition and later slides down the mountain on a large pizza pan in the middle of a skiing event. Everyone will chuckle with glee at Curious George's unforgettable winter adventure on the slopes!

- Would you like to have Curious George as a pet? Explain your answer.

- Choose a favorite winter sport. Draw a picture of all the equipment you would need to use in this sport.

- Create a billboard picture to advertise this sport.

VALENTINE RACE

To practice some of the harder addition facts, copy the valentine number pairs, one set (pages 174-175) on red paper, one set on white paper. Laminate them, cut them out and attach a small piece of magnetic tape on the back of each. If you do not have a magnetic chalkboard, put a roll of masking tape on the back of each small valentine. You might need to use new tape each time the game is played.

How to Play

1. Before the party, draw eight large valentines on the board. Number the valentines 11 through 18.

2. Divide the class into two teams. If you have an odd number of students, ask a volunteer from the larger team to be the umpire, watching to see that no one runs and that no students start before their number is called. The umpire gets a prize no matter who wins.

3. Pass out red number pairs to one team and white number pairs to the other team. If the teams are small, give several valentines to each student.

4. Use a stopwatch or a clock with a second hand to time the teams.

5. Have each student figure out the answer to the addition problem on the valentine he or she was given. If you are just starting addition, go around the room and check to see that each one has the correct answer in mind.

by Marilyn Hein

6. The red team goes first. Call out 11. The red team students with number pairs that equal 11 walk quickly to the front of the room and put the magnetized valentines into the large valentine with the 11 at top. They move to the side of the room and return to their desks by way of the back of the room.

7. As soon as the small valentines have been stuck to the board, the teacher calls out 12. Continue until all numbers have been called.

8. When the last student places the small valentine on the board, call time and write down the time for the red team. Add one second for each student who ran or started before his or her number was called. Add one second for each answer placed in the wrong place.

9. Repeat the process for the white team. Pass out the number pairs again and repeat as many times as you wish, keeping track of times. The team with the fastest time wins. Prizes may be pencils, small erasers, candy or gum.

$$5 \atop +6$$ $$4 \atop +7$$ $$3 \atop +8$$

$$5 \atop +7$$ $$4 \atop +8$$ $$3 \atop +9$$

$$5 \atop +8$$ $$4 \atop +9$$ $$7 \atop +7$$

$$6 \atop +6$$ $$6 \atop +7$$ $$6 \atop +8$$

5
+9

7
+8

6
+9

8
+8

7
+9

8
+9

9
+9

The Valentine Virus

On February first,
Ann woke up in a tizzy.

She didn't have fever,
She didn't feel dizzy.

She hadn't a cold
And her throat wasn't sore.

But something inside her
Was screaming for more—

More love, more attention—
She just wasn't sure.

So Ann called her mom,
Hoping she'd have a cure.

"Well it sounds like the
Valentine Virus," Mom said.

"Don't worry a bit.
Now just hop out of bed."

"Will I live?" Ann inquired.
"Is it fatal . . . or worse?

"And how did I get it?
From bad food . . . or a curse?"

"Now, now," said Ann's mother,
"I'll explain it to you.

"But it's not at all like
Chicken pox or the flu!

"The doctor's quite useless,
And they don't make a pill.

"But I do know, my dear,
Why you're feeling so ill.

"Valentine's Day is soon
And the hearts are all out.

" 'In store windows, on TV;
Why they practically shout,

" 'Who loves you?' 'Who cares?'
'Whom do you admire?'

" 'Is your heart all aglow
With a passionate fire?'

" 'Do you yearn? Are you yearned for?'
" 'What cards will you buy?'

" 'Will someone send chocolates?'
And if not, then why?'

" 'Will your friends send you cards?'
And if so, how many?'

"And how will you feel
If you never get any?' "

"Yes, yes!" Ann agreed
"It all sounds quite perverse.

by Rachel Karff Weissenstein

176

Quick, tell me the cure,
Before I get any worse!"

"The cure," said her mom,
Is the simplest thing.

It will make your heart soar,
And your spirit will sing!

The 'Look Who Loves Me' necklace
Is the best remedy.

The virus will vanish
And it's even pain-free!

We'll make it, one day
At a time," said her mother,

And you'll soon have a necklace
Unlike any other!

Each day we'll add one heart
With one special name

Of someone who loves you.
No two hearts the same!

By Valentine's Day,
You'll have quite a collection

Of hearts on a string
Symbolizing affection.

You can count them, and touch
them,
And they'll always remind you

Of all of the people
Who are standing behind you.

"'You go, girl!' they'll shout.
'We love you! We do!'

"'On Valentine's, New Year's,
And April Fools', too!'

"'On each day that is special,
And each day that is plain'

"'You are loved and admired
From New Jersey to Spain!'

"'So each day remember . . .
And don't ever forget

"That your necklace keeps growing.
It hasn't stopped yet!

"Your 'Look Who Loves Me' necklace
Will only grow longer

"As your love for yourself
Gets stronger and stronger!"

On February 14th,
Ann woke up in a hurry.

Her heart was racing,
But from joy, not from worry!

She put on her necklace
And jumped out of bed.

She picked out a red dress
And a bow for her head.

Today is the day
To declare it out loud!

"Look at me! Look who loves me!"
Ann was feeling so proud!

"And look who I like,
Who I love and admire!

"I can shout from the rooftops!
I can sing in the choir!

"You and you . . . Oh, and you!
Happy Valentine's Day!

"I've got such love to spare,
I'll just give some away!"

So, Ann raced to school
With her bag overflowing

Full of valentines to share
And a heart that's still growing!

Directions for Making the "Look Who Loves Me" Necklace
Supplies

pink, red and white heavyweight paper
red or pink plastic lanyard string
assorted beads
permanent black marker
scissors
hole punch
heart-shaped cookie cutter
pencil

Directions
1. Trace five to ten hearts onto the paper, using the cookie cutter as your guide.
2. Cut out the hearts and punch a small hole in the center of each heart near the top.
3. Write the name of someone who loves you on each heart (write the same name on both sides).
4. String the hearts on the lanyard, putting one or two beads in between each heart.
5. Now tie it into a necklace and wear it proudly! Touch and count and remember those hearts (and the love they represent) whenever you feel scared or sad or lonely.

Pop-Up Heart Card

Materials

one 8½" x 11" sheet of scrapbooking
   or computer paper
floral paper bag
white place mat size doily
glue stick, transparent tape
pencil and eraser
scissors
eraser
colored pens, pencils or crayons

Directions

1. Fold an 8½" x 11" sheet of paper into fourths.

2. Open the sheet so the open folds are facing up. Trace the half heart pattern in pencil on the fold with the top of the heart pattern ¾" from the top of your paper.

3. Decorate the front of the card with scraps from the floral paper bag. Be creative. Cut and glue the designs on the front of the card, leaving room for your message.

4. Write a message in the space you left, such as "Be My Valentine."

5. Open the card. Fold it the long way with the traced heart showing. Starting at the top of the heart, cut on the line you traced. Be sure to leave the heart attached at the bottom. Put transparent tape at the base of the heart on the back of the card, just below your cuts. Carefully erase your pencil line.

6. Decorate the inside of the card with a heart cut from the paper bag scraps. Make it ¼" bigger than the pop-up heart. Glue it to the front of the pop-up heart. Write your message inside and sign your name. Or you could use a red heart doily or an old valentine to glue onto the pop-up heart.

7. Fold the card so you see the heart inside. Pull the heart forward so it forms a parallel line with the bottom of the card. As you close the card, holding the heart parallel, press the heart flat at the base.

8. Cut the place mat doily 6¼" from the end. Fold it in half and insert it inside the card. It will stick out over the edges on the top and sides. Glue the doily in place at the corners.

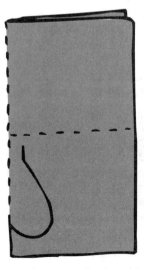

by Louise Monohon

178

Musical Fun

Celebrate National Music Month in February by
involving students in some fun musical activities.

Echo Song

Divide students into two groups and have them stand at opposite ends of the room to sing this song. The second group softly echoes what the first group sings. Let the groups take turns being the echo.

To the tune of "Are You Sleeping, Brother John?"

Group 1:   As I'm singing,
Echo: As I'm singing,
Group 1:   Loud and clear,
Echo: Loud and clear,
Group 1:   Someone else is singing.
Echo: Someone else is singing.
Group 1:   Can you hear?
Echo: Can you hear?

Group 1:   How annoying!
Echo: How annoying!
Group 1:   Go away!
Echo: Go away!
Group 1:   Go and find your own song,
Echo: Go and find your own song,
Group 1:   OK then, stay!
Echo: OK then, stay! Stay! Stay! (fading out)

Make Your Own Kind of Music

Bring a variety of materials to class for making musical instruments: covered containers of various sizes and shapes, large and small rubber bands, beads and beans, wood blocks, paper plates, metal cans, bottles, etc. Also have on hand glue, string, scissors, paper, cardboard, paper clips, stapler and staples and markers.

Let students use their creativity to make musical instruments. Explain that they don't have to limit themselves to familiar instruments, but they can invent anything that will make music of some kind.

When the instruments are done, ask students to demonstrate them. Then play a song on tape and have everyone play along on their instruments.

Name That Tune!

Take students into a room with a piano and seat them on the floor. Ask someone to play familiar tunes on the piano and let children guess what they are. The first child to recognize a tune must jump up. Watch carefully to see who gets up first. Call on that person to name the tune. If the answer is correct, that person gets a point. If the answer is incorrect, all the children sit back down and another tune is played. That tune may be played again later to give students another chance. (This will keep you from the unenviable task of figuring out who stood up second, third and so on.) Make a list of tunes for the pianist to play, including the following:

"Jingle Bells"
"If You're Happy and You Know It"
"This Old Man"
"Pop Goes the Weasel"
"London Bridge Is Falling Down"
"The Star-Spangled Banner"
"Yankee Doodle"
"Bingo"
"Old MacDonald Had a Farm"
"My Country 'Tis of Thee (America)"

If a pianist is not available, tape songs on cassette before class.

by Mary Tucker

Name _____

Music, Music, Music

February is National Music Month. Look at the top picture. Then look at the second picture. Can you find eight things in the bottom picture that are not in the top one?

Honoring Black History

In the year 1976 February was officially established as Black History Month! Here's a bulletin board idea that will help your children learn about and celebrate black history. You'll need to get the following materials: black and white butcher paper, black and white construction paper, black marker, white yarn, scissors, and glue. Then follow these simple steps.

1. Cover the top fifth of the board with white butcher paper that you have cut to have a scalloped bottom edge. Cover the remaining area with black butcher paper.

2. Use black construction paper to cut out letters that say "Celebrate Black History." Staple them across the white space. (If you're short on time you, can use a black marker to write this title.)

3. Cut oval shapes from white construction paper to make balloons. On each, use a black marker to write the name of a famous African American. You may want to assign the names to the students. They can research what outstanding achievements or contributions these people have made to black history. This information can then be written on the balloons, also. Put white yarn beneath the balloon for string.

4. Cut out black and white stars and confetti pieces. Glue the black items on the white area and white items on the black area. In the end you should have a striking display that will attract attention to black history!

by Becky Radtke

Three Cheers for
Presidents' Day

Hip . . . hip . . . hooray, it's Presidents' Day. We celebrate this holiday the third Monday in February to honor two famous U.S. Presidents—George Washington and Abraham Lincoln. Get everyone in the spirit for this patriotic holiday with these motivating activities!

There's Music in the Air!

Spark enthusiasm for Presidents' Day by having a Stars and Stripes Song Fest. Brainstorm with your class and compile a list of patriotic songs that they would like to sing for the event. Some suggestions are: "Grand Old Flag," "My Country 'Tis of Thee" and "Yankee Doodle." After practicing the songs, invite another class to join you for the song fest.

Presidents' Day Trivia Time!

Have your class help make a trivia game featuring questions about George Washington and Abraham Lincoln. Give your students blank red, white and blue construction paper cards and ask them to write both the trivia question and answer on each card. They can use encyclopedias, reference books or the internet to help gather information about the two men. Decorate a plain gift bag with red, white and blue stars to hold the trivia cards. Have fun playing the trivia game during those spare minutes of the day!

Lincoln's Bow Tie Game

Have each child trace and cut out a bow tie from construction paper, using the pattern on the right. Next ask them to decorate the ties with crayons or colored pens.

Now the fun begins! Each child will be blindfolded and take turns trying to tape the bow tie to Lincoln's collar on the picture of Abe (page 184). Give prizes to the children who place the bows closest to the center of the collar.

by Mary Ellen Switzer

All-Star Presidents Fun Cards

Celebrate Presidents' Day with these cards featuring activities with a U.S. Presidents' theme.

Read *Arthur Meets the President* by Marc Brown, (Little Brown and Co.). In the story, Arthur wins the "How I Can Make America Great" essay contest. Make a list of four ways you could make America great.

Design a billboard to encourage Americans to "Celebrate Presidents' Day."

 Pretend you are President for a day. Write a "Dear Diary" entry to tell about your unforgettable day.

Make a list of all the words you can think of using the letters in ballot box.

Design a ballot box using a patriotic theme. Use red, white and blue colors in your picture.

Conduct an "All-Star Presidents Survey." Ask classmates, relatives and friends to name their favorite U.S. President. Create a graph to show the results of your survey.

Be a White House expert! Use an encyclopedia, reference book or the internet to help in your research. Make a picture book with facts and illustrations about this historical place.

"Scramble" the letters in the names of four U.S. Presidents. Give them to a friend to unscramble.

The Washington Monument was built to honor George Washington. This famous landmark is located in Washington, D.C. Make a picture puzzle of this popular monument.

The beautiful Lincoln Memorial in Washington, D.C., was built in honor of Abraham Lincoln. Find out more about this well-known landmark. Create an advertisement featuring information about this memorial.

**Abe Lincoln Picture
for Lincoln's
Bow Tie Game**

Abe Lincoln's Hat

Read the story *Abe Lincoln's Hat* by Martha Brenner (Random House) to your students. The story tells about how Abraham Lincoln would forget important papers. When Mr. Lincoln was a lawyer, his papers were very important to him. He solved his problem by putting his papers in his hat. After reading the story, let students make Mr. Lincoln's hat.

Materials Needed

black paper cup (or white paper cup and black construction paper to cover it)
circle pattern on page 186
8½" x ¾" strip of black paper
scissors
glue
stapler and staples

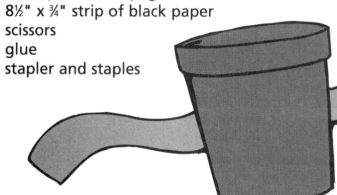

Directions

1. Give each student a black cup (or white paper cup and a piece of black construction paper to cover the cup).
2. Give each student a copy of the circle on page 186 to trace onto black construction paper and cut out. (Make sure they cut out the circle in the center, also.)
3. Have them place the black circle around the top of the cup just below the rim and staple the circle together at the ends to form the hat brim.
4. Cut an 8½" x ¾" strip from black construction paper and give it to each student or let them cut the strips themselves.
5. Have students wrap the black paper strip around the cup just above the brim and glue it in place for the hat band.

by Christine Fischer

Abe Lincoln's Hat Pattern

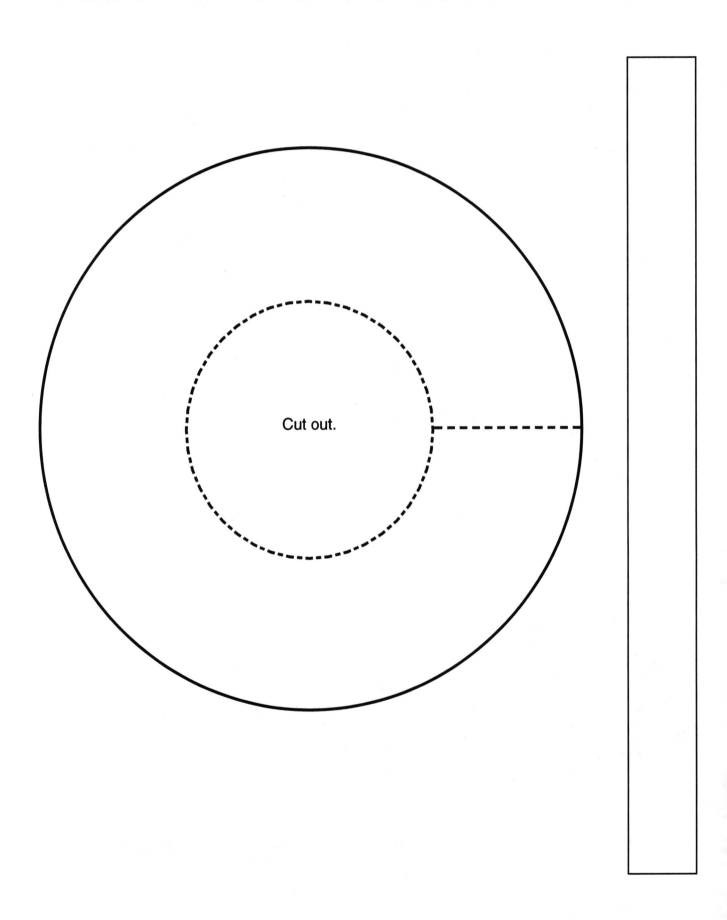

Cut out.

Washington Quiz

To celebrate George Washington's birthday, copy the following questions, cut them apart and hide them around the room. You may want to put the question slips in small envelopes with stickers of Washington on them to make them easier to find. Let students look for the questions. As soon as a student finds a question, he or she must try to find the answer. Set up a table with encyclopedias, history books and books about Washington on it for the children to use. The student may not look for another question until the answer to the first one has been written on the back of the question slip. (If you have a large class, you'll need to write additional questions so you'll have plenty.) When time is up, have students share their questions and answers about Washington. Keep track of who has the most questions and correct answers. Give that student a small prize such as cherry Lifesavers™ or some stickers.

1. George Washington was called the Father of _____.

2. What was the name of George Washington's estate?

3. After being President, Washington went to live in what state?

4. What was George Washington's wife's name?

5. How many years did Washington serve as President?

6. On what coin does Washington's face appear?

7. When was George Washington born? (month, day and year)

8. What was Washington's rank when he fought in America's War for Independence?

9. What kind of job did Washington have before he became a soldier?

10. Did George Washington come from a poor or a wealthy home?

11. Who became President after George Washington?

12. How much money was Washington paid for being commander in chief of the American forces?

13. Who was Washington's vice president?

14. How old was Washington when he died?

15. When Washington became President, what was the (temporary) U.S. capital?

by Mary Tucker

Holiday newsletter

Celebrate American Health Month in February by reminding your children of the importance of eating a healthy breakfast. Breakfast provides the body with the fuel it needs to progress through the day's work. According to the American Dietetic Association's Child Nutrition and Health Campaign, children who eat breakfast perform better in school because of increased problem-solving ability, better memory, more creativity and better verbal fluency. Children who have breakfast before they begin their day are also less likely to be absent. A good breakfast can help to fuel the fire of learning.

Simple Science

Invite your child to collect coins to commemorate Presidents' Day in February. Ask your child which coins should be collected. Experiment with the coins to learn about the surface tension (skin) of water. You will need two cups of the same size, water, pennies and quarters. First fill the cups to the brim with water. Notice that the water does not overflow. What holds it in place? Its "skin" or surface tension. Ask your child to guess how many pennies/quarters can be added to each cup before the water overflows. One at a time, carefully add pennies to one cup, quarters to the other. As your child adds coins, the surface tension of the water will stretch, higher and higher, until it breaks and the water overflows. Have your child count the coins used and compare the actual results with the estimates.

On the Move

Challenge your family to a winter game of ice hockey. Use wrapping paper tubes as hockey sticks, a foam ball or crumpled newspaper lightly taped as a puck, and a cardboard box placed on its side for a goal net. Have the players take turns guiding the puck around the "ice" then shooting for goals. Keep a tally of each person's score, or divide your group into teams and tally team scores.

Creative Kitchen

Clever snacks do not have to take all day to prepare. Invite your child to sculpt and eat warm snowpeople this winter using frozen bread dough that has been thawed, and raisins. You will also need a little flour, a cookie sheet and non-stick spray with which to coat the sheet. Sprinkle a little flour onto your working surface. Coat everyone's hands with flour. Divide the bread dough into portions and shape the portions into snowpeople. Decorate with raisins; then bake the snowpeople for 8-10 minutes at 375°F degrees. Serve warm with butter, margarine or jam.

by Marie E. Cecchini

Communication Station

This January, in honor of National Soup Month, challenge your family to create a recipe for Silly Soup, using the letters of the alphabet. Proceed through the alphabet from A to Z and have the family members take turns naming an ingredient for your soup that begins with that letter. For example, mom will add something that begins with A, dad B, brother C and sister D. Then it will be mom's turn again for E, and so on. Continue until you have listed 26 ingredients.

Mathworks

Collect empty gelatin and pudding boxes and use them to make your own Valentine Domino game. Cover each box with white or pink paper. Add a red marker line across the center of both sides of each box. Place red heart stickers of various counts above and below the red lines to serve as domino "dots." Challenge your favorite sweetheart to a game.

Poetry in Motion

February is Dental Health Month. Buy your child a new toothbrush to celebrate, and the next time your child sees the dentist for a checkup, ask the dentist to show your child the correct way to brush teeth. Share the following dental health song with your child and talk about what foods and habits help us keep our teeth looking their best. Talk about why our teeth are important to us.

Smile
To the tune of "Jingle Bells"

Brush your teeth,
Watch those sweets,
Keep cavities away.

See your dentist,
Drink your milk,
Wear a healthy smile each day.

Reading Room

Books make great valentine gifts. Share them with someone you love.

A Great Big Valentine by Lillian Hoban, HarperTrophy.
Candy Hearts by Rita Walsh, Troll.
Honest Abe by Edith Kunhardt, Greenwillow.

GUNG HAY FAT CHOY!

Happy Chinese New Year!

Good Fortune

I Love to Brush!

It's Groundhog Day!

In 200_, I resolve to:

_____

_____

_____

_____

_____

_____

_____

_____

signed

New Year's Resolution Form

Clip Art for Winter

Happy New Year!

CELEBRATE!

Have a "Cool" Winter!

Brrr!

"Peas" Be My Valentine!

A Valentine for You!

Sweetheart!

Presidents' Day

We have a dream!

Celebrate Kwanzaa!

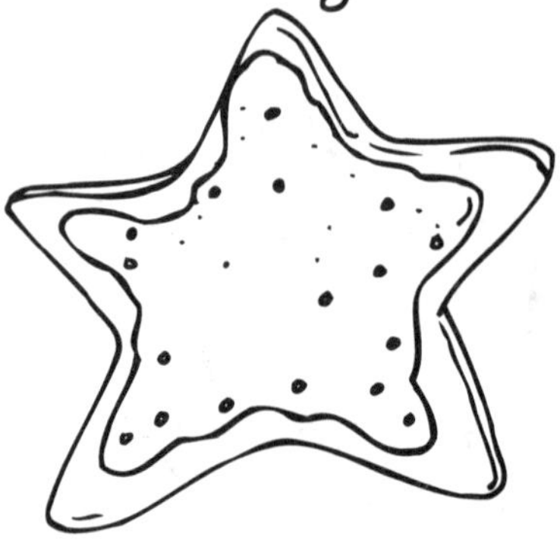

"Sealed" with Holiday Wishes for You!

May Your Holiday Be Bright!

Happy Hanukkah!

Clip Art for Winter

Tis the Season!

North Pole

Ho!
Ho!
Ho!

Merry

Christmas

"Chris Mouse"
Reading List

1. _____
2. _____
3. _____
4. _____
5. _____
6. _____
7. _____
8. _____
9. _____
10. _____

Name _____

Clip Art for Winter

Happy Holidays

In-Between Time

"Just what's so great about springtime?" Jeremy
	wanted to know.
"You can't ski or skate or go sledding, the sun has
	destroyed all the snow!

"You can't roller-skate or use skateboards—there are
	puddles wherever you go.
Your fingers freeze if you play marbles. What's good
	about spring, I don't know.

"A kite should be right for the springtime—a kite was
	disaster for me!
The wind was too strong and it blew it away, and left it
	up high in a tree!"

"You've got it all wrong," said Nathaniel. "You're thinking
	of things you can't do.
But springtime is just a between-time. Come on, and I'll
	show it to you!

"Out in the yard is a robin, he's tired
	and in need of a rest.
He flew all the way from the southland, and soon he'll
	be building a nest.

"See the fat buds on the maple? They'll open up one of
	these days,
When the time is just right for the leaflets
	to soak up the sun's golden rays.

"The plants in the garden are starting
	to push their heads out of the ground,
All of the time you were sledding, they waited for
	spring to come 'round."

"I know all that stuff about springtime," said Jeremy.
	"Sure I can see
It's fine for the robins and maples, but not much fun
	for kids just like me."

"Then why don't you go ask the robins?" Nathaniel
	asked. "Use each spring day
To get yourself ready for summer, when weather is per-
	fect for play."

"Oil up your bike and your skateboard, get busy and
	make a new kite.
Prepare in the spring in-between-time to play when the
	time is just right."

"I guess I was wrong about springtime," said Jeremy.
	"Now I can see
It's really a time to get ready, just like a plant or a
	tree.

There are games you can play in the springtime, if the
	weather is sunny and clear.
But it really is just a between-time to prepare for the
	rest of the year!"

by M.D. Howitt

198

CELEBRATE SPRING

It's Spring

Come, let's go running.
The sun is sunning.
The snow is going
and grass is growing.
It's spring!
It's spring!
It's spring!

The squirrels are whirling.
Leaves are unfurling.
Seedlings are sprouting
and children are shouting.
It's spring!
It's spring!
It's spring!

Rain is falling.
Worms are crawling.
Birds are winging
because spring is singing.
It's spring!
It's spring!
It's spring!

Hey, Hills!

Hey, hills!
I have something to say.
Winter's leaving
and melting away.
The snow white blanket
once covering you
is patched with grass
and dirt pools too.
So throw off those covers!
Let flowers grow!
Hey there, hills!
There's no more snow!

by Jennifer Jesseph

Tulip Time

Create your own tulip mania.

You will need

> empty egg cartons
> green construction paper
> scissors
> pencils
> green and yellow paint
> paintbrushes
> dirt
> empty round butter or cottage cheese container
> glue

1. Paint a pencil with green paint for a stem and let dry.

2. Paint pencil point yellow and let dry.

3. Paint round container red for tulip pot and let dry.

4. Cut egg cartons apart into separate cups. Shape the tops into petal points like a tulip.

5. Paint the egg carton sections a bright tulip color and let dry.

6. Using the scissors, make a hole in the bottom of the tulip and push the pencil point through about ¾". The point should be in the center of the tulip with the yellow part showing.

7. Cut out two green leaves for each tulip.

8. Glue leaves onto the pencil, about two to three inches from the bottom.

9. Fill painted container with dirt and plant your pencil (tulip stem) in the pot.

Your pot can hold more than one. Would you like to make more?

Centuries ago in Holland, tulip bulbs were so few that they became valuable and were traded like gold. Tulip mania had struck! Tulip exchanges were set up and as their popularity increased, people sold their land and houses just to buy one bulb. Some became rich overnight. Tulip mania lasted only a few years. As the bulbs became plentiful, they lost their value. Those left with many tulip bulbs often had no home or garden in which to plant them. Lives were ruined and the government had to step in to settle disputes.

England and France also found this beautiful flower valuable. Gardens of the wealthy grew full with many unique varieties of tulips. If you were too poor to buy a bouquet of tulips, you could have an artist paint a picture of them. Tulips have been used often in design and are found blooming on dress fabrics, curtains, pottery, and children's toys.

Today tulips can be enjoyed by all. They grow best in a cool climate from bulbs planted in the fall. The different types of tulips number into the thousands and come in many sizes and shapes. Given as a symbol of love and friendship, the tulip is as popular as the rose.

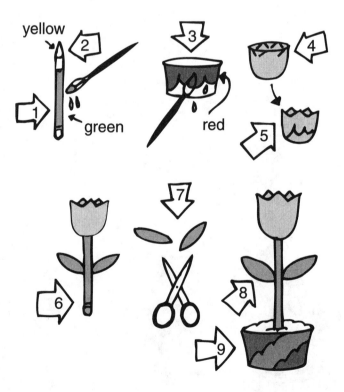

TLC10299 Copyright © Teaching & Learning Company, Carthage, IL 62321-00

Name _____

Barnyard Mothers and Babies

Draw a line from each rhyme to the baby animal it describes.
Write the name for the baby animal on the line.

Baby _____ begins to whinny,
Because its legs are long and skinny.
It wants to stand and run and play.
A nudge from mother shows the way.

Baby _____'s a furry ball,
Soft and silky, very small.
Its mother keeps it close to her.
That feels so good. Just hear it purr!

Baby _____, all round and yellow,
Such a fluffy little fellow.
Mother doesn't hear a peep
From her baby, fast asleep.

Baby _____, it's time for bed,
Wobbly legs and nodding head.
It shuts its eyes with a sleepy sigh
To its mother's "Moo-llaby."

Baby _____ falls in the mud,
Disappears with a squishy thud.
"Oink" says Mother. "Time to eat.
Here's a tasty little treat."

by Mary Prescott Moya

Name _____

Spring Things

Find each spring word in the puzzle and circle it.

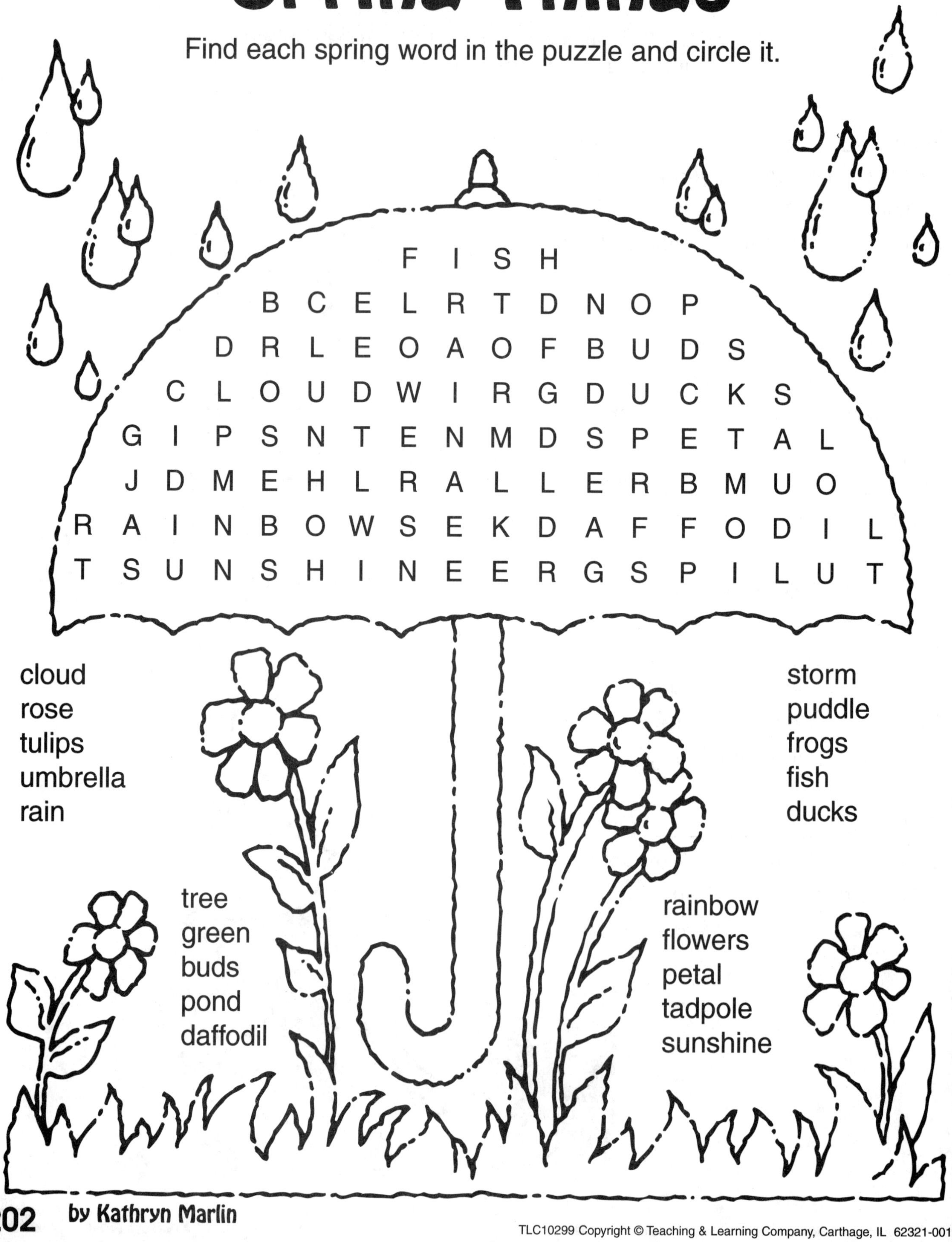

```
            F I S H
        B C E L R T D N O P
        D R L E O A O F B U D S
      C L O U D W I R G D U C K S
    G I P S N T E N M D S P E T A L
    J D M E H L R A L L E R B M U O
    R A I N B O W S E K D A F F O D I L
    T S U N S H I N E E R G S P I L U T
```

cloud
rose
tulips
umbrella
rain

tree
green
buds
pond
daffodil

storm
puddle
frogs
fish
ducks

rainbow
flowers
petal
tadpole
sunshine

by Kathryn Marlin

Windy Weather

*Take your students outside on a wonderful, warm, and windy spring day.
Enjoy the breeze and play in the wind. Let nature blow all around you.*

How Windy Is It?

Gather the students to discuss the workings of wind.

- The wind carries pollen and seeds to new places.
- Trade winds push sailing ships across the ocean.
- Wind powers windmills, which generate electricity.
- The wind helps to cool us off on a hot summer day.
- Some days are more windy than others. On April 12, 1934, three weather surveyors at an observatory on Mt. Washington in New Hampshire recorded the highest natural wind velocity ever measured on Earth. Would you believe 231 miles per hour?
- The windiest place in the world is found in Antarctica. Average wind velocity in Commonwealth Bay, King George V Coast is 70 miles per hour, reaching 200 miles per hour during storms!

Race the Wind!

*Pick a warm and windy day
to have some blustery fun.*

You Need
- stopwatch or wristwatch
- windy day
- start and finish lines

What to Do
1. Have children line up at the starting line. Note which direction the wind is blowing.
2. "On your mark, get set, GO!" Have the children race to the finish line. Time the fastest child or randomly choose various children to time.
3. Turn the race around. Have children line up at the finish line and race in the other direction.
4. Compare the results.

Discuss
- Why did it take longer to run into the wind? Was it easier or harder to run with the wind at your back? Did you need to use more energy to run the same distance?

- Air is always on the move. When air moves, it moves other things. What kinds of things do you think are moved by the air?

by Robynne Eagan 203

Let's Go Fly a Kite

What could be better on a windy day than flying a kite?

A Bit of History

- Some experts believe the craft of kite flying started in China over 2000 years ago. Kites were used in battle by armies in an effort to scare the enemies. These painted kites hummed and shrieked as they flew overhead.

- It is thought that kites were introduced to Japan between the sixth to eighth centuries by China and Korea. The early Japanese kites were called "paper hawks" and were primarily flown for religious purposes. The basic rectangle of the Chinese kite took on many forms such as cranes, dragons, fish, and turtles. Some were thought to bring good fortune, while others frightened away evil spirits.

- In the 15th century, Leonardo da Vinci developed a method for spanning a gorge with the help of a kite. Later, in the 1850s, his method was used at Niagara Falls to make possible the construction of one of the first large suspension bridges.

- Benjamin Franklin, in June 1752, flew a kite in a rainstorm in order to prove that lightning had the same properties as the electricity that was being generated in the laboratories. When lightning struck his drenched kite, fiery streaks sparked around the key, which was attached to the line. He had proven his theory!

- Years of kite flying led the Wright brothers to the invention of the airplane in 1899.

Kites are *aerodynes* and they overcome the pull of gravity and stay aloft by the force of the wind. This aerodynamic principle is called "lift." For a kite to fly, the combined lifting forces must be greater than the weight of the kite. When the wind dies, so does the kite.

Visit the National Kite Month web page at
http://www.KiteTrade.org/NationalKiteMonth/

Kite flyers have to be careful of a few things.

1. Never fly a kite in a storm or if there is danger of lightning.
2. Never fly a kite near electrical wires or transmission lines.
3. Never fly a kite near an airport.

Make Your Own Wind

Mimic nature by making your own wind.

Paper Fan

You Need

- paper
- markers or crayons
- stickers (optional)

What to Do

1. Decorate the paper using the markers and stickers.
2. Fold the paper in accordion fashion.
3. Attach tape to the bottom part of the folded paper.
4. Gently spread open the paper.

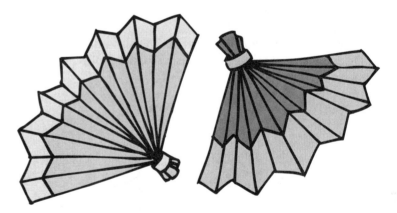

Paper Clip Yacht

Make a lot of these tiny yachts and sail them in a puddle or wading pool.

You Need

- paper clips
- white paper
- crayons or pencil crayons

What to Do

1. Bend up the inner curved end of a paper clip so that it stands straight and forms a "J" shape.
2. Cut out squares of paper, no taller than the top of the "J" to make little sails. Color them; then slip them into the paper clip.
3. Using your own wind power, blow your tiny yachts across the water. Happy sailing!

204

Blow the Cup Race

Set up the game area for as many teams as you would like; then put the students on teams and get ready as they make their own wind.

You Need
- cone-shaped paper cup for each team
- string (approximately 5 m (15 ft.) long for each team)

What to Do
1. Pull the string through the bottom of the paper cup. Tie the sting to something stationary such as a piece of furniture, doorknob, or nail so that it is stretched tight.
2. Line up the teams, behind each string, with the open end of the paper cup facing the students.
3. At the start signal, have the first student start blowing into the paper cup, moving along with it as it is blown along the string. When the cup reaches the other end of the string, have the student push it back, by hand, for the next student to blow. The first team to finish wins, and it could be said that they have the most hot air!

Stay Up, Feather

You Need
- feather for each group or for each student
- stopwatch or a watch with a second hand

What to Do
1. Divide the students into groups and have them hold hands in a circle. One student per group will be the leader.
2. Have the leader throw the feather up in the air.
3. Just by blowing, ask each team to try to keep their feather up in the air the longest.
4. Have the leaders time their own group.
5. The team that keeps the feather up the longest wins!
6. Have the students take turns being the leader.
7. This game can be played individually as

well.

Let's Make a Paper Airplane

You Need
- 8½" x 11" (21 x 27 cm) paper

What to Do
1. Fold the sheet of paper in half lengthwise.
2. Fold the two front corners down toward the inside of the plane. Help the students ensure the edge of the paper meets the fold.
3. Next, fold down the sides again, this time making the edges of the fold meet each other in the center.
4. Finally, fold the sides in again as shown, and the airplane is ready for flying.

Let's Play
Have the children bring their paper airplanes outside to enjoy another windy adventure.

You Need
- paper airplane
- windy day
- measuring tape

What to Do
1. Have the children bring their paper airplanes outside.
2. Have each child throw their airplane into the wind.
3. Measure how far it has traveled.
4. Throw the airplane again, this time with the wind behind it. Compare these results.

Discuss
- A commercial airplane will reach its destination more quickly if there is a strong tail wind. What are the benefits of a strong wind? When is a strong wind a disadvantage?

- Strong winds can become storms. A hurricane is the biggest and most powerful kind of storm. Hurricanes are circular and vary in size with wind speeds of 125 mph (200 km/h) and diameters of 400 miles (650 km).They can last up to 10 days.

- Tornadoes are the most violent of all windstorms. Tornadoes are smaller than hurricanes, but their winds are more powerful. A tornado can be no wider than a house, but it can cause buildings to explode and cars to fly through the air.

KiTe BookMark

*Children will enjoy using their coloring and
knot tying skills to make this project.
The yarn tail on their kite will hang out of
the book to mark their place.*

Materials

    diamond-shaped pattern at the right
    white construction paper
    scissors
    markers
    yarn in a variety of colors
        (4" piece, five 1" pieces)

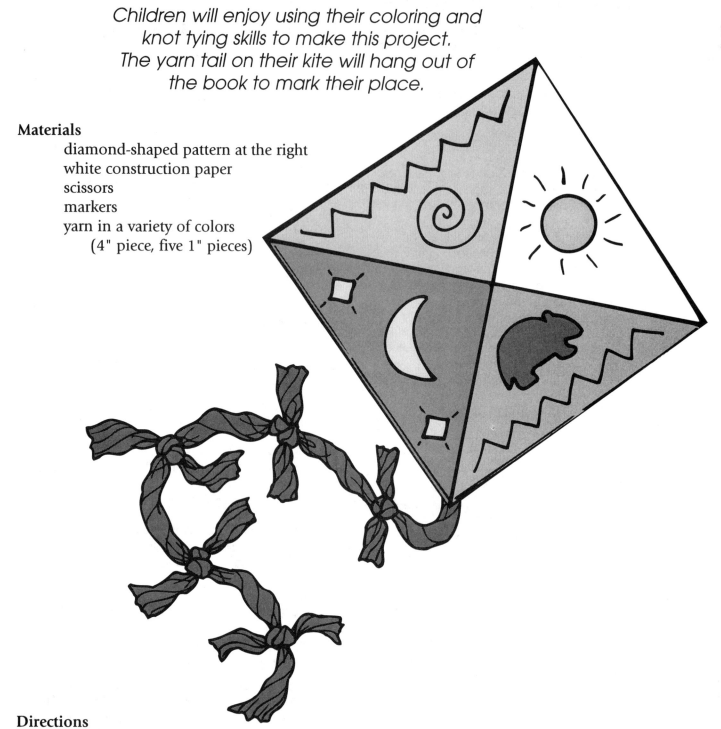

Directions

1. Trace the diamond shape onto white construction paper.
2. Cut out the shape.
3. Divide the diamond into fourths and color each section. Make each section different. Repeat on the other side of the diamond shape.
4. Glue a 4" yarn tail on the bottom point of the kite.
5. Tie five 1" pieces of yarn along the tail. Fly the kite bookmark in a book to keep your place.

by Carol Ann Bloom

206

It's Raining Cats and Dogs!

When it's raining cats and dogs,
The rain's coming down very hard.
So don't think when you look outside
There'll be cats and dogs in your yard!

But what would happen if someday
When there's a rainstorm in your town,
Instead of raindrops falling,
Cats and dogs came tumbling down?

Yes, cats and dogs have landed!
There's not a space left on the ground!
With fluffy tails and floppy ears,
They're scampering all around!

"It's raining cats and dogs!" you shout.
But if friends shake their heads in doubt,
Invite them all to come and get
A furry, playful, animal pet!

by Estelle Feldman

207

Rainy Day Blues

Outdoors, outside
Why, oh why does the sun have to hide?

Indoors, inside
I'm going to search far and wide.

Upstairs, downstairs
Till I find a way to scare—

Away my rainy day blues.

Musical Sunshine Game

Capture some sunshine in this sunny version of musical chairs.

Object of the game: Capture the sun by being the last person standing at the end of the game.

Materials
- music
- yellow construction paper
- tape

Directions
Cut sun shapes out of construction paper. (You will need one less sun than the number of participants.) Tape the sun shapes on the floor in a circle. When the music starts, everybody walks around the circle on the suns. Whoever is not standing on a sun when the music stops is out. Remove a sun and repeat until only one person is left standing.

Sunny Yummies

Ingredients
1 cup peanut butter
2 tablespoons honey
⅔ cup nonfat dry milk powder
¼ cup toasted wheat germ
chocolate syrup
pretzel sticks

Directions
1. Use a spoon to mix peanut butter and honey together in a small bowl.
2. Stir in the dry milk powder and wheat germ till well blended.
3. Lay waxed paper on a baking sheet.
4. Using about a tablespoon at a time, shape the peanut butter mixture into circles and flatten them onto waxed paper.
5. Dip a toothpick in chocolate syrup to decorate the suns with eyes and big smiles.
6. Press pretzel sticks around the sides to form rays of the sun.
7. Chill in refrigerator at least 30 minutes. Makes about 2 dozen. Eat and enjoy. (Sunglasses optional.)

Cloud Attack

Get rid of the thunderclouds before you're drenched.

Object of the game: Toss back the thunderclouds as fast as you can. The side with the fewest remaining clouds at the end will win.

Materials
- timer
- several sheets of white paper
- masking tape

Directions
1. Crumple paper into 50 or so balls (thunderclouds).
2. Place masking tape down the center of the room.
3. Players divide up evenly and go to opposite sides of room.
4. Pass out an equal number of thunderclouds to each group.
5. Set the timer for two minutes and let the attack begin.
6. Count the number of thunderclouds on each side. The smallest number wins.
7. "Dry off" and play again.

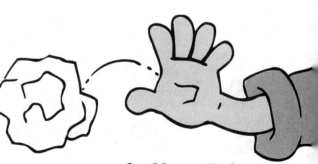

by Nancy Ralston

TLC10299 Copyright © Teaching & Learning Company, Carthage, IL 62321-001

Name ______________________________

Rainy, Rainy Day Fun!

Here is something you can do,
for rainy, rainy day fun.

Part of a word is missing—
look below and find which one.

Write the word, color the pictures.
Have rainy, rainy day fun!

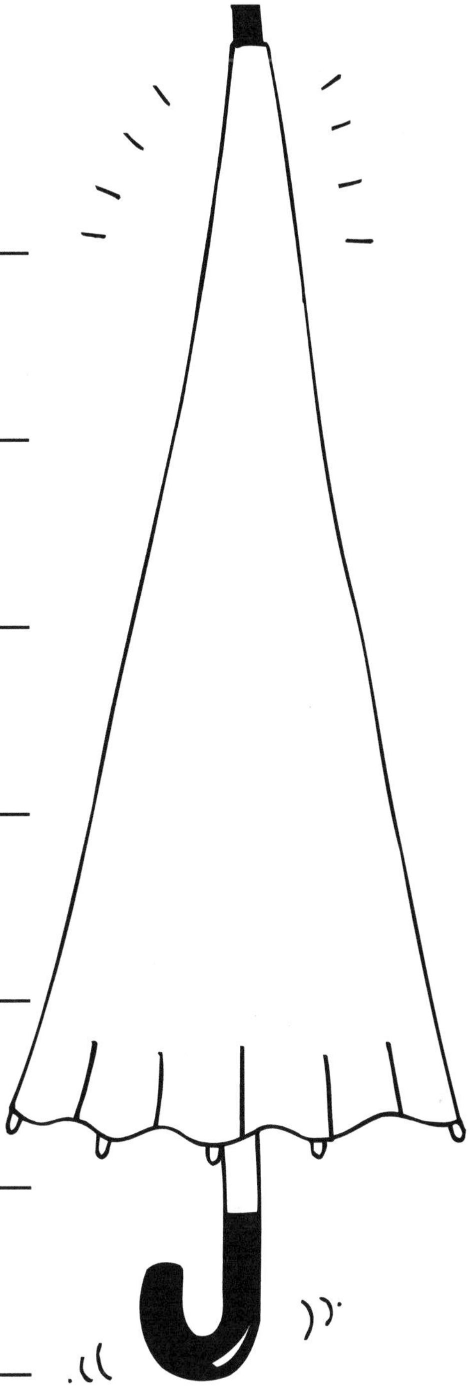

rain + 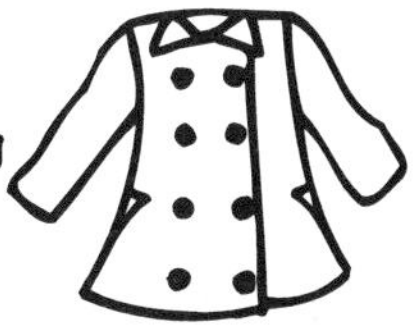 = ______________________

rain + 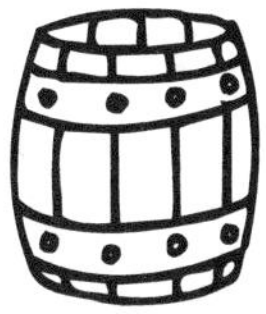 = ______________________

rain + 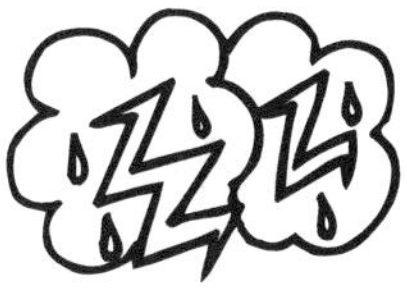 = ______________________

rain + 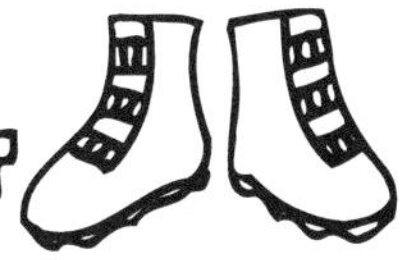 = ______________________

rain + 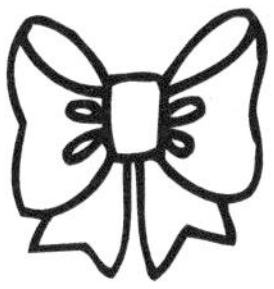 = ______________________

rain + 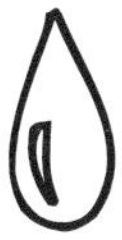 = ______________________

rain + 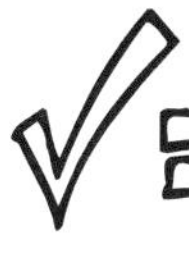 = ______________________

by Ann Richmond Fisher

Name _____

Rainy Day Math

Solve the problem in each umbrella and write in the correct answer.

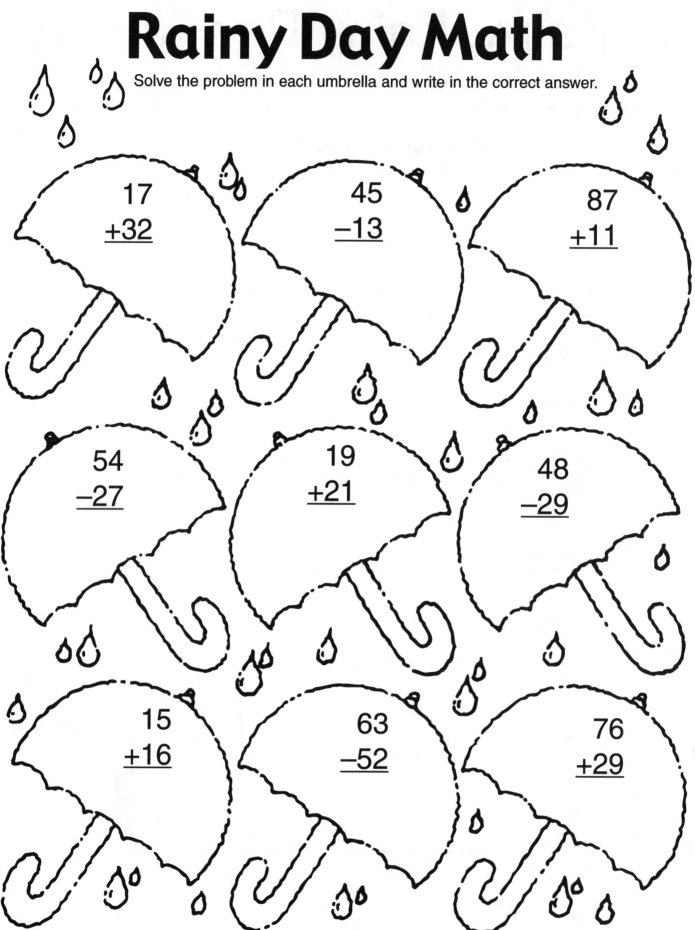

17
+32

45
−13

87
+11

54
−27

19
+21

48
−29

15
+16

63
−52

76
+29

by Kathryn Marlin

National Peanut Month

March is National Peanut Month. Americans eat an average of seven pounds of peanuts a year. Much of that is in the form of peanut butter. So don't forget to celebrate Peanut Butter Day on March 1. (Be aware that some children may have peanut allergies.)

Peanuts on the Map

Peanuts grow in Asia, Africa, Australia, India, China, North America, and South America.

Nearly 10% of the world's peanuts are grown in the United States. Georgia, Texas, Alabama, North Carolina, South Carolina, Florida, Oklahoma, Virginia, and New Mexico are the peanut states.

Help students locate these states on an outline map. Have them draw a peanut shape on each of the peanut-producing states.

Peanuts by Any Other Name

Peanuts are not nuts. They are legumes. Legumes grow in pods like peas or beans. Peanuts have been called ground nuts or ground peanuts because they grow in the ground.

They have also been called goobers or goober peas—from *nguba*, the Congo word for "peanuts."

Give students a few goobers to munch for inspiration. Then challenge them to write a poem about peanuts, goobers, ground nuts, or ground peas.

Traveling Peanuts

Peanuts were grown in South America and Mexico by the time the Spanish came to the New World. The Spanish explorers carried peanuts back to Spain. Explorers and traders carried peanuts from Spain to Africa and Asia.

Africans, brought to North America as slaves, carried peanuts with them.

Use a large world map or globe to trace the travels of peanuts from South America to Spain to Africa and Asia, and from Africa to North America. Have students identify the cardinal directions, countries, and continents as the peanuts traveled.

Read About Peanuts

Life and Times of Peanuts by Charles Micucci, Houghton Mifflin.
Peanut Butter (How It's Made) by Arlene Erlbach, Lerner Publications.
Spill the Beans and Pass the Peanuts: Legumes by Meredith Sayles Hughes, Lerner Publications.

by Linda Masternak Justice

Peanut Butter History

A physician in St. Louis, Missouri, invented peanut butter as a health food for his patients in 1890. In 1895, Dr. John Harvey Kellogg patented the peanut butter process he used for his patients in Battle Creek, Michigan. George Washington Carver, an African American agricultural scientist, developed a spread very much like peanut butter. He discovered some 300 additional uses for peanuts, peanut oil, and peanut shells.

Plant a Peanut

A peanut plant grows about 20 inches tall. Flowers bloom on the bottom half of the plant. When the flowers are fertilized, a "peg" (the fertilized ovary) grows down into the soil. A peanut embryo is in the tip of each peg. It grows in the soil to become a peanut. The kernels in the peanut shell are the seeds for future peanut plants.

You can grow a peanut plant from a raw peanut kernel! First soak some raw peanut kernels overnight. Then make a soil mixture of ⅓ sand and ⅔ potting soil. Peanuts like sandy soil. Fill a plastic cup with soil to 1" from the top. Place three kernels in the soil about one inch deep. Keep the soil moist, but not too wet.

The peanuts will sprout in about a week. Place in a sunny window. Decide which peanut plant is strongest and thin out the other two. The plant will need to be transplanted outdoors or into a bigger pot eventually. It may bloom in about 45 days. If you give it enough room, your plant may produce peanuts in about four months.

Peanut Butter Taste Test

Wrap four jars of peanut butter in paper to hide the brands. Label each jar A, B, C, or D. Allow children to taste each brand and make a note of their favorite. Let them have a bite of unsalted crackers between each taste.

Graph the Results

Divide poster board into four columns. At the bottom of each column write A B, C, or D. Leave some space to write the real name of the peanut butter later. Give each child a peanut in the shell. To make a bar graph, have each child glue his peanut in the column for his favorite peanut butter. Finally reveal the real brand names.

Count the Peanuts

There are an average of 1000 peanuts in a 28-ounce jar of peanut butter. Have 10 groups of children count out 100 peanuts. Put them all together to see what 1000 peanuts look like. Compare the pile of peanuts to the 28-ounce jar.

212

Picture a Peanut Person

Duplicate the peanut shape below on brown or tan paper for each child. Have children cut out the shapes and design peanut people. The shape can be the head, the head and body, or just the body of a peanut person. Use paper scraps, yarn, pipe cleaners, felt, buttons, and glitter to make arms, legs, features, and clothing for your peanut person.

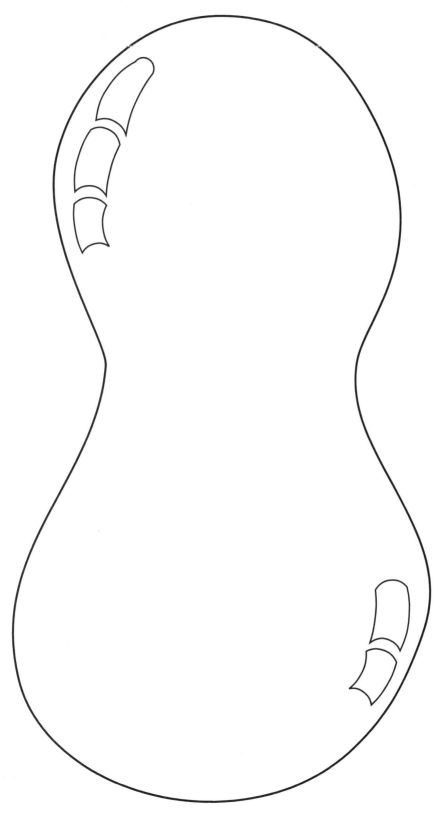

FOOD, GLORIOUS FOOD!

We wish many things for our children's future, not the least of which is good health. Nutrition is a key factor in good health. These fun classroom activities will help celebrate National Nutrition Month in March and help instill in students the importance of good nutrition by reinforcing the food guide pyramid.

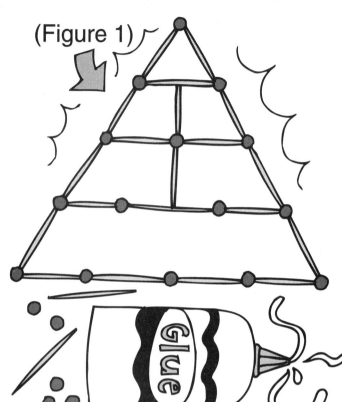

(Figure 1)

FOOD PYRAMID

Introduce the unit by having students make food pyramids with toothpicks and canned peas. Each pyramid requires 20 toothpicks and 15 peas.

1. Gently push soft peas onto the ends of round toothpicks, connecting 18 of them in the shape of a pyramid with four levels.
2. Divide the two middle levels in half with the two remaining sticks to separate the fruits/vegetables and meat/dairy groups. (See Figure 1.)
3. Let dry overnight. The peas will harden and hold the toothpicks in place.
4. Secure when dry by adding a drop of white glue to joints. Attach the top and bottom of the vertical divider with a drop of glue.

DECORATIONS

Prepare for the party by having the students make classroom decorations. Decorate the walls with shapes of fish, wedges of cheese, and other food shapes cut from construction paper. Hang plastic fruits and vegetables and plastic eggs from the ceiling. String garlands of cereal or pretzels around the room.

Make a creative bulletin board border using foods like dried apples or other fruits, beans, uncooked pastas, crackers, beef jerky, eggshells, nuts, raisins, vanilla wafers, kernels of corn, bagels, or English muffins. Create shapes of hands and, with one or more of the foods, spell out the caption, *Our Health Is in Our Hands.*

Stick cooked, wet spaghetti to the chalkboard to write *Food and Fitness: Build a Healthy Lifestyle*, the National Nutrition Month slogan for 2001. After the party is over, the dry spaghetti can be easily removed with a rubber spatula and the chalkboard cleaned with cold water.

BY SARAH KAYE

214

PLACE MATS

Students can make their own place mats using the instructions below. They can use them on their desks during the party and take them home afterwards. Give students bonus points or a healthy treat if they bring in food labels from each of the food groups. They can then use the labels on their place mats, if desired.

The basic supplies needed to make the place mats are: poster board; food labels, old magazines, catalogs, grocery ads or flyers, old greeting cards; anything with pictures of food; scissors, glue, and clear self-adhesive paper (optional).

Once you have your supplies gathered, just follow these simple steps:

1. Cut the poster board in half and cut four inches off the end of each half so it's place mat size.
2. With a marker, divide the poster board into three sections, drawing a diagonal line from the center top to each bottom corner. The center section should form a pyramid shape.
3. Divide the pyramid into four levels, making each level 3½ inches wide. Divide the two center sections in half to separate the fruits/vegetables and meat/dairy groups. (See Figure 2.)
4. Label each level and glue pictures representing the foods in each of the four groups. Be sure the edges of the pictures are glued down smoothly and firmly. Allow to dry completely. (It is wise to lay out the collage on the poster board before gluing it down.)
5. Use a frozen concentrated juice lid to trace a "coaster" for a drink in the upper right-hand section.
6. To finish and waterproof the place mat, laminate it or, if desired, cover front and back with clear self-adhesive paper. Trim away excess and enjoy the finished product. Using the food pyramid as a guide, these hints and activities provide fun ways to celebrate National Nutrition Month, reinforcing the importance of food nutrition.

LUNCH PARTY

One afternoon, instead of having everyone go to the cafeteria for lunch, have an informal lunch party in the classroom. Assign each student a food group and have him bring in a dish to share that represents that food group, including a list of the main ingredients. As an activity, have students identify which dishes would fit more than one food group.

Name _____

Favorite Foods

Look at the food pyramid. In each section, write your favorite food in that category.

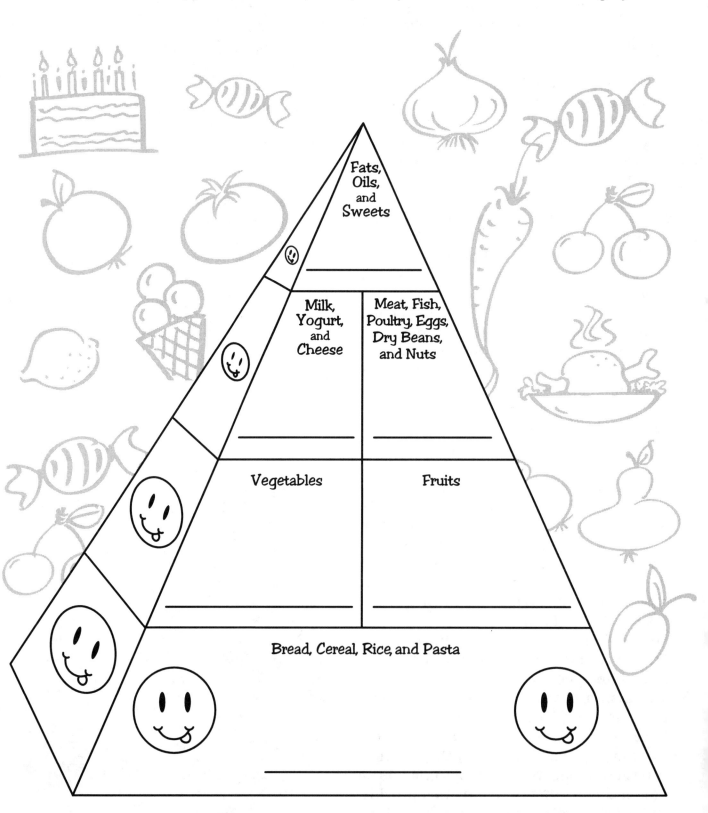

Fats, Oils, and Sweets

_____

Milk, Yogurt, and Cheese

Meat, Fish, Poultry, Eggs, Dry Beans, and Nuts

_____   _____

Vegetables

Fruits

_____   _____

Bread, Cereal, Rice, and Pasta

_____

by Mary Tucker

Name _____

Celebrate Dr. Seuss Day!

Here's a fun activity in honor of Dr. Seuss Day! Have you had the pleasure of reading the famous *The Cat in the Hat* book? (If not, visit your school or public library to find it and many other titles by Dr. Seuss. Write the names of those you read on the cat below.) Color all the hats that have words that rhyme with *cat*!

by Veronica Terrill

Name _____

Rhyming Titles

The Cat in the Hat is a good title for a funny story. The title is short and has a pair of rhyming words. Think of other titles to fit the same pattern. First finish these titles that are started for you.

1. A Bug in the _____

2. The Ape in the _____

3. The Fly in the _____

4. The _____ in the Log

5. The Bear in the _____

6. The Fox in the _____

Now try some more of your own.

7. _____

8. _____

9. _____

10. _____

by Ann Richmond Fisher

The Story of St. Patrick's Day

Why do we celebrate March 17 as a special holiday? That's the day a man named St. Patrick died. Patrick was born more than 1600 years ago in England. When he was 16 years old, he was kidnapped and taken to Ireland where he lived as a slave for six years, taking care of sheep. One day, Patrick managed to hide on a boat going to France and he escaped.

When Patrick returned home, he thought a lot about Ireland. You might think he would have been very angry at what those people had done to him, but he wasn't. In fact, Patrick decided he wanted to go back to Ireland as a missionary to help the people there. And he did! He spent the rest of his life in Ireland, his adopted land.

There are many legends about St. Patrick, such as the one about him driving all the snakes out of Ireland. But the true facts of his life are more interesting than any legend.

Today, St. Patrick's Day is celebrated with parades, Irish music and dancing, and special food such as corned beef and cabbage. The shamrock, which is the national flower of Ireland, is seen everywhere, and everyone, Irish or not, tries to wear something green. It's a high-spirited day for everyone, especially the Irish.

St. Patrick's Day Song

Sing this song together and do the foot-stomping and hand-clapping actions. Make sure each child is wearing something green or has something green, such as a paper shamrock, to hold up.

To the tune of "If You're Happy and You Know It"

St. Patrick went to Ireland long ago
(Stomp, stomp)
To teach the people what they ought to know.
(Clap, clap)
March 17th is the date
That we love to celebrate,
And green is the color that we show.
(Hold up a green shamrock or point to green clothes you're wearing.)

by Mary Tucker

Holiday Sing Alongs

by Mabel Duch

Early on St. Patrick's Day

To the tune of "Mary Had a Little Lamb"

Early on St. Patrick's Day,
St. Patrick's Day, St. Patrick's Day,
Early on St. Patrick's Day,
I met a little man.

He said "I am a leprechaun,
A leprechaun, a leprechaun."
He said "I am a leprechaun.
Catch me if you can."

"They say I have a pot of gold,
Pot of gold, pot of gold.
They say I have a pot of gold
I can give to you."

"But I don't have a pot of gold,
Pot of gold, pot of gold.
I don't have a pot of gold.
That story isn't true."

"Better than a pot of gold,
Pot of gold, pot of gold.
Better than a pot of gold,
I'll grant a wish or three."

"I can grant you any wish,
Any wish, any wish.
I can grant you any wish
If you can capture me."

Background

St. Patrick's Day, March 17, honors St. Patrick who brought Christianity to Ireland almost 1600 years ago.

Leprechauns, tiny little men dressed in green, are one of the legends connected with Ireland and St. Patrick's Day.

Legend says leprechauns hide pots of gold at the ends of rainbows, and that they can, if they choose, grant wishes.

Discussion

1. What would you wish for if you had three wishes?

2. Suppose the wish rule said only one wish could be for you and the other two must be for other people. What would you wish for someone else?

3. Is there anything you can do to make your wishes come true? There is an old saying, "Be careful what you wish for. It might come true." The following folktale illustrates what happened when some people were careless with their wishes.

Once upon a time, a man and his wife helped a leprechaun and thereby received three wishes between them.

The man was very hungry, so he said "I wish for a great big juicy sausage." No sooner had he said that than there appeared in his hands a delicious-looking sausage.

His wife was very angry. She bellowed, "Why have you wasted a valuable wish on a sausage?! You could have asked for gold. I wish that sausage was on the end of your nose!"

Lo and behold, the sausage appeared on the end of the poor man's nose. What did they do with the one wish remaining? That's right. They wished the sausage off the man's nose, and were no better or no worse off than they were before.

4. Have you ever been granted a wish, then regretted making that wish?

Activity

Make up stories about wishes that people later regretted, or wishes that had to be reversed. Here are some ideas:

1. A boy might wish to be the tallest person in the school. If his wish comes true, what problems could he experience?

2. A girl might wish she was so smart that she would never have to study. If she gets her wish, could this be a bad thing?

Enjoy role-playing some of the stories.

St. Patrick's Mobile

1. Cut out top hat and shamrocks from green poster board.
2. Cut out beard and mustache from orange poster board.
3. Cut out eyes from white poster board and color the eyes.
4. Glue mustache to beard and shamrocks as shown.
5. Using string, tie beard and eyes to hat.

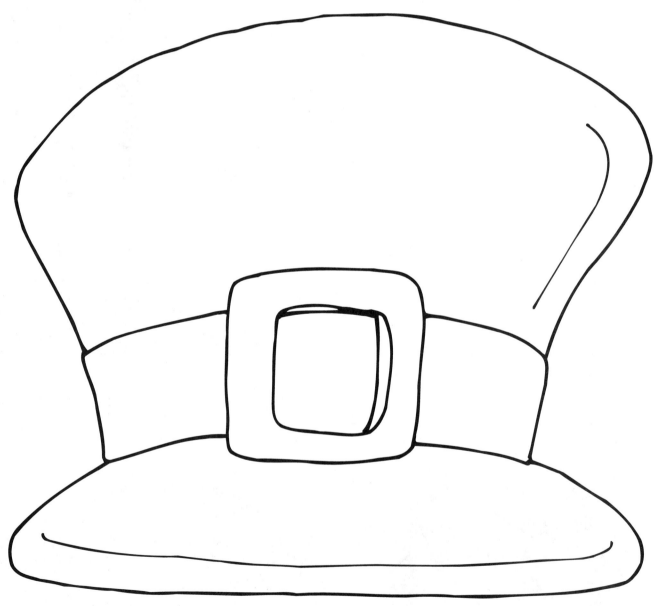

by Twilla Lamm

Leo Leprechaun

Meet Leo the Leprechaun. Someone started making sketches of him. Sharpen your pencil and finish drawing each so they all look like him!

by Becky Radtke

CRAFT CORNER

Nephoscope

A nephoscope is an instrument that helps to determine the direction in which clouds are traveling.

Materials

   piece of Plexiglas™ about 5" x 10" (13 x 25 cm)
   piece of black paper the same size as the Plexiglas™
   heavy cardboard about 12" x 18" (30 x 45 cm)
   plastic tape, 1 inch (2.5 cm) wide
   magnetic compass
   paints and a paintbrush

Let's Make It

1. Lay the black paper in the center of the cardboard and place the Plexiglas™ on top of it, so that the paper is completely covered by the glass.
2. Carefully tape the glass and paper to the board. Cover all edges of the glass with tape.
3. Paint the letters *N, S, E, W, NW, NE, SW,* and *SE* on the board in the same positions they appear on a compass. A parent helper or teacher should ensure the students paint the compass headings correctly.
4. To use the nephoscope, head outdoors. Hold the board so that N points north when the board is held flat. Look in the glass and you will see a reflection of the sky. As you watch the clouds float across the glass surface, you will be able to determine the direction in which they are moving.

Lucky Leprechaun

Materials

   piece of sturdy cardboard 10" x 6" (25 x 15 cm)
   ¼ ball of green yarn for each student
   1 ball of thick black yarn for the entire group
   scissors
   ruler
   stick-on eyes
   red and gold fabric paint
   pennies

Let's Make It

1. Wrap the green yarn around the long side of the cardboard about 25-50 times, depending upon the thickness of your yarn.
2. Slide the yarn off of the cardboard.
3. About 2 inches (5 cm) from the top of the yarn, tie a piece of black yarn to form the leprechaun's hat. Wrap the black yarn around this area several times to resemble a hat.
4. Move down another 2 inches (5 cm) from the hat and tie a green piece of yarn to form the head.
5. Cut all of the looping ends at the bottom so they hang free.
6. Separate some yarn on either side of the form leaving some in the middle, and tie halfway up the figure to make arms. Cut off the remaining ends and tie the hands together.
7. Wrap black yarn around the middle several times to form a belt at the waist.
8. Separate the remaining yarn into two bundles to form the legs. Tie these at the feet with green yarn. Trim off the ends to resemble feet.
9. Use craft glue or a hot glue gun and glue sticks to attach eyes and a penny where the hands meet.
10. Use red fabric paint to make a smiling mouth.
11. Use gold fabric paint to add gold buckles to the shoes and belt.

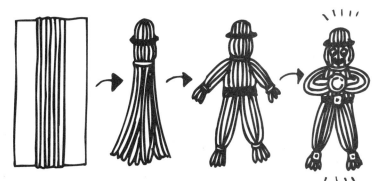

by Robynne Eagan

Spring Quilt

An old-fashioned quilt is a colorful way to teach your students about pioneers. Welcome spring in your class with this variation of a historical handicraft.

Discuss

Quilts are wonderful works of art made from scraps of clothing, bedding, and flour sacks. These works of recycled cloth helped to keep a family warm and passed on family memories, stories and quilt patterns. Pioneer women often worked together on quilts at social events called quilting bees. Today Mennonite and Amish people make quilts in much the same way.

Common Quilt Patterns

Have your students investigate some common quilt patterns.

Friendship Star	Shooting Star
Log Cabin	Four Patch
Fan	Nine Patch
Hourglass	

Let's Make It!

1. Photocopy pattern pieces or supply uniform-sized paper for each student.
2. Have students decorate the samples given or create their own pattern. Fabric paints, drawing or coloring tools, and ribbons or buttons, and paste will work well. Invite students to create patterns that represent spring.
3. Have your own quilting bee as you join the pieces together by gluing the blocks to a large piece of mural paper.
4. Display your spring quilt on a bulletin board or in the hall for all to see.

Create a school quilt to hang in the front foyer.

Invite each family in your school to become part of the school family by contributing a square to the school quilt. Distribute blocks to interested families. Invite families to sew, quilt, stitch, embroider, transfer, or paint on their block. Hang the school quilt in the front foyer of your school.

Try This

Share the book *Selina and the Bear Paw Quilt* by Barbara Smucker, illustrated by Janet Wilson, Lester Publishing, 1995. A bond between little Selina and the grandmother she leaves behind during the Civil War was forged through the stitches of a quilt.

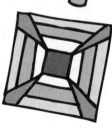

226

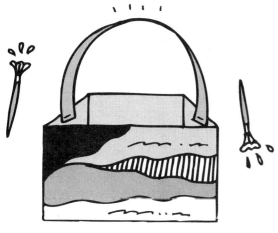

Easter Baskets

Materials
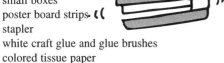
small boxes
poster board strips
stapler
white craft glue and glue brushes
colored tissue paper

Let's Make It!

1. Apply a layer of glue to the outside of a box and then cover with tissue paper. When that layer is dry, apply another layer. Continue until you have a nice effect.

2. Use a stapler to attach a poster board strip as a handle.

Easter Stained-Glass Picture

This simple craft will produce two end products, the beautiful stained-glass Easter picture and the eggs that were used as tools to create the pictures.

Materials
hard-boiled eggs
wax paper
large box
acrylic paint in various spring colors
construction paper or poster board
scissors

Let's Make It!

1. Lay the wax paper on the bottom of the box.

2. Dab spoonfuls of different colored paint on the wax paper.

3. Roll the eggs around inside the box until the paper is completely covered with paint.

4. Allow the paper to dry completely.

5. Using the poster board or construction paper, cut out a frame to hold the wax paper "stained glass" artwork. Display these wonders in the window for everyone to enjoy.

Cotton Ball Clouds

Explore the wonder of clouds on a fluffy-sky spring day!

Materials
3 blue construction paper cloud shapes
glue
cotton balls

Let's Make It!

1. Have students pull cotton balls apart until they are thin and wispy. Have them glue the wispy cotton onto a blue cloud shape to make a cirrus cloud.

2. Next, have them make a stratus cloud by first pulling the cotton balls in all directions to flatten and lengthen them. Have them glue these onto a blue cloud shape in flat, even layers.

3. Finally, try cumulus clouds. Leave the cotton balls as they are. Have students glue them onto the blue cloud shape in clusters or piles for a heaped effect.

Try This

After making your clouds, venture outdoors, find a dry spot to lie down, and look up. Search for the types of clouds you just made as you discover the joy of becoming a cloud watcher.
(Caution: Remind students of the dangers of looking directly at the sun.)

Spring

Knock-knock! Who's there? It's just a lively group of very funny bunnies taking you on an Easter egg hunt in *Easter Crack-Ups: Knock-Knock Jokes Funny-Side Up* by Katy Hall & Lisa Eisenberg (HarperFestival, 2000). This entertaining book features some hilarious knock-knock jokes—just lift the flaps and the answers will appear. After sharing this book, ask your youngsters to create their own answers to the questions in each riddle.

Need the perfect craft for spring? *Papercrafts: Origami, Papier-Mâché, and Collage* by Judith Hoffman Corwin (Franklin Watts, 1988) offers an array of unique projects for your budding young artists. Many of the materials can be easily found around the house or school. Some crafts perfect for spring include folded fan flowers, nesting birds collage, and six bunnies in a row.

Fun Factory by Lyndsay Milne (Reader's Digest Kids, 1995) features craft ideas for games and toys from household junk. This fantastic book is brimming with appealing projects, such as puppet-making, puppet theaters, an island town, castle, masks, costumes, and much more. Turn your classroom into a fun factory!

Fluffy's Spring Vacation
by Kate McMullan
illustrated by Mavis Smith
Scholastic, 1998

Fluffy, the lovable guinea pig in Ms. Day's class, gets the adventure of his life, when he goes home with Emma during spring vacation. First, Fluffy manages to escape from Emma's two frisky cats who want to "play" with him, and then it's on to a beauty shop to do some exploring. To top it off, at the end of spring break the adventuresome guinea pig ends up at the airport, after hiding in a briefcase at Emma's house. Luckily, Fluffy gets a taxi ride from the airport back to school just in time for roll call!

- Write a story about the day Fluffy visited your classroom.

- Be a pet detective! Find out all about guinea pigs. Look in an encyclopedia, animal book, or on the internet to help with your research. Create a poster report with facts and information about this popular pet.

- Divide a plain sheet of paper into four parts. Draw four things you would like to do on spring vacation.

Danny and the Easter Egg
by Edith Kunhardt
Greenwillow Books, 1989

Danny's Easter season is full of fun and surprises. First, he enjoys dyeing eggs with his friend. On Easter, he finds a special gift during an egg hunt—a new Easter coat hanging from a tree. To top it off, he visits his grandmother and presents her with a special Easter egg.

- Danny found a special surprise during his egg hunt. Draw a picture of a surprise you would like to find on a hunt.

- Draw a design for a special egg to give to a relative or friend.

- Be an artist! Design a new book cover for *Danny and the Easter Egg*.

by Mary Ellen Switzer

Book Nook

The Bird's Gift: A Ukrainian Easter Story

retold by Eric A. Kimmel
illustrated by Katya Krenina
Holiday House, 1999

This touching Ukrainian legend tells the story of how the beautifully decorated pysanky eggs originated long ago. In the legend, a young girl convinces some villagers to save hundreds of little birds when winter comes too early one year. The villagers bring the birds to a church for refuge, where they stay until the end of winter. After being released, the birds fly away, only to return at Eastertime with a special reward for the villagers—lovely pysanky Easter eggs. Also included in the book is some fascinating information on these unique eggs.

- Write a list of three facts you have learned about pysanky eggs from the "Author's Note" at the end of the book.

- Draw a design that you would like to create for a pysanky egg.

- You're an author! Write your own legend called *The Rabbit's Gift*. Draw a picture about an event in your story.

The Best Easter Hunt Ever

by John Speirs
Cartwheel Books, 1997

Here's a holiday book that's fun and educational, too! The reader will get to participate in an Easter hunt and sharpen math skills at the same time. First read the rebus directions on each page, which tell what hidden treats to look for in the picture. After finding the hidden items, keep track of how many Easter treats each of the children in the story find on every page. At the end of the book, add up the number of items found by each child and "presto"—you will know the winner of the egg hunt!

- Help Wanted! Pretend that the Easter Bunny needs a new artist to paint eggs. Write an ad for this new job.

- Draw a picture of your school playground or a park with hidden eggs and treats. See if a friend can find all of the hidden items.

- News Flash! You find the biggest Easter egg in the world. Draw a picture of what the egg looks like. Tell what you would do with the egg.

The Very Best Easter Bunny

by Ann Braybrooks
illustrated by Josie Yee
Golden Book, 2000

Easter is coming to the Hundred-Acre Wood. Rabbit unexpectedly decides he's much too busy planting his garden and can't deliver Easter eggs this year. Winnie the Pooh, Tigger, and his other friends try to become the perfect substitute for Rabbit, but soon decide no one can measure up to the job. Finally, the group of friends come up with an "eggs"traordinary plan—they will all help Rabbit plant his garden. Will their clever idea work in time for Easter?

- Winnie the Pooh and his friends try to become the perfect substitute for Rabbit. Draw a rabbit costume that one of them could wear to deliver Easter eggs.

- Surprise! Help Rabbit design the best garden at the Hundred-Acre Wood. Draw a "map" showing your idea of a perfect garden.

- Create a picture book called *My Best Spring Garden* with pictures and information about your new garden plan at the Hundred-Acre Wood.

Poetry Corner

April is National Poetry Month. Delight your youngsters with some sensational poetry this spring. Give springtime a rousing welcome by sharing the poems in *Month-by-Month Poetry, March, April, May & June,* compiled by Marian Reiner (Scholastic, 1999). This wonderful collection of more than 60 poems is the perfect springboard to creative writing and other classroom activities. Also included in the book is an "Activities Ideas" section with some top-notch ways to extend the poems into your curriculum.

Let's Celebrate: Festival Poems
compiled by John Foster
Oxford University Press, 1989

Animal Trunk: Silly Poems to Read Aloud
by Charles Ghigna
Harry N. Abrams, Inc., 1998

Confetti: Poems for Children
by Pat Mora
Lee & Low Books, Inc., 1996

The 20th Century Children's Poetry Treasury
selected by Jack Prelutsky
Alfred A. Knopf, 1999

The Rebus Treasury
compiled by Jean Marzollo
Dial Books, 1986

What Rhymes with Moon?
by Jane Yolen
Philomel Books, 1993

Kids Pick the Funniest Poems
selected by Bruce Lansky
Meadowbrook Press, 1991

Leprechaun Gold

by Teresa Bateman
illustrated by Roseanne Litzinger
Holiday House, 1998

A good-hearted man named Donald O'Dell hears the cries of a drowning leprechaun and bravely saves the little man from the raging stream. When the grateful leprechaun offers Donald gold as a reward, the man refuses, saying that he already has enough money for his needs. The determined leprechaun cleverly devises a plan and repays Donald with a special surprise, even more valuable than gold.

• How did the clever leprechaun repay Donald in the story?

• Using the letters in *Leprechaun Gold,* make a list of all the words that you can think of.

• Cut out a large shamrock shape from a plain sheet of paper. Write a poem about St. Patrick's Day on one side of the shamrock. Create an illustration about your poem on the other side.

• Learn more about leprechaun legends and St. Patrick's Day traditions in *Shamrocks, Harps & Shillelaghs, The Story of St. Patrick's Day Symbols* by Edna Barth (Clarion Books, 1997). This informative book gives the history and background of this green-letter holiday.

Computer Zone

Software
KidWorks Deluxe
Davidson
Win/Mac CD ROM
Put your budding young writers to work creating their own stories, poems, and other types of creative writing activities using this superb software. There are excellent story starters to help even the most reluctant writer get started on the way. Some of the writing activities include an autobiography, interview, letter, and newsletter. You can print their masterpieces and even e-mail the work to friends and relatives.

Web Sites
Spark enthusiasm for Earth Day in April with the help of www.earthday.wilderness.org/ This helpful site is sponsored by the Wilderness Society and features information about Earth Day, as well as children's activities such as a picture and coloring books. You can also enjoy checking out links to other sites and sending on-line postcards.

For more ideas for Earth Day activities, click on over to the National Wildlife Federation web site www.nwf.org/kids. Ranger Rick's Kids Zone is loaded with amazing wildlife trivia, riddles, games, quizzes, and helpful information on conservation and saving the environment.

Need ideas for the Easter season? Here's a site brimming with lots of holiday ideas: www.kidsdomain.com/holiday/easter/ You'll find clip art, games, crafts, mazes, puzzles, and cards at this site.

For additional Easter activities, try www.holidays.net/easter/ Some of the sections include a history of the holiday, coloring sheets, and recipes. Also featured is a directory for other Easter web sites.

Seasonal Science

Try these super science activities for springtime learning fun.

Donna

Double Vision

Activity

Invite your students to explore the tricks mirrors can play on our eyes in honor of April Fools' Day. Make use of a large classroom mirror or several small unbreakable ones. First, have the students write their names on index cards or paper. Let them hold their name cards up to the mirror and describe what happens to their names. Encourage the students to try to write their names so they will look correct in the mirror. Next, make use of cards from an old playing deck. Have the students observe as you cut a few of the cards in half. Hand each student one card half and invite individuals to hold their card halves next to the mirror. What happens to each half picture? The cards will appear whole in the mirror. Finally, use three small mirrors, taping them together to form a standing triangle shape. Let the students choose small objects from around the room to place in the center of this mirror tripod. How do the mirrors reflect each object? Talk with the students about how mirror images are formed when beams of light are reflected.

Project

Have the students work in pairs so one child can mirror exactly what the other child does. Have the partners face each other; then as the first one moves, the second must mirror the action exactly. Have the students take turns being the leader and the mirror. Follow up by letting the students use mirrors for reference as they draw pictures as they look today.

by Marie E. Cecchini

Hooray for Chocolate!

The second week of March each year is American Chocolate Month. Give your children a special treat by relating their lessons to chocolate for one day with these suggestions.

Counting Chocolates

Give each child several small chocolate candies (preferably with a hard candy coating to avoid messy fingers). Have each child count his or her candies, then print the number on the chalkboard. Ask children to look at the numbers to discover who has the most candies, who has the least, and how many children have the same number. Ask children to figure out how many more candies each child should be given in order for all the children to have the same number as the person with the most. Hand out that number of candies to the children. Challenge children to divide their candies into two equal groups. If there is a leftover candy, the child may eat it. Then let the children eat their candies. If some children don't like chocolate or are allergic to it, provide non-chocolate treats for them.

A Chocolate Experiment

Bring to class some unsweetened cocoa, sugar, a measuring spoon, a bowl, and a chocolate candy bar.

Let each child taste the unsweetened cocoa. They will not like the bitter taste. Ask them what is wrong with the chocolate. Why doesn't it taste like chocolate usually does? Someone may mention that it doesn't have sugar in it like the chocolate we usually eat. Try mixing some sugar with the cocoa in a bowl. See how much sugar it takes to make the chocolate taste good. Hold up the candy bar and point out to the children that the first ingredient listed is sugar. Discuss why too much chocolate candy (and sugar) is not good for us.

by Mary Tucker

232

Chocolate Words

Ask children to think of words to describe chocolate (*yummy, brown, sweet, delicious, good,* and so on). Print the words on the chalkboard. Then ask them to name as many different chocolate treats as they can think of (chocolate milk, chocolate candy bar, chocolate shakes, chocolate ice cream, hot chocolate, and so on). List these on the board, too.

A Chocolate Adventure

Begin telling a story about a child having an adventure with chocolate. Stop after a few minutes and ask a volunteer to make up some more of the story. After a minute or so, let another child take over where that child left off. Continue until everyone has had a chance to add to the story. Finish the story yourself.

Story Starter Suggestion: Avery loved chocolate more than almost anything. He ate it whenever he could. He dreamed about it at night and thought about it when he was supposed to be doing his schoolwork. Whenever he got money for his birthday or Christmas or for doing work for his parents, Avery spent it on chocolate. His mother told him too much chocolate wasn't good for him, but Avery couldn't imagine that anyone could ever have too much chocolate. He sometimes wished that everything in the world was made of chocolate. Wouldn't that be great?

One morning when Avery woke up, he got out of bed and went into the bathroom to get ready for school. He took his toothbrush out of the cabinet and squeezed toothpaste on it. Then he looked at his toothbrush more closely. The toothpaste was brown. What was wrong with it? He took a little taste. It was chocolate! Wow! Chocolate toothpaste. What could be better? He began brushing his teeth, but instead of spitting out the toothpaste, he swallowed it. Yum!

When Avery was dressed, he went downstairs. In the kitchen, another surprise was waiting for him . . .

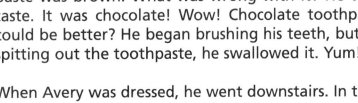

Look! Up in the sky! It's the moon . . . a star . . . a meteoroid!

It's Astronomy Week!

The first week of April is Astronomy Week. It's a good time to send your students' imagination to the moon and the stars.

I See the Moon

Call attention to the phases of the moon by making a moon phase calendar. Give each child a blank calendar page. Write in the dates and use a counting chip to lightly trace a circle for each day. Ask the children to look at the moon each night and to color in the shaded part of the moon circle. Here are the standard symbols.

● new moon (just a dark circle)

◐ first quarter

○ full moon (fully lighted)

◑ last quarter

You can make an exciting classroom moon phase calendar by cutting the shapes out of silver paper or painting them with glitter. Use a large poster-sized calendar. After several days, ask students to predict what the next night's moon will look like. Do this for at least one full cycle of the moon.

Have students use a dictionary to find out the difference between **meteors, meteoroids** and **meteorites**.

Moon Craters

Craters of the moon were formed when meteorites crashed into its surface. Students can make a classroom model to help them understand this process.

Materials
plaster of Paris mix
large bucket or bowl
measuring cup
shallow cardboard box (about 12" x 14" x 2")
deep cardboard box (chest high on students)
goggles or old sunglasses
water
stirring stick
newspapers

Directions
1. Cut the top and bottom off the deep box.
2. Mix plaster of Paris in large bucket according to package directions. Pour in shallow box. Place on newspaper-covered floor.
3. Place large box around the shallow box to act as spatter shield.
4. Allow students to throw meteoroids (foil balls, rocks) into the plaster. Remove meteorites before plaster hardens.
5. Observe the resulting craters.

Craters on the moon have names. You may want to have students name their craters. Write the names on the craters with permanent marker when the plaster has dried.

by Linda Masternak Justice

234

✩ A Handful of Stars

Show children pictures of transparencies of the constellations and tell their stories. The constellations we are familiar with take their names from Greek mythology—Orion, Scorpio, Lyra. Other cultures had their own stories of the constellations. Read some of these stories to your students. *The Heavenly Zoo: Legends and Tales of the Stars* by Allison Lurie and Monika Benson is a multicultural look at the stories of the stars. *Find the Constellations* by H.A. Rey has wonderful drawings of the traditional constellations.

Then give each child a dark blue paper and a handful of stars—five to nine tiny star stickers. Ask the students to drop the stars on the paper. Connect the stars to make a picture. Name the new constellation and write a story to tell about it.

Write shape poems. Write one word on each line in a star shape. The first word is STARS. Then list three adjectives to describe stars. Finally, write two verbs. Brainstorming a list of adjectives and verbs may be helpful.

Cut out the star. Run glue and glitter along the edges. Display on a bulletin board covered with dark blue paper. Title the display "A Galaxy of Poems by Star Students."

Out-of-This World Books

Amanda Visits the Planets by Gina Ingoglia, Inchworm.
Grandpa Takes Me to the Moon by Timothy R. Gaffney, Tambourine Books.
Maria's Comet by Deborah Hopkinson, Atheneum.
MoonTellers: Myths of the Moon from Around the World by Lynn Moroney and Greg Shed, Rising Moon.
One Giant Leap: The Story of Neil Armstrong by Don Brown, Houghton Mifflin.
The Magic School Bus Lost in the Solar System by Joanna Cole, Scholastic.

Did You Ever See a Rabbit?

To the tune of
"Did You Ever See a Lassie?"

Did you ever see a rabbit,
A rabbit, a rabbit—
Did you ever see a rabbit
Hop this way and that?
Hop forward, hop backward,
Hop forward, hop backward—
Did you ever see a rabbit
Hop this way and that?

Did you ever see a rabbit,
A rabbit, a rabbit—
Did you ever see a rabbit
Hop this way and that?
Hop leftward, hop rightward,
Hop leftward, hop rightward—
Did you ever see a rabbit
Hop this way and that?

Did You Ever See a Robin?

To the tune of
"Did You Ever See a Lassie?"

Did you ever see a robin,
A robin, a robin—
Did you ever see a robin
Fly this way and that?
Fly northward, fly southward,
Fly northward, fly southward,
Did you ever see a robin
Fly this way and that?

Did you ever see a robin,
A robin, a robin—
Did you ever see a robin
Fly this way and that?
Fly eastward, fly westward,
Fly eastward, fly westward,
Did you ever see a robin
Fly this way and that?

Background

As the children sing the songs, have them hop like rabbits and move arms like birds' wings.

Before singing the robin song, label the north, east, south, and west sides of the room.

Discussion

For discussion, bring in maps (city, county, state, and if necessary, a world map).

1. Can you find on a map where your grandparents live? (Give help as needed.)

2. What direction (north, east, south, or west) do you go to get there? Can you show us? If it's an in-between direction (northeast, southeast, southwest, or northwest), tell the student the name of that direction. Show and name the other in-between directions.

236

Activities

Even adults can have trouble giving and following directions and reading maps. The following exercises are designed to help students develop these skills.

1. Duplicate copies of your school district's map and/or your city or town's map. Have each student draw lines and arrows on an appropriate map, showing how to get to his or her home. (Before beginning, take your class outside and point out north, east, south, and west.)

2. Pair up children. Have one child, without showing his map but using it as a guide, give step-by-step directions to his or her home. (For example: "Go three blocks north on School Street until you come to Elm. Turn right on Elm and go one block to Fairfield. Turn left on Fairfield. My house is in the middle of the block on the east side of the road.") The other child draws lines and arrows on the same kind of map, showing the way to the first child's home. Have them compare maps to see how well the first student gave directions; then switch roles and repeat the activity.

3. Put the names of children who walk to school in a bag and pull one out. Have that child give oral directions to his or her home. Write down the directions. Take your class on a walk to that home. (If a parent is home, be sure to let them know you are coming.) Along the way, see how well your students remember the directions. (For example, When you leave the school ask, "Who can remember what direction we go? How far do we go?" And later, "What direction do we turn?") The "walker" whose home you selected should remain quiet, unless you get lost along the way.

4. Hide treats somewhere on the school grounds. (You may want some parental help with this.) Divide your class into four groups. Give two groups maps, a different map for each group, directing them to the treats by different routes. Give the other two groups different sets of directions, directing them to the treats by different routes. The treat-seekers should not touch the treats until everyone arrives. The winning group can help hand out the treats.

237

EASTER RiDDLE Activities

Because young children like riddles and jokes, they have a surprising capacity to learn them. The following riddle activities capitalize on the aptitude and motivation of young children and reluctant older readers to read and write riddles and jokes.

Place each of the following Easter riddles on its own sheet of chart paper. On the back of the chart paper or on a separate word card, write the answer. Number each riddle and its answer so you don't get them mixed up. Have the students read the following riddles and try to guess the answers. Record the suggested answers with each question on chart paper. Then present the answers, having a student reread the question and another student read the answer. Record who, if anyone, got the answer correct. You may wish to have prizes for the best guesses.

When questions and answers have been shared, have students create their own riddle books, copying the question at the top of a page and the answer upside down at the bottom. Have students illustrate each page. Use half-page-sized books so the illustrations do not have to be large. Or you may prefer to use large 18" x 24" sheets, letting each child paint a picture to illustrate the riddle. Then collate the entire book into a *Classroom Riddles Big Book.* If time permits, students may be encouraged to find or write their own Easter riddles.

BY GAiL LeNNoN

THE RiDDLES AND ANSWERS

1. How does the Easter Bunny stay healthy? (He "eggs"ercises.)

2. What do you call Easter when you are hopping around? (A hoppy Easter)

3. What do you get when you find a rabbit with no hair? (A hairless hare)

4. Why are people always tired in April? (They just finished a March that lasted 31 days.)

5. Why did the Easter egg hide? (He was a little chicken.)

6. What do you call a duck who plays basketball? (A slam duck)

238

7. What do you call a bunny with a large brain? (An egg head)

8. Why did the Easter Bunny cross the road? (It was the chicken's day off.)

9. What do you call a bunny with a dictionary in his pants? (Smarty pants)

10. What do you call 10 rabbits marching backwards? (A receding hareline)

11. Why was the rabbit rubbing his head? (He had an eggache.)

12. How do you catch a unique bunny? (Unique up on him.)

13. Why did the Easter Bunny hop down the road? (He was making the movie *Here Comes Peter Cottontail*.)

14. What do you call the Easter Bunny after a hard day's work? (Tired)

15. What did the rabbit say to the carrot? (It's been nice "gnawing" you.)

16. What did the Easter Bunny put over his sore? (An eggage)

17. What do ducks have for lunch? (Soup and quackers)

18. Knock, knock . . . Who's there? . . . "Ether!" . . . "Ether" who? (Ether Bunny!)

19. Why did the other rabbits say that the Easter Bunny was peculiar? (He was "egg"centric.)

20. When does Valentine's Day come after Easter? (In the dictionary)

21. What's the difference between the Easter bunny and a lumberjack? (One chews and hops and the other hews and chops.)

22. How does the Easter Bunny say "Happy Easter"? (The same way you do!)

23. Why did the magician have to cancel his show? (He had just washed his hare and couldn't do a thing with it!)

24. What type of movie is about water fowl? (A duckumentary)

25. What is at the end of Easter? (R)

26. What do you call a duck that just doesn't fit in? (Mallardjusted)

27. Why is the letter A like a flower? (A bee [B] follows it.)

28. What do you call rabbits that marched in a long sweltering Easter parade? (Hot, cross bunnies)

"Egg"citing Activities

No one knows for sure why eggs are associated with Easter. There are several theories. According to legend, the goddess Easter saved a bird whose wings were frozen. She gave the bird a new life by turning it into a hare—a magical hare that could lay eggs. Another old tale that dates back to at least 1682 tells of an Easter Hare laying eggs and hiding them in a garden. Not wanting to miss out on a good thing, European children built nests with their caps or bonnets which they placed in secluded spots, hoping the Easter Hare would leave them eggs and candies. During the 1700s German immigrants brought this custom to North America. During Easter week in Germany, dyed hollow eggs are hung from trees and shrubs. In North America we have continued this custom.

For children eggs hold mystery and intrigue. This interest is, no doubt, connected with Easter eggs, egg hunts, Easter Bunnies, and egg decorating. In non-Protestant religious faiths, the egg holds appeal because of its association with life, baby chicks, and with rebirth.

The following activities are designed to capitalize upon children's natural fascination with Easter eggs. The activities may be completed as whole-class projects, as small group experiences, or as individual pursuits. They may be set up as centers through which students rotate in cooperative groups of three to four students.

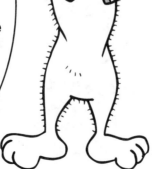

Easter Egg Hunt

Cut six eggs each out of four different colors of paper. Hide the eggs throughout the school. Divide students into four teams. Give each team a written clue or directions to help them find their first egg. On the back of the first egg, write a clue or directions to the second, and so forth. The winning team is the first to find all six of their eggs and return to the classroom.

Mystery Egg

Purchase plastic Easter eggs. Fill each egg with a different substance—sand, coins, paper, candy, rocks, grass, and so on. Have students try to guess what is inside each egg by asking questions. (Is it soft or hard? Does it taste good? Is it something usually found outside? And so forth.) A variation is to tell one student what is inside the egg. That student must then answer questions.

240   **by Gail Lennon**

Scrambled Eggs

Cut egg halves out of paper. On the back of each half, write a word or draw a picture. On the other half, write or draw its opposite (hot/cold, big/little, over/under, and so on). Label the halves A and B. When students arrive, give each one two mismatched egg halves (one A half and one B half). Students must find their matching half by asking other students questions in English. When the students make a match, the student holding the A half keeps the match. The winner is the first student to give away his B half and find the match for his A half. (This activity may also be done with rhyming words, numbers/number words, pictures/vocabulary words, and so on.)

Easter Treat!

Beat a dozen eggs with ½ cup milk. Lay pieces of bread in the bottom of a flat dish. Cover with half of the egg mixture. Add grated cheese, diced ham, green peppers . . . whatever you want. Lay another layer of bread on top and cover with remaining egg mixture. Top with cinnamon, nutmeg, and grated cheese. Refrigerate to let the egg mixture soak into the bread. You may want to add additional eggs before cooking the next day if the mixture seems dry. Bake in a 350°F oven until the top is golden brown. Cut and serve on warmed plates. It's delicious with maple syrup!

Confetti Eggs

You need: eggs, straight pins, food coloring or egg dyes, vinegar, bowls, large spoon, egg carton, confetti, and tape. Poke a small hole in one end of the egg and a larger hole in the other end. Blow the contents of the egg through the small hole and into a bowl. Save for another project. Place the shells in vinegar mixed with food coloring or egg dyes. Soak until shells are dyed. Remove from dye with a spoon and place on inverted egg cartons to dry. Slightly enlarge the hole at the end of each egg. Using a funnel, fill the egg shell halfway with confetti. Close the holes in each end with tape. These eggs can be squeezed or tossed at an opportune moment at an Easter party or used in a game of Easter egg toss.

Synonym Eggs

Copy basket pattern on page 56 onto several sheets of brown construction paper. Beneath each basket, print an adjective. Copy egg shapes onto colored paper, cut out, and laminate.

Put basket sheets, egg shapes, wipe-off markers, and a children's thesaurus in a learning center. Have students select a word, write as many synonyms as they can think of on eggs, then place eggs on the basket. Students may then compare the synonyms they came up with to those which appear in the thesaurus or on a teacher's answer sheet. Encourage children to keep a record of how many synonyms they found for each word. Give each child a plastic Easter egg filled with goodies when he or she completes all of the word baskets in the center.

Who Has the Egg?

Note: This game is best played outside. If you must play inside, make sure nothing breakable is in the playing area.

Have students form a straight line. Choose one student from the line to be the mother hen. The mother hen will stand 15 to 20 feet in front of the line, with his or her back to the remaining students. Mother Hen then throws an "egg" (ball) over his or her shoulder to the rest of the class. Students scramble to catch it. When one of them has caught it, they form a line again, and all students place their hands behind their backs to make it look as if they have the egg. After everyone is back in position, they begin to call, "Cheep, cheep, cheep!" Mother Hen must guess who has the egg. He or she may ask five yes/no questions (Does a girl have it? Does someone wearing blue jeans have it? and so on,) before making a guess. If Mother Hen guesses correctly he or she gets another turn (maximum three turns). If Mother Hen guesses incorrectly, the person holding the egg becomes the next Mother Hen.

Naturally Dyed Easter Eggs

You need: hard-boiled eggs, saucepans, water, frozen spinach (for green), blackberries (for purple), onion skins (for tan), coffee bags or used coffee in a filter (for yellow), beets (for pink), carrots (for peach), plastic or Styrofoam™ containers for each color, a large spoon, and egg cartons. In separate saucepans, boil the natural dye substances until each saucepan is brightly colored. Drain food items from the water and place the colored water in separate Styrofoam™ or plastic containers. Place a hard-boiled egg in each of the containers with the spoon. Let soak until the egg is the desired color. The longer you leave them in, the brighter the colors will be. Let eggs dry on inverted egg cartons. Decorate the dry eggs by adding features with fine-tipped markers, or stickers, lace, ribbon, or felt. Glue on google eyes, sequins, glitter, yarn . . . Be as creative as you wish!

Easter Egg Cookies

Create your favorite sugar or peanut butter cookie recipe. Roll dough into one-inch balls and place two inches apart on a cookie sheet. Make a thumbprint indentation in the top of each cookie and place three jelly beans or small candies in each indentation. Bake the cookies as directed.

Ukrainian Easter Eggs

For this project you need brushes, paints, and illustrations of Ukrainian painted eggs, plus hard-boiled eggs for decorating. Using illustrations of Ukrainian eggs as models, design your own creations and paint the eggs.

Easter Egg Treasure Hunt

Create a map and hide Easter eggs throughout the neighborhood. Have prizes for finding certain hard-to-find Easter eggs, for the most eggs found, and for other unusual features of the hunt.

"Eggbert the Easter Egg"

Obtain a recording or copy of the lyrics for "Eggbert the Easter Egg." Learn the song and have your students perform it for other classes. Consider costumes, choreography, and sets for their performance. If time permits, create your own original verses for this song.

Easter Egg Mobile

Using a purchased hoop, a coat hanger or other base, have students create egg mobiles using small Styrofoam™ egg shapes and decorating them with acrylic paints.

Egg Collage

On a large tagboard egg shape, have students glue magazine pictures, sketches, and/or photos with an Easter theme.

Ceramic Eggs

Have students shape eggs from clay, paint them with glaze, and fire them in a kiln. If one is not available, they can use air-dried clay and paint the dried eggs with acrylic paints.

Egg Muppets

At this center, have students create egg puppets using socks or paper bags or papier-mâché frames. Have them create a skit using their puppets and present it for the rest of the class.

Building a Better Egg Carton

At this center have students experiment with the creation of an egg carton which will keep a raw egg safe from breakage when dropped from the roof of a one-story building. Have a test day for the egg cartons and award prizes for the least expensive, most unusual, most aesthetic, most effective, and most cumbersome cartons.

The Enormous Egg

At this center, have a tape or book copy of *The Enormous Egg* by Oliver Butterworth. Have each student create his or her own story about enormous eggs. When the stories are completed, compile them into a big book or picture book for younger children.

The Egg Book

Have students collect egg facts from this unit and other sources. Have them select their 12 best facts and create an egg-shaped book to share their information.

The Egg Game

Have students use various resources to collect facts about eggs and egg production. Then have them use these facts to create a board game, trivia game, or card game to share their information.

Easter Clothes Logic

Suzanne has a new outfit for Easter. Use the clues to find out which one it is.

1. Suzanne's new outfit is a dress.

2. It does not have buttons on the front.

3. It does not have stripes.

4. It does not have flowers.

Circle Suzanne's new Easter outfit.
Then color all the clothes.

by Ann Richmond Fisher

Easter Egg Math

Solve the math problems below.
For each even answer, color the egg a solid color.
For each odd answer, color the egg with stripes.

$$27 + 10$$

$$54 + 12$$

$$43 + 21$$

$$70 + 17$$

$$14 + 8$$

$$32 + 16$$

$$25 + 21$$

$$91 + 3$$

$$84 + 9$$

$$65 + 37$$

$$39 + 11$$

$$42 + 49$$

$$16 + 52$$

by Veronica Terrill

Name _____

EARTH DAY DOT-TO-DOT

Can you complete the dot-to-dot below and help our rain forest monkey find a home?

BY VERONICA TERRILL

My Earth Day Pledge

I want to do what I can to make the Earth
an even better place to live, so I pledge to

- be careful, not wasteful, with the natural resource of water.
  Here's how I will do that:

  _____

- not litter, and pick up litter when I see it.
  Here are the places I will pick up litter:

  _____

- help care for the birds and animals around my home.
  Here's how I will do that:

  _____

_____   _____
my name   date

Name _____

Arbor Day

(The word *arbor* comes from the Latin language and means "tree.")

Mr. J. Sterling Morton lived in Nebraska
Over one hundred years ago.
He loved the beauty of nature
And wanted to keep nature just so.

There were not many trees
In the Nebraska land.
So he thought, "I will take
This matter in hand."

"Dear people in this treeless land,
I have something important to say.
Please do something about this.
Plant a tree on Arbor Day."

So in Nebraska on the first Arbor Day,
April 10, 1872,
Many trees were planted,
And they grew and grew and grew.

The people were happy
And gave Mr. Morton a cheer.
"The trees look so nice in our land,
We'll keep Arbor Day year after year."

This practice is still alive
All over the U.S. of A.
Think about it my friend.
Plant a tree on the next Arbor Day.

by Sister M. Yvonne Moran

Poplar Tree

A. We planted a tree on Arbor Day.
   After a year or so it looked this way.

B. The tree grew helped by the rain and
   the sun.
   To watch it grow was a lot of fun.

C. The best time of all
   Was when the tree was nice and tall.

A. A.

B. B.

C. C.

B. B.

A. A.

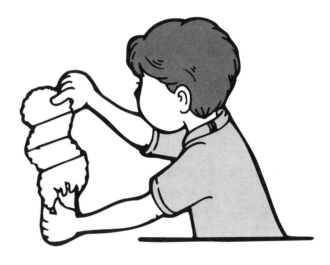

Directions

1. Fold the paper on dotted line C.

2. Open the paper and fold it on dotted line A. Make the 4 As come together.

3. Open the paper, then fold it on dotted line B. Make the 4 Bs come together.

4. Open the paper and see your nice tall tree.

Seasonal Science

Jets

Activity

Jet engines provide thrust to move aircraft. They suck in air at one end and force it out at the other at a much greater speed, pushing the aircraft in the opposite direction. A simple experiment will demonstrate this action. First, blow up a balloon to make it firm and hold the neck of the balloon closed to prevent the loss of air. Now release the balloon and observe that the balloon moves forward as air rushes out from behind. The gases that escape from the back of a jet engine work in the same manner, providing thrust to push the aircraft forward.

Project

Have your students write a few paragraphs about where they would choose to travel in a jet aircraft. Why would they like to visit this place? What would they expect to do and see there? How would this place be different from home? How would it be the same? What would the people be like? Encourage students to illustrate their work and share their imaginary trip with the class.

Parachutes

Activity

Parachutes are designed to use air resistance, or drag, to reduce the speed of falling objects, providing them with a safe landing. Your students can experiment with large sheets of cardboard to feel the effect of drag. Remove the sides from several cardboard cartons. Have the students take turns running while holding a sheet of this cardboard in front of them. As they run, they will feel the air push against the cardboard, slowing them down. Help them to conclude that a parachute works on the same principle. As the air pushes against the underside of the parachute canopy, the speed of the falling object or person is reduced.

Project

Use the cardboard sheets from the experiment along with magazines, pamphlets, newspapers, catalogs, and brochures to create collages of all types of things that fly. Divide the students into groups and have them search for pictures of seeds, kites, blimps, balloons, helicopters, airplanes, and so on to cut out and glue to the cardboard.

by Marie E. Cecchini

Airplanes

Activity

Aircraft wings are streamlined to reduce air resistance. Experiment to demonstrate how a curved, streamlined shape (as the wings of an airplane) helps air flow. You will need a soda can, a piece of cardboard the same height and width as the can, a candlestick, a small plate, a little clay, and matches.

Procedure

1. Secure the candlestick to the center of the small plate with clay. Use additional clay to secure the cardboard to a table or desk, placing the cardboard next to one side of the plate. Light the candle, stand about a foot back, and blow at the card to try and put the candle flame out.

2. Extinguish the candle. Fill the soda can with water to weigh it down. Remove the cardboard and replace it with the water-filled can. Relight the candle, stand back, and blow. What happens to the flame? Help the children conclude that the cardboard broke up the flow of air (your breath) and prevented it from putting out the flame. The flame went out in part two because the air was able to move smoothly around the sides of the can. Note: Experiments using lit candles need to be directly supervised at all times.

Project

Have the children keep a tally of how many airplanes and helicopters they see or hear each day during National Aviation Week. Record and total these daily on a classroom chart.

Balloons

Activity

Demonstrate how hot air balloons make use of warmed air to take flight. You will need an empty plastic soda bottle, a party balloon, a bowl, and hot water. Stretch the neck of the balloon to fit securely over the top of the bottle. Pour the hot water into the bowl; then hold the bottle in the hot water. Prompt the students to observe and discuss the following:

1. Although the bottle appeared empty, it was filled with air.

2. As the air was warmed, it moved upward and expanded, thus inflating the balloon. It is this same process that fills the nylon envelopes of colorful hot air balloons the students may have seen. Also note that the pilots of these airborne balloons do not control the direction of their flight. It is controlled by the direction of the wind.

Project

Make hot air balloons out of paper plates to suspend from the ceiling. Materials: paper plates, paper cups, tissue paper or newspaper, brown construction paper, yarn, markers, paper punch, scissors, stapler, tape.

Procedure

1. Use markers to color the back sides of two paper plates. Staple the plates together, color out, around the edges, leaving a small opening for stuffing. Stuff lightly with tissue or newspaper; then staple the opening closed. Punch a hole at one end. Thread yarn through the hole and knot the ends of the yarn together to make a hanger.

2. Use tape to secure brown construction paper to the paper cup to make a basket for the balloon. Punch two holes at the top of each cup on opposite sides.

3 To attach the basket to the plate balloon, punch two holes at the bottom of the balloon. Cut two lengths of yarn. Thread each piece of yarn through one cup hole and one plate hole, then knot the yarn ends together.

April Showers

Activity

A mirror can also help you demonstrate for the students how rainbows are formed after April showers. A rainbow is colors of light seen in the sky when sun rays strike the falling raindrops. They are curved because raindrops that reflect the light are curved. Set a small mirror into a glass or fishbowl of water. Place this so the sun will shine on the mirror. Turn the glass or bowl until a rainbow is reflected on the wall. Have the students find the colors. The water in the glass or bowl, just as in raindrops, separates the colors that are always present in sunlight. Rainbow colors are red, orange, yellow, green, blue, indigo, and violet (Roy G. Biv).

Project

Provide the students with white paper and fine-point markers or colored pencils. Challenge them to write rainbow-shaped poems about the colors of light.

Up or Down

Activity

Passover is the Festival of Freedom celebrated by Jewish people in April. Matzo, or unleavened bread, is an important part of the observation of this holiday. The story of Passover tells how matzo originated thousands of years ago when the Hebrews fled Egypt in a great hurry without taking time to allow their bread dough to rise. This event is remembered by using matzo during Passover. Experiment with yeast to discover how it is used to make bread rise. Fill two glasses half full of warm water. Stir some flour into one glass. Dissolve a little yeast in the second glass, then stir in a little flour and a pinch of sugar. Set the glasses in a warm place for about an hour, then observe what has changed. Yeast is a fungus, dormant in its dry form. Providing it with warmth (the water and warm spot) and food (sugar) reactivate it, allowing it to produce bubbles of carbon dioxide, which causes bread dough to expand. When bread is baked, it stops rising because the yeast is killed by the heat of the oven.

Project

Let the students make their own matzo by mixing and kneading 3½ c. flour with 1 c. water. Roll the dough out on a floured surface, cut to desired size, then place the matzo squares on a cookie sheet. Use a fork to poke holes in the bread squares. Bake at 475⁰ until lightly browned, about 10-15 minutes.

252

Holiday newsletter

This Earth Day discuss ways your family can make a difference for all living things. Learn to conserve whenever you can by using only what you need of things such as water, soap, and electricity. Make use of reusable containers whenever possible. Start seeds to plant your own garden. Grow vegetables and fruit you can eat. Plant flowers to attract birds and butterflies. If you feel the need to use chemicals for your garden or lawn, choose ones that are safe for the environment. Finally, when shopping, buy products made with recycled materials. Refuse to buy products that have a lot of packaging. Think of every day as Earth Day.

Simple Science

Experiment with raindrops during the shower month of April. Use a medicine dropper to closely observe water drops. What do they look like before they fall? How do they look when they fall onto a hard surface? Into a puddle? Try making your own raindrops. Fill a baking dish with about 2 inches of flour. Hold the pan outside to collect a few raindrops. Allow the flour to dry completely, then carefully sift out your raindrop shapes. Do raindrops come in different sizes?

Look where you put your shoes.

Creative Kitchen

Turn an ordinary sandwich into a "fun"wich during the windy month of March. Let your child trim two slices of bread into diamond shapes. Help your child prepare tuna salad, egg salad, or other sandwich filling. Spread the filling over one kite-shaped bread slice and top it with the second slice. Add strips of cheese, potato sticks, or a licorice whip for a kite tail.

On the Move

Plan to have a rabbit scavenger hunt this year for Easter. Have your child help draw or trace and cut out several rabbit shapes from construction paper. You can also buy rabbit-shaped note paper at a craft or teacher store. Use markers to add facial features to the rabbits. On each rabbit, write a clue directing the child to the next clue. Print the clue and write simple words your child will be able to read with little to no assistance. Place the clues around the house or yard where appropriate. Explain the rules of the game and hand your child clue #1. Have the final clue lead your child to a stuffed or chocolate rabbit.

by Marie E. Cecchini

253

Communication Station

April showers may mean days of indoor play, so bring out the board games and settle in for an afternoon of fun. Games can be an important learning tool as they help children improve their reading and writing skills. Games teach children that there is a sequence to things, which relates to the reading sequence in which letters are used to make words, then words are used to make sentences. Games also encourage children to use their imaginations, which lays a foundation for creative writing and thinking. Games teach children to follow directions. They also reinforce reading and thinking skills. So pull out your favorites and turn a rainy afternoon into an opportunity to have some fun while you're helping to reinforce basic skills.

Poetry In Motion

Celebrate Earth Day by inviting your child to make up a song or jingle to remind everyone about the importance of taking care of our environment. The song might be about littering, recycling, or planting trees.

For example:

Earth Day Song
To the tune of "Frére Jaques"
Please don't litter,
Please don't litter,
Our green Earth, our green Earth.

Every day is Earth Day,
Every day is Earth Day,
Keep it green, keep it green.

You may want to suggest such a project to your child's teacher or principal. Have the PTA make arrangements to award each child who participates a package of seeds, and then publish the songs, poems; and jingles in their school newsletter.

Mathworks

April showers sometimes become thunderstorms, and thunderstorms can become a math lesson. First have your child observe the sky and tell which comes first, the sound of the thunder or the sight of the lightning. Since light travels faster than sound, we see lightning first. Secondly, you can work with your child to find out approximately how far away the storm is. You will need

a stopwatch, pencil, and paper. Use the stopwatch to time the number of seconds between seeing the lightning and hearing the thunder. Divide that number of seconds by 5 to figure out how many miles away the lightning is. Sound travels through air about a mile's distance in 5 seconds.

Reading Room

Celebrate National Library Week this April with spring stories from your local library.

Arthur's April Fool by Marc Brown, Little, Brown & Co.

Easter Crafts by Judith H. Corwin, Franklin Watts.

In the Tall, Tall Grass by Denise Fleming, Holt and Co.

Lunch Bunnies by Kathryn Lasky, Little, Brown & Co.

We Celebrate Spring by Bobbie Kalman, Crabtree Publishing Co.

254

Marvelous

Every day in the month of May can be special with the following calendar of events to spice things up in the classroom! Parents will need a copy of the calendar in order to help with the projects that require homework. Keep extras on hand for lost or misplaced calendars. Enjoy!

MAY

1 Make May baskets from recycled materials you bring from home.
2 Wear two different socks for Socks Day.
3 Bring a pen from home today.
4 Bring a rubber ball to school today.
5 Bring your favorite chips for sharing at snacktime today.
6 Stamp Day—bring one from home.
7 Backwards Day! Do the school day backwards!
8 Write a thank-you note today.
9 Bring your favorite book today.
10 Wear your shirt backwards today.
11 Crazy Socks Day
12 Collections Day—bring your favorite collection to school (with parents' permission only).
13 Pet Day
14 Boxing Day. Create something new from an old box and bring it to share.

15 Boat Day—build a boat with your parents or a friend. Bring it for smooth sailing in the classroom pool.
16 Grandparent or Aunt and Uncle Day.
17 Write a letter to a classmate. Bring it today.
18 Write a thank-you note to your teacher.
19 Draw a picture of your teacher and bring it today for sharing.
20 Be kind to your brothers and sisters today.
21 Surprise your parents by doing something without being asked.
22 Bring your favorite snack to school today.
23 Cleanup Day begins at home and continues at school. Clean up the environment!
24 Colored Pencils Day— bring one or several from home.
25 Splash Day! Wear your swimsuit under your clothes and bring a towel and/or beach bag.
26 Sunglasses Day all day!

28 Happy Hat Day!
29 Stripes Day
30 T-shirt and Game Day— bring your favorite board game.
31 Bring a car today. Race time will be provided.

Using a calendar grid, write the ideas on the days you desire, adjusting the schedule to your classroom needs and putting things on the weekends that are appropriate. Hopefully, every day will be a fun day in the merry, merry month of May!

by Mary Ruth Moore

May Day Flowers

You can't let May Day (the first day of May) pass without flowers! By May most gardens have blooms. Depending upon where you live, the blossoms may be in full bloom, or they may just be peeking out for the first look at spring.

Turn your classroom into a burst of spring color by collecting as many flowers as you can for this exciting day. Cut garden flowers and wild-flowers, lilac or apple blossom blooms. Potted flowering plants and purchased cut flowers will also help bring spring indoors. Use baskets, rubber boot vases, children's sand pails, and other bright containers to display your array of flowers.

Take a Hike to Collect a Picture Bouquet!

Take a flower hike to admire wild and domestic flowers in you area. Use a Polaroid™ camera to capture the flowers on film Make a bouquet of the photographed flowers.

Encourage children to respect the wildflowers and bring in on a few flowers if the plants are plentiful. Discuss how the cuttin of blossoms means that some plants will be unable to releas seeds and others won't last as long.

The May Day Tradition

True to the May Day tradition, flowers should be given to thos you care about on this day. Use the flowers that decorate yo classroom to make bouquets for the children to take home someone special—or give the whole basket of bouquets to retirement home, community helpers, or others you feel wou appreciate the beauty!

Dear Parent/Guardian:

Take a moment to smell the flowers with your child! We will be celebrating spring with a burst of color and fragrance on May Day. If possible, please have your child bring one flower (or more) to class on _____. The flower can be from your garden, nature's garden, or a potted plant.

These flowers will be used to enhance our study of spring and plant growth. We will study the flowers, admire their beauty, and make graphs about the flowers that are brought to class.

Thank you for your contribution!

Sincerely,

by Robynne Eagan   TLC10299 Copyright © Teaching & Learning Company, Carthage, IL 62321-0

Seasonal Science

A child's awareness of his or her physical body is an important step in the development of a healthy self-concept and a sense of physical coordination. One way to develop this awareness is by learning about the various parts of our bodies, how they function, and what they are capable of. Invite your students to learn about the human body as you celebrate National Physical Fitness Month in May.

Muscles

Activity

Explore how muscle contractions create movement. Stretch and release a rubber band to demonstrate how muscles stretch and contract. Discuss how muscles pull our bones so we can move. Invite students to see and feel their muscles in action. Have them bend over and place their hands on their calf muscles (back of lower leg). Tighten and release these muscles. What do they look and feel like? Have the students place their hands on their faces, then alternately smile and frown. Can they feel the movement of the muscles? Invite students to contribute ideas on what jobs muscles help us do. Prompt them to include muscles used in breathing, swallowing, and circulating blood.

Project

Divide students into small groups. Challenge each group to invent a game to share with the class that requires them to use their muscles. Have them name their games, write a list of rules, and list any equipment needed to play. Keep their games on file and select one a day to play during recess.

Health

Activity

Part of keeping physically fit is making sure we take healthy actions for our bodies. Have students name actions we should take to keep our bodies performing at their best. Prompt them to include ideas on exercise, eating habits, cleanliness, rest, and germs. What activities would help us get exercise? What kinds of foods are good to eat? What can we do to keep ourselves clean? Why is this important? Why do our bodies need rest? Where do germs come from, and how do we prevent them from attacking our bodies?

Project

Have students make use of the shared answers from the above discussion to make Healthy Life Books. Let them cut pictures from magazines, catalogs, and newspapers to illustrate exercises, healthy foods, keeping clean, and resting. Label a book page for each of these aspects of health, and glue the appropriate pictures to each page. Have them write a sentence or two about each topic and make covers for their books. Bind the books with staples or yarn.

by Marie E. Cecchini

Bones

Activity

Demonstrate how bones give our bodies support. Build a simple structure with blocks (the bones). Drape a cloth (skin) over the structure. Note how the block skeleton supports the cloth to give it shape. Take a second cloth and drop it next to the first structure. Note what happens to the cloth with no support system. Have students feel their bodies to discover bones under their skin (skull, ribs, spine, hands, and so on). Discuss how some bones (skull, rib cage) protect vital organs. Note how some bones move (ankles, wrists, fingers, and so on). What allows them to move? Dig out your movable Halloween skeleton to demonstrate how joints work. If possible, provide students with real bones from chicken, pork, or fish to observe. Soak the bones in a bleach-water solution overnight to sanitize them.

Project

Let students examine an actual X ray or pictures of X rays from a book. Provide tracing paper and white crayons. Have them draw their own X-ray pictures. In order to view these X rays, have students brush-wash their pictures with watered-down black paint.

Body Jobs

Activity

Invite students to explore the various jobs our bodies do, contributing ideas on how our bodies work for us. Encourage them to use descriptive words and name body parts (heart, lungs, muscles, and so on). when they can. Prompt students with questions like, "What body parts help you lift your backpack? Hold your pen? Run a race? Hear a siren? Read?" Have students place a hand next to their necks and feel their throats as they swallow water and talk. Have them scratch their scalps and listen to what they hear. Make use of a stethoscope so the students can listen to their heartbeats and to what their stomachs sound like when they swallow food or liquid. Let them place the stethoscope next to their cheeks and listen as they chew. What sounds can they make with their tongues, lips, and cheeks? Use a latex glove to demonstrate how our skin fits our bodies. Use a balloon to show how air moves in and out of our lungs. Place a small amount of food into a self-sealing plastic bag and mash it into smaller and smaller pieces to demonstrate the action of our stomachs. Help the students conclude that our bodies are constantly working, even if we are not always aware of it.

Project

Divide the class into small groups. Invite them to trace and cut the body shape of one group member from butcher or craft paper. Have them use markers and collage materials to add body parts inside the shape. Let the students borrow library books to help with the location of the organs, bones, and so on.

258

The Chinese Dragon Boat Festival

Cultures, customs, playtime, and craft time can be intertwined to extend a child's awareness of the world around them. Taking part in a custom will invariably ensure a keener understanding of a different culture.

The Chinese Dragon Boat Festival

On the fifth day of the fifth lunar month, the Chinese Dragon Boat Festival, or Tuen Ng, is celebrated around the world.

The Dragon Boat Festival is one of the three most important of the annual Chinese festivals. The other two are the Autumn Moon Festival and the Chinese New Year. The history of this colorful summer festival rests with the failed attempt to rescue a famous Chinese scholar-statesman, Chu Yuan, who drowned on the fifth day of the fifth lunar month in 277 B.C. The unsuccessful rescue attempt is a part of what the Dragon Boat Festival commemorates each year.

The dragon boats can be 30-100 feet (10-34 meters) long and feature the head and tail of a dragon, which are affixed to the boat for the races and then removed. A dragon boat team consists of 22 people. There are 20 paddlers, a drummer who keeps the paddlers in time, and a sweep who steers the paddlers in the right direction. It takes teamwork to paddle such a long boat through a course that is between 750-3000 feet (250-1000 meters) long.

by Robynne Eagan

Get Ready for Your Own Dragon Boat Races

- Discuss the importance of teamwork when it comes to playing games or competing as a team.
- Discuss the importance of the drummer and the sweep in a Dragon Boat Race.
- Demonstrate how counting out loud helps to keep groups moving in unison.
- Have students take turns being the drummer while others march in unison to the beat.
- Have students march and "paddle" in unison.

School Yard Learning Adventures

Dragon Drum

You Need
- plastic containers with lids
- wood dowels (about 12" long)
- masking or electrical tape
- acrylic paints and paintbrushes or squeeze-on fabric paints
- paper streamers

What to Do
1. Have children place the lid on the container and paint the container to look like a Chinese drum.
2. When the paint has dried, have students remove the lid, place one end of each of the streamers in the container and replace the lid, leaving the remaining portions outside the container. The flying ends will look spectacular streaming behind the drummer.
3. To make the drumstick, have each child wrap tape around one end of the wooden dowel. This end will create an interesting sound when banged on the drum.

Make a Dragon Boat

You Need
- open-ended cardboard boxes, large enough for students to stand inside and hold above the ground
- construction paper or poster board
- paint and paintbrushes
- markers, crayons
- scissors
- streamers, ribbons, sequins for decorating
- packing tape

What to Do
1. Divide the class into groups of 5-10 students. (The number of boxes that make up the body will be determined by how long you want your dragon to be.) Have each group decide which boxes will become the head, tail and body of the dragon. Next develop simple designs. Supply books and posters to inspire ideas. Encourage students to use creativity and cooperation throughout this exercise.
2. Have students paint all the boxes to look like parts of the dragon boat. When the paint is dry, have children add details to the head and tail using construction paper, poster board, and other decorations.
3. The decorated boxes will form the body of the dragon. The head and tail should be added to the body using packing tape
4. Have children practice standing inside the boxes and moving together to make the dragon move.

Host Your Own Dragon Boat Races

- Set a date for the festival. (Include a rain date or two as soggy cardboard just won't work!) Invite spectators to enjoy your dragon boat races.
- On the big day, have students parade the finished dragon boats before other classes. This gives students the opportunity to take pride in their creations and demonstrate knowledge of the origin of the Chinese Dragon Boat Festival.
- Have teams assemble their dragons at the starting line. Encourage team members to use their counting skills as they walk and pretend to paddle to the finish line. Spectators will enjoy watching the dragons march in time to the beat.
- Just for fun, include a backward race and a tricky course with bends and curves marked by blue water-colored obstacles.

260

TLC10299 Copyright © Teaching & Learning Company, Carthage, IL 62321-00

Cinco de Mayo Flower Quilt

Can you color this quilt for Cinco de Mayo? Count the flowers and color each square following the key.

2 flowers = yellow
3 flowers = blue
4 flowers = green
5 flowers = pink

by Veronica Terrill **261**

A Mother's Day Gift

Allison wanted to give her mother something special for Mother's Day. She wanted her mother to know how much she loved her, but Allison did not know what to give her.

Allison's brother Jimmy also wanted to give his mom something for Mother's Day, but he did not know what.

Let's get her something together," suggested Jimmy.

"Okay," agreed Allison. "How about a doll?"

"No," said Jimmy, "Dolls are for little girls. Mom is a big girl. She needs things like . . . tools!"

"Tools are for Dad," argued Allison.

"I've got it!" shouted Jimmy, raising his hands high in the air. "Let's go upstairs to our toy closet and see if we can find something there for her."

They raced upstairs to the closet. "Wow!" said Allison. "This closet is a mess. We'll never find anything in here."

Jimmy looked around, up and down, left and right. From the top to the bottom, from the beginning to the end, toys were scattered everywhere in the closet.

"I have an idea," said Jimmy. "If we clean out this closet, then maybe we can find something to give Mom for Mother's Day."

"Okay," agreed Allison. "But where do we start?"

Thoughtfully, Jimmy scratched his head. "Let's get the baby-sitter to help us. Maybe she can even help us find something in this messy closet to give Mom for Mother's Day."

Allison and Jimmy hopped downstairs, got the baby-sitter, and dragged her upstairs to help clean their closet. They were determined to find something in that messy closet to give their mother so she would know how much they loved her.

"You must hurry," explained the baby-sitter. "Today is Mother's Day, and your mother will be home soon."

Together, Allison, Jimmy, and the baby-sitter cleaned the closet. They put all the puzzles in one corner and all the instruments in another corner. Their chalkboard and school supplies were placed at one end of the closet and their stuffed animals were at the other end.

Allison's doll clothes were neatly packed in a suitcase. Jimmy's cars and trucks were neatly parked in a toy garage. All the other toys were put in big boxes. The sitter threw away all the old, used, broken pieces of crayons and other things

which could no longer be identified.

But they didn't find anything in the closet to give Mother for Mother's Day.

Allison and Jimmy were sitting in their clean closet, trying to think of where to look next, when their Mother walked in.

Disappointed and unhappy that they had no gift to give her on Mother's Day, Allison and Jimmy looked at the sitter. But it was too late for her to help them. She only shrugged. Mother was standing in front of them, staring and smiling!

"Oh, how wonderful!" praised Mother. "Allison, Jimmy, you cleaned your closet. What a wonderful Mother's Day present! I love you both very much."

by Lynn Renee Wise

Gifts for Mom

Mother's Day Hat Planter

While your class is learning about spring, seeds and growing things, start a project that will be ready to take home for Mother's Day.

Materials
- small plastic plates and bowls
- stapler
- potting soil
- pebbles
- flower seeds (alyssum, marigold)
- paper
- pattern
- crayons or markers
- ribbon
- craft knife

Directions

1. Prepare part of this project ahead of time by cutting out the bottom of the bowl with a craft knife.
2. Place the bowl upside down on the plate and staple the edges together. It will look like a hat.
3. Have students put pebbles in the bottom so the water can drain; then add the potting soil, seeds, and a bit of water.
4. Place the planters in a sunny spot and water them regularly.
5. When Mother's Day is near, finish this project by tracing the face shape on appropriately colored paper. Have children decorate the face to look like their mothers. Add yarn hair, if desired.
6. Attach the face to the bottom of the plate near the edge so that it can sit on a shelf and the face will hang down in front. Your students may want to decorate the hat a bit by winding some ribbon around the base or adding a paper bow.

by Sheila M. Hausbeck

Mother's Day Stationery

This project will turn out best if children brainstorm first and make a plan on scrap paper before proceeding.

Provide each child with an 8½" x 11" sheet of paper. Fold the paper into four equal parts as if it were a greeting card. Then open it and lay it flat.

In each section of the paper, let children design a different border for Mom's stationery. In order to personalize the notes, urge them to think of their mother's interests, hobbies and so on.

Emphasize that they must not draw too close to the edges. If they leave about a finger's width from each edge, it will make it easier to copy and cut apart later. It is also important to check that the pencil drawing is dark enough to copy well. If it is too light, have the child trace over the design a second time. Remind children NOT to color their designs—this can be done after the notes are copied.

by Karen Bjork

It will make it easier for the teacher to identify notes if children are instructed to initial or sign each note in a bottom corner before copying.

Four copies of each sheet will make a total of 16 notes for Mother to use as reminders, grocery lists, messages to teacher, and so on. Notes can be cut apart individually by the child using scissors, or if time is of the essence, the teacher can align notes and use a paper cutter.

Upon returning the copied stationery, give children the option of coloring their designs.

A construction paper stationery holder can be easily designed from a 9" x 12" sheet of construction paper to contain the notes for safe keeping and transported home. If available, a photo of the child is a nice addition to the cover. Notes may be made for Dad, Grandma, an aunt, or a caregiver if a mother is not in the home.

264

CRAFT CORNER

Mother's Day Card

Make a special Mother's Day card for a very special Mom.

Materials
- food coloring
- water
- small bowls
- white paper towels
- construction paper
- scissors
- crayons or markers
- green pipe cleaners
- glue

Let's Make It

1. Put some water and a few drops of food coloring in a small bowl. Repeat in separate bowls for as many colors as you want to have.
2. Fold the paper towel into a small square. Dip each end of the paper towel into a different bowl of colored water. Continue dipping until the paper towel is completely wet with colored water.
3. Carefully unfold the paper towel and allow it to dry.
4. Fold a piece of construction paper in half.
5. Cut a cone shape with a radius of approximately 3 inches (8 cm) from the dry paper towel. This will be the flower. Twist a green pipe cleaner around the bottom of the flower. Have each student make three or four flowers, depending on the size of each flower.
6. Use a small piece of pipe cleaner to keep each bouquet in place. Poke the pipe cleaner through the front of the card, wrap it around the bouquet and poke it back out on the other side. Twist the ends together on the inside of the card. Be sure to hide this with the vase.
7. When there are enough flowers for a small bouquet on the card, cut a triangle shape from another color of construction paper to make the vase. Glue the vase to the card, making sure the pipe cleaner stems are in the vase.
8. On the inside of the card, write the following message:
   Happy Mother's Day, Mom!
   I love you a bunch!

Happy Mother's Day, Mom! I love you a bunch! Mandy

Mother's Day Wind Chimes

A gentle breeze on a spring day will have Mom thinking of her little one, as her Mother's Day wind chimes sing to her.

Materials

    clay flowerpot
    scissors
    rope
    fishing line
    paintbrush
    acrylic paints
    broken pieces of pottery or seashells

Let's Make It

1. Wash and dry the clay pots.
2. Cut a piece of rope about 3 feet (1 m) long for each student. Have students tie several knots on top of one another at one end of the rope. The knots should form a large lump.
3. Thread the unknotted end of the rope from the inside, out through the hole in the bottom of the pot. The knot should be large enough to stop the rope from coming out of the pot.
4. Cut a piece of fishing line about 8 inches (20 cm) long for each student. Have students tie one end of it to a piece of broken pottery or shell.
5. Have students reach into the pots and pull the knotted rope out so they can tie the other end of the fishing line to it. Adjust the length of the fishing line so that the bottom edge of the clapper, (shell) hangs out of the pot about 1 inch (2.5 cm).
6. Using the acrylic paints, have students paint designs on the bells. Have children write *Happy Mother's Day!* and the year on their designs. Encourage students to be creative.
7. When the paint has dried, have children wrap the chimes well and place in a gift bag.

A Pat on the Back for Dad

A Dad card, and remembering to tell Dad why he deserves a pat on the back will make Dad feel great.

Materials

    large sheets of construction paper
    white bond paper
    markers or crayons
    tempera paint
    scissors

Let's Make It

1. Have students brainstorm reasons their dads deserve pats on the back. Record their ideas on chart paper.
2. Fold the construction paper in half to form a card.
3. Have students draw the shape of a T-shirt on the white paper. The T-shirt should be large enough to enclose the child's handprint.
4. Spread paint on each child's hand and have him or her make a handprint on the front of his or her T-shirt shape.
5. While the handprint is drying, students should print *You Deserve a Pat on the Back* in big letters on the front of the card.
6. When the paint is dry, have students glue the T-shirt shapes to the inside right half of the card.
7. Inside, on the left-hand side of the card, students can write the heading *Why You Deserve a Pat on the Back*. Beneath the heading, students can write thoughts about why their dad is special. Refer to the recorded thoughts but encourage individuality. Have children finish by writing *Happy Father's Day!* and signing the card.

GIFT IDEA FOR DAD

Here's a simple Father's Day gift that children will enjoy giving and dads will enjoy all year long.

Materials

small container with a lid (box or jar)
paint and paintbrushes or decorative adhesive paper
small photo of the child
glue
dark marker
typing paper
pen or marker
scissors

You laugh a lot.
You take me fishing.
You read to me.
You help me.
Dad, you're special to me because . . .
You are fun.
DAD

Directions

1. Paint the container and its lid a bright color, or cover it with decorative adhesive paper.

2. Glue your photo (or a copy of the photo) on the container.

3. Draw a speech balloon above your photo. Print in the speech balloon, *Dad, you're special to me because . . .*

4. Cut out several small strips of paper.

5. On each strip of paper, print something about your dad that makes him special. (You are fun. You take me fishing. You read to me. You laugh a lot. You help me.)

6. Fold each paper strip and put them in the container.

7. Give the gift to your dad and tell him to take out one of the paper strips each day as a reminder of why you love and appreciate him.

by Mary Tucker

267

End-of-School Activities

You know you've had a successful school year when your students are feeling sad about leaving you and their friends. This is a good time to reinforce the value of friendship. Hold a classroom discussion on friendship. Recite this poem together, using actions to show the emotions.

So Long

It's always sad to say good-bye,
But summertime is here.
It's not "good-bye," it's just "so long,
See you in the next school year."

"Remember Me" Projects

Have students make these friendship gifts to exchange with class-mates. If possible, let students choose what they will make.

Doorknob Sign

1. Cut a 4" x 7" rectangle from poster board.
2. Draw a circle at the top of the rectangle large enough to go over a doorknob. Draw two crossed lines across the circle, one verti-cal and one horizontal.
3. Do not cut out the whole circle; just cut along the two lines inside the circle.
4. Use a yellow crayon or marker to draw lines around the circle to make it look like the sun.
5. Print on the lower half of the rec-tangle, When this you see, please think of me.
6. Color the rest of the rectangle with interesting designs, flowers, shapes, and so on.
7. Write your name at the bottom and give the sign to a friend.

Friendship Bracelets

1. Choose three colorful pieces of yarn, long enough to go over your hand and fit loosely around your wrist.
2. Braid the yarn and tie the ends together to make a bracelet.
3. Give the bracelet to a friend.

Dear Brittney,
I am so glad we are friends!
See you next year!

Shelly

School Pictures

Write a short message (or the "So Long" poem) on the back of one of your school pictures and sign your name. Give the photo to a friend.

by Jo Jo Cavalline & Jo Anne O'Donnell

Flag Day

Children will need scissors and an 8½" x 11" sheet of paper. Show them how to fold the paper according to the numbered drawings.

Old Glory, the Stars and Stripes, the Star-Spangled Banner . . . no matter what you call it, June 14 is the day to celebrate our country's flag.

Betsy Ross sewed the first American flag in 1776. George Washington suggested a six-pointed star, but Betsy showed how a five-pointed star could be cut with just a single snip of her scissors. Here's how she did it.

1. Fold in half.

2. Fold in half again, both ways, then unfold this part.

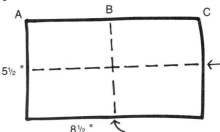

A   B   C

5½ "

8½ "

3. Bring corner A to the long crease and fold.

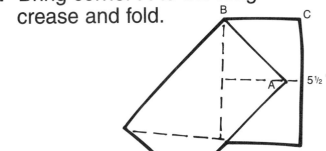

B   C

A   5½ "

4. Fold A back on itself toward the left.

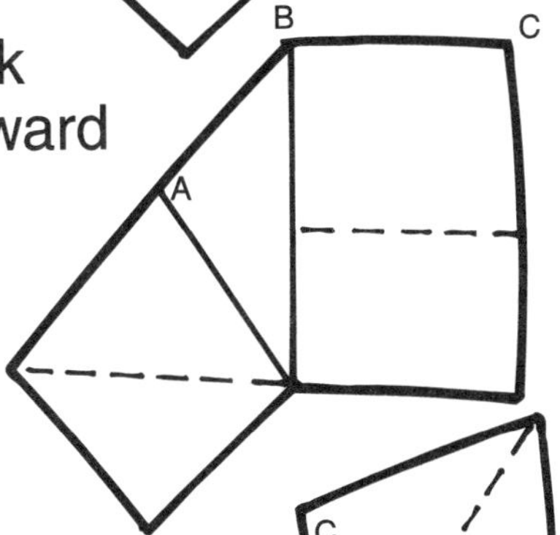

B   C

A

5. Fold flap C toward the left over A.

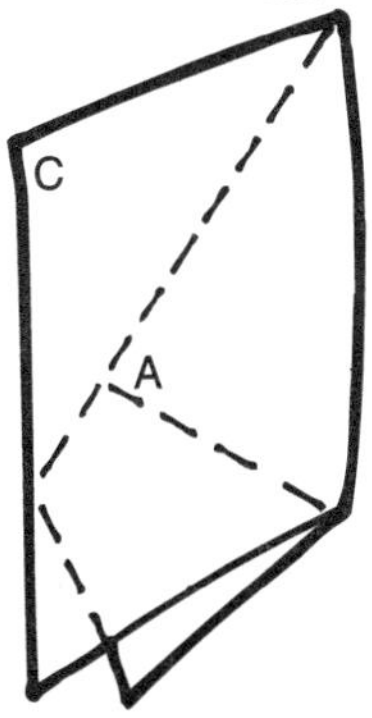

C

A

6. Fold C over itself, back toward the right.

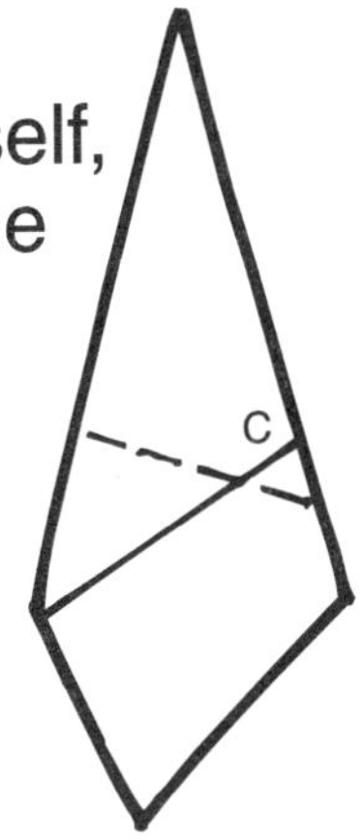

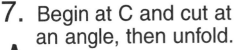

C

7. Begin at C and cut at an angle, then unfold.

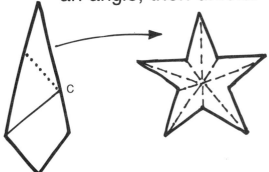

C

It may take a little concentration and practice; but after the first few, you can cut stars by the dozen. You can make them any size. Just be sure to use a similar rectangle to begin.

by Linda Masternak Justice

269

Now that your kids can cut stars like Betsy Ross, put everyone's stars together to make a flag. Try a model of the flag Betsy made—13 stars in a circle and 13 alternating red and white stripes.

Flag Birthday

June 14th was officially proclaimed Flag Day by President Truman in 1949, but the celebration of "Flag Birthday" was originated by a school teacher, B.J. Cigrand, in 1885. Early Flag Day celebrations involved having each child carry a small flag and parade around the school grounds while singing patriotic songs. Plan a Flag Day celebration at your school.

☆ Start before Flag Day with a school-wide door decorating contest with a patriotic theme.

☆ Set aside a few moments for the entire school to recite the Pledge of Allegiance. It was written in 1892 by Francis Bellamy and published in a magazine called, *Youth Companion*.

I pledge allegiance…

☆ Give each child a small flag and have a parade as you play a Sousa march.

☆ Listen to "The Star-Spangled Banner," one of the few national anthems dedicated to a flag.

☆ Read a book about Betsy Ross. Here are some to choose from.

Betsy Ross by Alexandra Wallner, Holiday House Publishers.

Betsy Ross: Designer of Our Flag by Ann Weil, Aladdin Paperbacks.

A Flag for Our Country by Eve Spencer, Raintree/Steck Vaughn.

270

The Longest Day of the Year

"I'm celebrating the longest day;
Summertime is here to stay.
The longest, sunniest day of the year,
June 20th is finally here!"

"I'm celebrating the longest day;
Summertime is here to stay.
The longest, sunniest day of the year,
June 20th is finally here!
Meet at the gazebo when the sun goes down
And we'll celebrate all around."

Franco the Frog delivered this message from his favorite spot by the side of the pond. He had just finished a delicious meal of earthworms and taken a quick dip in the warm water. While drying himself on a convenient shelf of mud, Franco noticed that the sun was located at the highest point in the sky, higher than it had been on any of the other days of the year. In nature, this is known as the Summer Solstice, and it is a special day.

Hearing Franco's announcement, Roxie the Robin flew over for a bit of conversation.

"I was going to make the announcement myself," began Roxie, "but I got detoured by a lovely new delivery of sunflower seeds in that feeder." She bobbed her head toward a bird feeder near the park's gazebo. "Those rude blue jays tried to steal all of it, but when they started fighting amongst themselves I darted in," she finished.

"Good strategy," agreed Franco. "But now that you're here, what are we going to do about the celebration?"

"I have an idea," a new voice chimed in. It was the voice of Rebekah Rabbit, who shyly approached the pond with her almost grown children beside her. "We can all meet at the gazebo at dusk when things are quiet and tell about our plans for the rest of the summer."

"And play!" added one of Rebekah's youngsters.

"That's a good idea," said Franco. "And we can let the other critters know about the celebration by singing my song."

Franco took this song around to animals living on the sides of the pond. He liked to stay near the rocks and water. It was his habitat and his protection. Leaping gracefully and darting into dark corners, he brought the message of the summer solstice to the family of beavers who lived on a wild, overgrown side of the big pond and to his closer neighbors, the lizards who lived under the small bridge.

Rebekah and her children preferred the tall grasses at the far end of the park. They shared the song with some squirrels they met on the way, but mostly Rebekah watched over her children. There had been some predatory cats around lately. "One would think that they had enough to eat at their fancy houses," thought Rebekah. But a baby bunny was too tempting. Mom had to be very vigilant.

It was Roxie Robin who got about the most. That was the advantage of wings. Roxie stopped and spoke to a pair of woodpeckers building in a rotting pine tree. Woodpeckers love a pine tree that has been hit by lightning; it is perfect for home building. She left a note for the opossum and raccoon clans. They were nocturnal critters, and spent the day sleeping and lounging. When they woke later on, they would learn about the celebration at the gazebo. Roxie thought about leaving the rude blue jays out of the celebration, but she sighed and swooped by with a quick song:

"I'm celebrating the longest day;
Summertime is here to stay.
The longest, sunniest day of the year,
June 20th is finally here!
Meet at the gazebo to celebrate.
Come at dusk and don't be late."

The day passed slowly, hot and humid. Do you know why that particular day was so long? The Earth revolves around the sun once during the 365 days of the year, but rotates every 24 hours on its axis. The movement of the Earth around the sun gives us the seasons. The turning of the Earth on its axis gives us day and night. The Summer Solstice occurs as the earth revolves around the sun, and around June 20th each year the Earth is tipped slightly toward the sun. This slight tipping gives our hemisphere a long look at the sun and gives us the longest day of the year. But what happens to the other part of the Earth while we are enjoying the long look at the sun? While it is summer in the northern part of the globe, it is winter in the Southern Hemisphere in countries such as Australia. Differences in climate and seasons make the Earth an interesting and wonderful planet.

It was dusk at the gazebo, almost 9:00 at night. The animals had enjoyed a leisurely day of eating, playing, and gathering food. They had to spend part of each day gathering food to save for winter. Though summer began officially on this day, they knew that in just a few months the days would become shorter and cooler, and food would be harder to find.

"If today is the longest day of the year, when do we have the shortest day?" one of Rebekah's children asked.
"Well, I'm not quite sure, it may be in November," Rebekah thought out loud.

"Not in November," Franco reminded her. "It is December 20th, six months from now. The Winter Solstice occurs near December 20th and our part of the Earth gets the shortest look at the sun, signaling the beginning of winter."

"But that leaves two more seasons," Roxie announced from her perch on a magnolia tree. She loved the fragrant scent of magnolias in the warm air.

"Right," said Franco, "but we don't call them solstices. In spring and fall we have equinoxes because the sun is at a middle height in the sky and day and night are just about the same length."

"That makes sense," agreed Rebekah. "*Equinox* means 'equal, or the same.' "

The animals had gathered near the gazebo. It was a good place to meet, nestled in trees, surrounded by flowering bushes and thick shrubbery. This gave good cover and lots of goodies to snack on. Meeting at dusk was a good idea, too, because the darkness kept people away from the paths of the park and the buzzing gnats and mosquitoes that swarmed when the sun went down.

The animals talked about their plans for the long summer days. Rebekah wanted to fatten up her babies and show them the best hiding places in the long summer grasses. Roxie planned to feast on fresh sunflower seeds in a garden planted near the gate of the park. Franco planned to sun and swim most of the summer. The opossum and raccoon families were looking forward to lots of food scraps, since human families often brought picnics to the park and left behind marvelous munchies in the trash cans. Peanut butter and honey sandwiches and apple cores were the best.

"Will today be the hottest day of the year?" one of the opossums asked Franco.

"I doubt it," he replied. "Those days don't come until August, when the Earth draws in a lot of heat from the sun. But today is the beginning of hot days."

"And big storms," added Roxie. "Look at that lightning." Sure enough, a yellow bolt of hot summer lightning lit up the park. "This heat stirs up some big storms. But that's okay too; we need the rain."

"Time to go, children," Rebekah gently nudged her babies toward home.

"See you tomorrow," Franco called out, heading for his rock.

"Happy summer to all of you!" sang out Roxie as she and the other critters sought shelter from the first big thunderstorm of summer rumbling into their park.

Language Enrichment

1. Encourage language fluency by introducing rich, new words to the children. Read the story first for pleasure, just to listen to the rhythm of the words and the message. Then move into analysis and discussion. Use a piece of chart paper and a bright, colored marker. Invite children to share new and unfamiliar words they encounter in the story *(convenient, solstice, announcement, bided, strategy, celebration, habitat, predatory, tempting, vigilant, advantage, nocturnal, humid, revolves, rotates, gazebo, swarm, axis)*. Find the places in the story where these words occur and read them aloud to the children. Show them how to use context clues to determine an approximate meaning for each word.
2. Copy page 274, "Notice My New Word," to help children build vocabulary and spelling skills.
3. Practice writing "announcements" for each of the four seasons of the year. Print on the board *Announcing a New Season*. Have children create sentences about each season. Discuss the purpose of announcements: to share important information in a quick, simple way. Combine children's announcements into a class season booklet.
4. For younger children, copy page 275, "By the Gazebo" coloring sheet. To encourage language flexibility, ask children to write or dictate what they think the characters are saying.

Science Enrichment

1. Use a globe and flashlight to illustrate the concepts of rotation and revolution.
2. Create "shoe box habitats." You will need clean, empty shoe boxes, glue, pieces of fabric, paper, magazine pictures, clay, and natural items (pine needles, stones, acorns). Discuss the concept of a habitat. Give examples from the story. Explain how different kinds of animals need habitats that offer food, protection, water, and climate that suit them. Make habitats that are realistic. Show water, shelter, protection, and clay animals or magazine pictures of animals taped to craft sticks.
3. Compare and contrast summer with the other seasons of the year. Use a plain white paper plate for each child to illustrate this discussion. Divide the plate into four sections of equal size. Invite children to draw or cut and paste magazine pictures of scenes and items unique to each season. Hang the plates from the ceiling using transparent fishing line.

Name _____

Notice My New Word

My new word is _____.

I looked this word up in the dictionary. It means: _____

_____

_____

_____

_____

_____.

Here is a sentence using my new word:

_____

_____

_____

_____

Here is a picture of animals from the story showing how they used the word.

Name _____

By the Gazebo

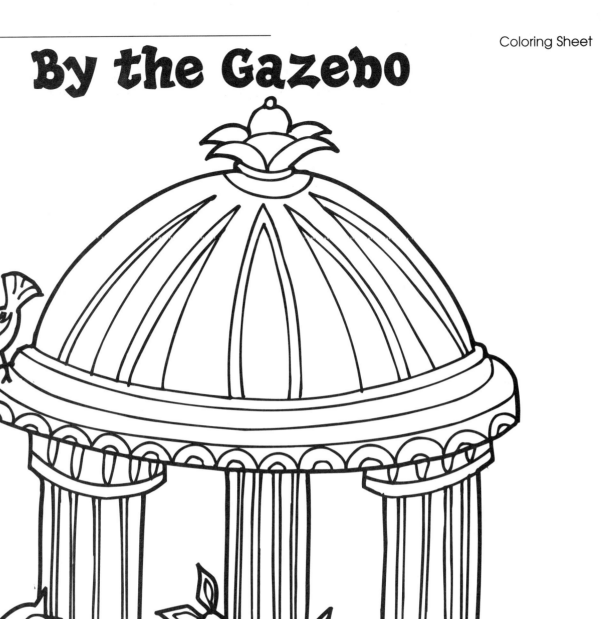

Bugs Can Dig in the Mud

Bugs can dig in the mud
And bugs can climb big trees.
They're very spry—some even fly—
They all do what they please.

Some bugs can glow in the dark!
Some bugs can swim with skill.
All run barefoot and always put
Away the food I spill.

Most bugs move fast (they have six legs).
They're brave and clever, too.
All this is why I wish that I
Was a big black bug . . .

don't you?

by Marcie Tichenor

276

Birds in Your Yard

Who said birds don't eat much? Try putting a feeder in your yard and you'll see that birds really do eat a lot. It doesn't matter if you live in the city or country, birds will find their way to your feeder. And when you make a special effort to feed them, you'll find yourself looking out your window at many different kinds of birds.

Build a bird feeder by having an adult help you put a large wooden post firmly in the ground. Then nail a square or round wooden tray securely on top of the post. You don't have to paint it because birds actually prefer plain wood. Maybe a roof could be attached, too. If you can't build a feeder, many are inexpensive to buy.

Now that you have your feeder, it's time to fill it with bird treats. Most birds love sunflower seeds, especially blue jays and cardinals. You can buy a mixture of bird seed at the store for your feeder, and feathered friends will go for it. If you want to attract mourning doves, juncos, or sparrows, put out cracked corn.

All birds love small bits of bread, dry oatmeal, crushed dog biscuits, chopped apple, nuts, or most any kind of cereal or chips, but avoid foods with salt.

Find a pinecone. Smear peanut butter on its hard petal parts; then tie a string on it and attach it to the underneath part of the feeder tray. Peanut butter is a fat and helps birds stay warm in the winter.

Another fat the birds love is suet. Ask an adult to buy some at the store. Then attach small pieces to a string and fasten them to the bottom of the tray. Suet especially appeals to woodpeckers, chickadees, starlings, and nuthatches.

If you want to learn the names of the birds that visit your feeder, you can go to the library and borrow a book with bird names and pictures. Many pet or farm supply stores have charts that show pictures and names of birds. Sometimes the charts are given free to the store's customers.

During the summer you can put a small dish of water in your feeder, but not in the winter of course, because it would freeze. Feed your birds during summer months so they'll remember your feeder's location when the cold weather comes.

It's fun to watch birds' activities, especially when it is too cold for you to go outside. Grab a pen and notebook and quietly sit by the window near your feeder.

Then take notes on which kind of birds are:

- most hungry
- the fighters
- most friendly
- group travelers

Then notice which ones:

- hop
- knock food to the ground
- make the most noise
- flutter their wings a lot

You may want to find stories about birds in old newspapers and magazines and add them to your notebook. It'll be fun to see how these bird stories compare with the ones in your notebook about your own yard birds.

by Jean Powis

277

Name _____

Birds in Your Yard

Starting with number 1, connect the dots and find something that chirps.

Birds of a Different Feather

Coming and Going Birds

Tweet! Tweet!
Squawk! Squawk!
Chirp! Chirp!
Bird talk.

Cheep! Cheep!
Cheerio!
Watch them
Eat and go!

Tweet Speak

Invite children to act like birds and teach them bird calls. Here are some examples from *A Field Guide to the Birds of Eastern and Central North America* by Roger Tory Peterson (Boston: Houghton Mifflin, 1980): *chip-burr* (scarlet tanager), *per-chik-o-ree* (American goldfinch); *sweet, sweet, sweet* (song sparrow); *chiv, chiv* (red-bellied woodpecker); *queedle, queedle* (blue jay); *fee-bee-ee* (black-capped chickadee); *who, who, who* (white-breasted nuthatch); *tea-kettle, tea-kettle* (Carolina wren); *kit-kit-kit* (brown-headed nuthatch); *weet weet weet tsee tsee* (yellow warbler). As children flap their "wings" they make bird sounds.

Ten Flying Visitors

To the tune of "Ten Little Indians"

One little, two little, three little feeding birds,
Four little, five little, six little drinking birds,
Seven little, eight little, nine little bathing birds,
Ten little visiting birds.

Bird Body

Teach children the parts of a bird. On self-adhesive labels, print the names for the parts of a bird (head, bill, wings, feathers, tail). Display a large picture of a bird. Call on one child at a time to stick a label on the correct bird part.

Eat Like a Bird

Have children help you set up a bird restaurant. Ask them to think up names for their restaurant. Vote on the choices. Show some of the things birds eat: sesame seeds, sunflower seeds, peanuts, beef suet, peanut butter, and bread crumbs. What will they put on today's menu for the birds to eat? Have children fill a bird feeder with their menu items. Hang the feeder outside your classroom window (or other suitable spot). Help the children identify the different kinds of birds that visit their restaurant.

by Jacqueline Schiff

Winging It

Copy the birds on this page and page 281. Have children color them; then ask children to cut out their favorite bird. Mount each bird on poster board, punch a hole, and tie a string through it so children can "fly" their birds around the room. Hang the birds from wire to make classroom bird mobiles.

Bird Words

Print the following bird names on the chalkboard. Ask children to fill in the missing letters from the word BIRD to complete each bird name. (Answers: 1. finch, 2. woodpecker, 3. lark, 4. robin)

1. F ___ N C H
2. W O O ___ P E C K E R
3. L A ___ K
4. R O ___ I N

"Winging It" Field Trip

Take a field trip in the neighborhood with your children and observe the birds. Bring binoculars. Ask children to listen for bird sounds. Can they imitate the sounds? Let children take turns looking through the binoculars. What colors are the birds they see? Can they spot any bird nests? When you return to school, ask children to draw or paint what they observed.

chickadee

robin

wren

woodpecker

Birds of a Different Feather Patterns

dove

cardinal

blue jay

goldfinch

Baltimore oriole

bluebird

Home Sweet Home Rebus

( ) looked out his ( ) . He saw a little ( ) under a

( ) . It could not fly. ( ) took the ( ) to a ( )

The ( ) fixed the ( ) wings. The ( ) told ( ) .

to keep the ( ) in a ( ) for a while. ( ) hung the

( ) in the ( ) near his ( ) . ( ) brought the

( ) ( ) and ( ) . Soon, the ( ) was well.

( ) opened the little ( ) in the ( ) and the

by Donnaleen Howitt

flew away. ◯ felt sad. One day ◯ looked out his ◯

and saw the little ◯ again. The ◯ was building a

◯ in the ◯ . "How nice!" said ◯ . "Even a

◯ can be a home if the ◯ is always open!"

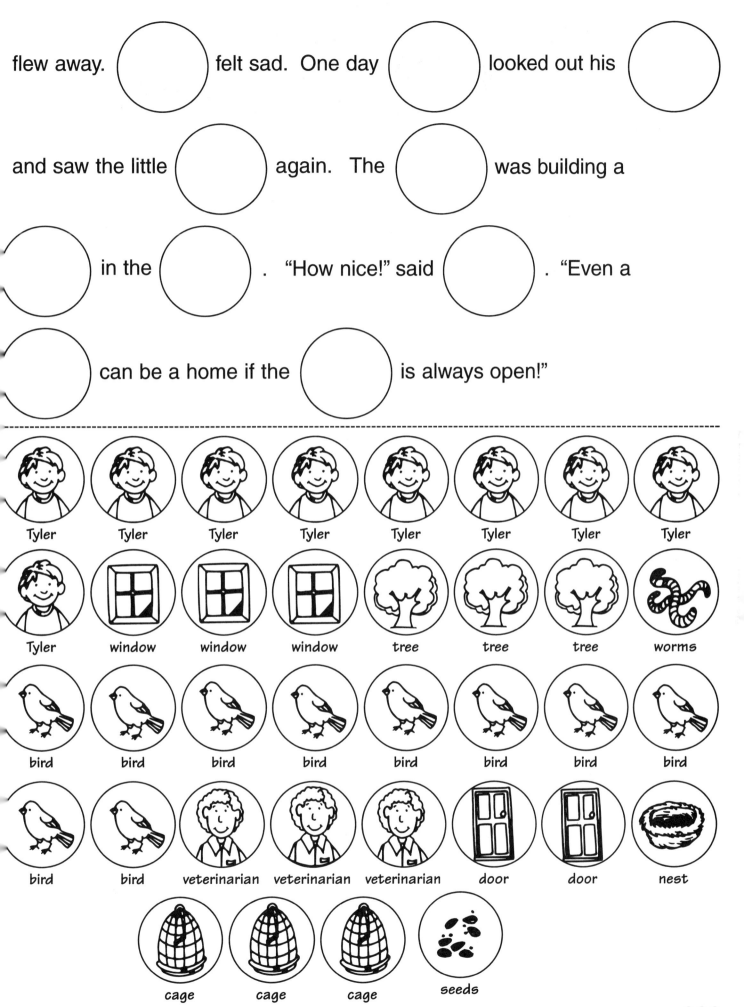

Tyler   Tyler   Tyler   Tyler   Tyler   Tyler   Tyler   Tyler

Tyler   window   window   window   tree   tree   tree   worms

bird   bird   bird   bird   bird   bird   bird   bird

bird   bird   veterinarian   veterinarian   veterinarian   door   door   nest

cage   cage   cage   seeds

Beautiful Butterflies

The butterfly is one of the most beautiful things we see in the spring and summer. It's hard to believe it was once a worm-like creature called a caterpillar. How, then, does a caterpillar become a butterfly? It goes through a process called *metamorphosis*, which is the four stages of a butterfly's life.

The first stage is the *egg*. The mother butterfly lays many eggs (about the size of the head of a pin) on twigs, leaves, or on the ground. A few days later, the eggs hatch and small caterpillars come out. This is the second, or *larva* stage.

Immediately, the caterpillar begins to eat. First it eats its own eggshell. Then it eats leaves and other foods. It eats and eats, and grows bigger and bigger. But its skin doesn't grow with the body. The skin becomes too tight. It splits open near the head and the caterpillar wiggles out wearing a new soft skin. In a few days, the caterpillar outgrows the new skin and again crawls out. This change of skin is called *molting*, and occurs four or five times over the course of two to four weeks.

When the caterpillar is fully grown, it stops eating and rests for a few hours. Then it gets to work. It finds a safe place (a twig or under a leaf) to turn into a *pupa*. It spins a sticky liquid thread from a small bump just below its mouth. This thread covers its body and holds the caterpillar safely in place.

The caterpillar's skin splits again. Now it is bare and in the *pupa* stage. A hard skin like a shell forms around the pupa. It doesn't eat and is very still. But inside the shell it's changing into a butterfly.

After several weeks or months, the butterfly is in the *adult* stage and ready to come out. A fluid from its body loosens it from the shell. The butterfly pushes hard and cracks the shell. In just a few minutes, the butterfly comes out. It hangs on the shell and pumps up its wings with blood. Once the wings are dry and large and strong enough, the butterfly flies away to drink a sweet liquid from flowers called *nectar*. And while butterflies fly from flower to flower, they make it possible for the flowers to develop into fruits and seeds by carrying pollen from one flower to another.

Butterflies do not grow as they become older. Small ones stay small and large ones are always large. But no matter what their size, they are the most beautiful and graceful of the insects.

by Judy Wolfman

284

Parts of a Butterfly

Because it is so small, we don't always see all the parts of a butterfly. If you can catch one and look at it with a magnifying glass, see if you can find these parts.

HEAD: the first part of the body. This is where the eyes, antennae, and mouth are. The mouth has a long, hollow tongue that curls and uncurls like a party blower. It is used like a straw to suck up the nectar from flowers. The antennae are used for smelling.

THORAX: the middle part of the body. It has three segments. A pair of legs grows from each. The front wings are connected to the center segment, and the rear wings to the last one.

ABDOMEN: the last part of the body. It has nine segments. Eight of them let air in so the butterfly can breathe. The abdomen also is like a stomach.

The whole body of the butterfly, including the wings, is covered with thousands of tiny, flat scales. The scales overlap like the shingles on a roof. This is what gives the butterfly its beautiful color and pattern. The scales are soft and rub off when something touches them. Then the butterfly looks pale and you can see through it.

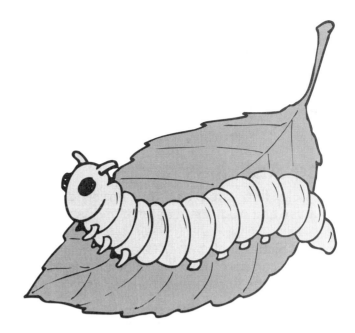

About Caterpillars

A caterpillar is a worm-like creature that usually has 12 segments, plus a head, on its long body. The head is at the front of the body and has six simple eyes. But the eyes don't see very well, so the caterpillar guides itself by using a pair of short feelers.

The caterpillar has six pairs of legs on the first three segments of its body. On the abdomen it has prolegs, that are really not legs at all. The "real" legs and feet are strong so the caterpillar can hold onto a leaf while eating it with his strong, biting jaws.

Caterpillars are not all the same. They can be long or short; thin or fat; smooth or bumpy; naked or covered with hairs, bristles, or spines.

Birds and some insects eat caterpillars, so they are not safe. They protect themselves in different ways. Some hide during the day, far from the plants they eat. Some roll into a tight ball and "play dead." Others are brown or green and look like the plant they live on. Still others smell or taste bad, or are prickly. And there are some caterpillars that fasten their silk thread to the end of a leaf or twig, then spin enough thread so they can hang down out of the enemy's sight and reach.

Caterpillars are heavy eaters and can be terrible pests. Caterpillars can strip trees and plants of their leaves, which is harmful to them. They also eat holes in fruits and vegetables, which make farmers angry.

Science Activities

1. If possible, find caterpillars, butterflies, eggs, and larvae and study them under a microscope.

2. Look at pictures of butterflies, or mounted ones, and compare them by color and markings. Notice the symmetry of the designs.

3. Use a net and catch your own butterflies. Put them in a bottle with holes in the lid. After studying them, release them.

4. Raise your own butterfly. In June or early July, look for monarch eggs. They can usually be found where milkweed grows, since this is what they like to eat. If you can't find monarch eggs, capture female butterflies. Keep them in cages in a warm, sunny place. Give them food plants and small amounts of sugar water. Many will lay eggs, which will hatch to caterpillars, change to pupae, and finally become adults. The children can observe the cycle.

Make Believe

1. As you describe the life cycle of a butterfly, have the children act it out. The following is a suggested narrative:
   You are a caterpillar curled up inside an egg. You are hatched. You crawl on the ground looking for something to eat. You find a leaf and eat it. You look for more food and keep eating. Now you are full. You attach yourself to a twig or leaf and make a pupa. After a long time, you come out of the pupa. Now you are a butterfly. You rest. Dry your wings and fly away. You fly from flower to flower, drinking nectar.

2. Have individual children act out one of the stages of the butterfly and caterpillar and have the class guess which stage it is.

3. After reading *The Very Hungry Caterpillar* by Eric Carle, have the children act out the story.

Butterfly and Caterpillar Art Activities

Random Butterfly

Fold a piece of white paper in half. Unfold. Drop different colors of paint on one side of the paper. Fold on the crease and gently rub the paper to let the paint drops spread. Unfold. When the paint dries, refold on the crease and trace around a butterfly pattern. Cut it out. Unfold the paper. Color the head black.

Clothespin Butterfly

Cut rectangles from several colors of tissue paper. Select two for each butterfly and squeeze them into the slit of a clothespin. Using paint or markers, color the clothespin black for the body. Draw eyes and a mouth on the head of the clothespin. Attach pipe cleaners on top for the antennae.

286

TLC10299 Copyright © Teaching & Learning Company, Carthage, IL 62321-0(

Stained Glass Butterflies

Cut out the outline of a butterfly from a black piece of paper. About a half-inch from the outside edge, cut out the wings. Glue colorful tissue paper on the back. Glue or staple a piece of string at the top of the butterfly's head and hang in a window so the light will shine through.

Styrofoam™ Butterfly

Draw a butterfly on a white Styrofoam™ meat tray. Cut it out. Color it with markers or crayons on both sides. Poke a hairpin or wire through the body and twist it to make it secure.

Styrofoam™ Caterpillar

Cut circles from a Styrofoam™ tray. Punch a hole through the center of each one. Tie a knot in the end of a piece of yarn and thread it through the holes. When you have a long caterpillar, knot the other end of the yarn. Leave a little bit for a tail. Draw a face on the first circle.

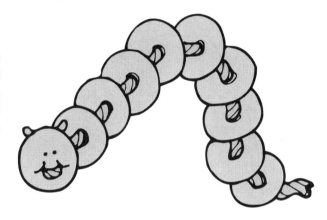

Egg Carton Caterpillar

Remove the cover from an egg carton. Cut the egg holder portion of the carton lengthwise. Cut one length into six separate cups. Trim the edges to make the cups even. Glue the cups to a long strip to make the caterpillar's body. Paint the caterpillar. With paint or construction paper, add eyes and colorful markings. For antennae, cut two strips of black paper and glue in place.

Mobile

Draw and cut out different pictures of butterflies, caterpillars, and/or the four stages of growth. Color and decorate them. Punch a hole near the top of each picture and tie a string through it. Hang each cut-out on a hanger, dowel stick, twig, or straws. Let them hang at different lengths. Hang the mobile where air can make it move.

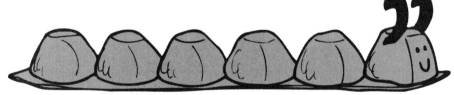

Murals and/or Books

This activity can be done individually or as a class project. On a long piece of paper, draw or paint the various stages of the butterfly (egg, caterpillar, pupa, butterfly). Fill in the area with appropriate background—trees, clouds, flowers, sun, bees, other butterflies, birds, and so on. Instead of a mural, make books using the same ideas.

What Happens First?

Color the pictures. Cut the boxes apart. Put them in sequential order.

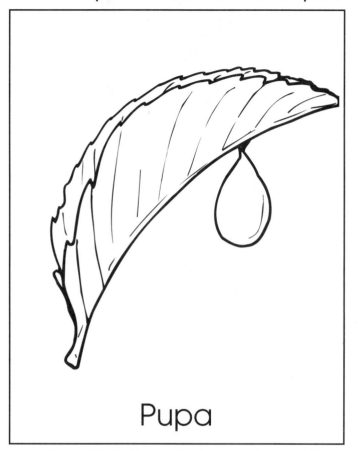

Pupa

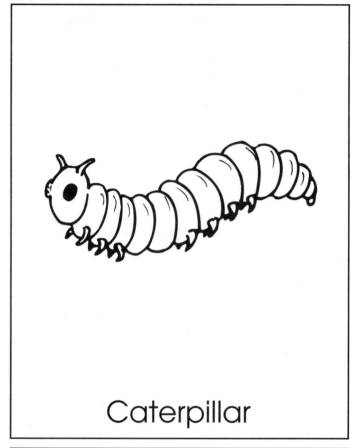

Caterpillar

Egg

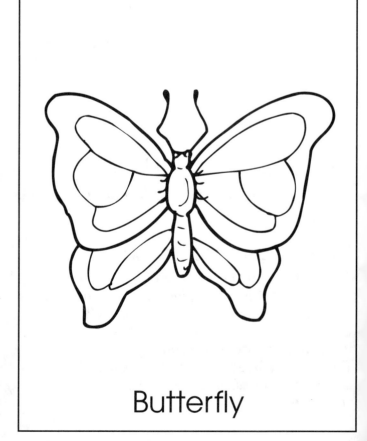

Butterfly

Dandelion Fun

Dandelion flowers
Are yellow as the sun,
But I like best to blow the puffs—
Each and every one!

A good "whoosh" sends them sailing
To float upon the breeze,
I love to stop and blow those puffs
Though Mom says, "Oh, no, please!"

Each tuft, she says, lands on the ground
And acts just like a seed
That grows another dandelion—
Precisely what I need!

A whole new crop of flowers
To turn into white puffs,
Grown just for me to gather up
And scatter all the fluff!

by Joan Welch Major

Kid Space
School Yard Learning Adventures

Have a Little Outdoor Summer Fun

The sun is shining, thoughts are wandering to summer days.
Why not burn up a little energy with some outdoor crafts and fun?

Super Crazy Ball

You Need
- about 15 thick rubber bands per student
- aluminum foil (one 8 ½" x 11" sheet per student)

What to Do
1. Scrunch the sheet of foil until it forms a solid ball.
2. Wrap a rubber band around the ball, twisting and turning it until it forms a tight wrap.
3. Wrap more rubber bands around the ball until the foil is completely covered.
4. Bounce and chase the ball—it won't go where you expect it!

Ribbon Ball

You Need
- small super-bouncy ball
- square of cloth
- rubber band
- 2 or more ribbons (24-36 inches in length)

What to Do
1. Wrap a ball in a square of cloth. Hold the four corners up with the ball resting in the center.
2. Hold the rubber band around the top of the ball and feed the ends of the cloth through the band. Move the band down to the ball and wrap the band around several times until the ball is held tightly in place. Tie the ribbons around the place where the rubber band meets the ball. Loop the rubber band around one more time to help hold the ribbons in place.
3. Throw the ball up and watch the tail flutter as it sails through the air.

Let's Play!
Use these balls for some traditional games of toss and catch, bounce and catch or wall ball, or invent some new games of your own.

290   by Robynne Eagan

SUMMER CELEBRATIONS

We line the curbs of Main Street
To cheer a proud parade
Of reds, whites, and blues,
So brilliantly displayed.

Brass-buttoned bands
March through sun and shade,
While we trick the heat
With snowcones and lemonade.

Afterwards we gather
To picnic in the park,
Play croquet and softball,
Till finally it's dark.

At last comes the time
We've all been waiting for,
Sparklers, whistling pinwheels,
Volcanoes, and much more.

Then, * **Boom** * *Crackle* * **Bang** *
Colors burst the sky!
What fun it is to celebrate
The Fourth of July!

by Paige Taylor

THE FIREWORKS

"Oh, no, Mom. Derek just told me that the fireworks were last night instead of tonight!" Sonia said as she ran in the door.

"But they always set off fireworks on the Fourth of July!" Mom exclaimed.

"Well, this year they changed it," said Sonia. "Now, just because we were away yesterday, we will miss our favorite part of July Fourth." She felt like crying.

"Maybe not," replied Mom. "Let's check the newspaper to see what other towns might have their fireworks tonight."

They found the name of another town about 10 miles away, but it didn't make Sonia feel any better. She didn't like things to change. She had watched the fireworks from Derek's back porch every year since she could remember. Their two families celebrated the holiday together, doing the same things each year.

Sonia's family had returned from their vacation in time for the afternoon's fun. Her father was making strawberry ice cream in the basement right now, her mom was trying to find everyone's baseball gloves, and her brother was hanging red, white, and blue streamers on the front porch.

"How will we find the best place to watch in a different town?" Sonia wanted to know.

"Don't worry," said Mom. "We'll just follow everyone else."

Sonia tried, but she couldn't enjoy the day quite as much as she usually did. The ice cream and the watermelon were the same as always. The baseball game and badminton set were the same. Playing with Derek and her brother was the same. But tonight, her favorite part of July Fourth would not be the same. It felt like something was missing, the way she felt when she outgrew her favorite red shirt.

by Linda McCollum Brown

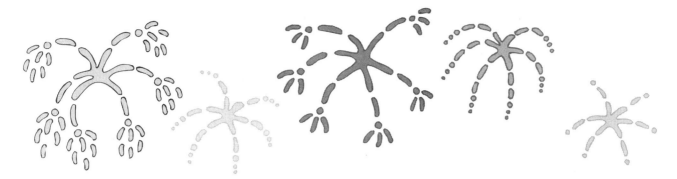

As the sun began to set, Sonia's family drove to the other town. More and more cars joined them on the road, all heading towards the fireworks. People were sitting in lawn chairs, and on blankets, and in the back of pickup trucks along the roadside.

"This looks like a good spot to stop," said Dad. They turned into the parking lot of a closed gas station. Lots of other people were around, getting settled.

"Where is the best place to watch the fireworks?" Mom asked a lady walking by.

"Oh, I know a great place," the lady answered. "Just follow us."

Sonia had to run to keep up because the lady and her children walked so fast. They went down a street behind the gas station to the playground of a small school.

Sonia felt dizzy as she looked to the top of a steep hill covered with trees.

"This is our special place to watch the fireworks," said the lady. "The fireworks are set off right above us, on the top of this hill. We discovered this spot years ago. It just wouldn't seem like the Fourth of July if we didn't come here."

Sonia helped Dad spread a blanket on the still-sun-warm blacktop near a basketball hoop. One of the lady's children came over to Sonia. "Do you want a sparkler? We have extras," she said.

"Okay, thanks," answered Sonia. "Do you do this every year?"

"Yeah," said the girl. "I like everything to be the same, don't you?"

Just then the fireworks began, lighting up the dark-curtained sky with one that looked like a giant burning pinecone. It was so big that Sonia almost felt like she was inside it—very different from seeing them from far away. Sonia smiled at her new friend. "Sometimes I do. But sometimes I guess it is fun to do things a little differently." She lay flat on her back to watch the rest of the fireworks spill over her head.

Summer

Journey through July and each month of the year with the wonderful collection of poems in *July Is a Mad Mosquito* by J. Patrick Lewis (Atheneum, 1994). This delightful array of poetry captures the seasonal sights and sounds for each month of the year. Read all about the "dreamsicle days" of July to the "feast of spring" in April.

The Twelve Days of Summer by Elizabeth Lee O'Donnell (Morrow Junior Books, 1991) is a captivating counting verse that will put everyone in the mood for a cool breezy day at the beach. A series of fun-filled visits to the sea are recounted by a girl who meets a group of lively ocean animals from strutting starfish to playful dolphins. After sharing the book with your class, have budding poets create their own versions of the poem. Compile their work into a classroom book entitled *Our Twelve Days of Summer*.

Down to the Sea with Mr. Magee
by Chris Van Dusen
Chronicle Books, 2000

Splash into summer with Mr. Magee and his little dog Dee as their "relaxing" boat ride in the ocean turns out to be quite an adventure. It all starts when the two encounter a pod of whales and suddenly, one of the whales gives their boat a "friendly" bump. The two sailors are soon in for a lively sea adventure they'll never forget! Put this humorous rhyming storybook at the top of your summer reading list!

- Make a list of all the ocean mammals you can think of. Draw a picture of the one that you like best.

- If you could talk to a blue whale, what would you say?

- A whale of a tale! Write another sea adventure that Mr. Magee and his dog Dee could have together.

Commotion in the Ocean
by Giles Andrea
illustrated by David Wojtowycz
Scholastic, 1998

Come on in, the water is fine! You'll love taking a "swim" through this picture book of humorous rhymes about some really neat ocean creatures. Meet dazzling dolphins, playful angelfish, jiggling jellyfish, a gigantic whale and a host of other sea animals. Enjoy a trip to the ocean this summer when you dive into this rhyming treasure.

- What's your favorite sea creature in the book? Write a riddle about the animal, giving four clues in complete sentences.

- If animals could talk . . . . Write a pretend interview with one of the sea animals in the book. First write four questions that you would like to ask the animal, then write the answers the animal might give.

- Write a tongue twister about a jiggling jellyfish.

by Mary Ellen Switzer

294

Book Nook

Stella & Roy Go Camping
by Ashley Wolff
Dutton Children's Books, 1999

Come along and join a fun-filled camping trip with Stella, Roy, and their mom as they hike to Lone Pine Lake. Have fun learning to identify the animal tracks of a coyote, raccoon, marmot, and black bear with the help of Stella's animal identification book. Find out if a black bear actually visits the family's campsite one night. Learn fascinating facts about woodland animals in a special section at the end of the book.

- Be an animal super sleuth! Choose one of the woodland animals from *Stella & Roy Go Camping.* Create an animal "trading card" with a picture and facts about your choice.

- Create a mystery animal track game and try to stump your friends with your "tricky" tracks.

- Be an author! Write a story about a camping adventure that YOU have with your family. Use these words in your story: *mountain, trail, tracks, cave, bear* and *forest ranger.*

The Super Camper Caper (The Fix-It Family)
by John Himmelman
Silver Press, 1991

Meet the amazing beaver family—Orville and Willa Wright and their children Alexander, Graham, and Belle. This family of inventors, nicknamed the Fix-It Family, enjoys repairing and inventing things. When Orville turns their truck into a super camper, the delighted family takes an unforgettable camping trip. The family soon finds their talent for inventing comes in handy even on vacation.

- If you were an inventor, what invention would you create to make the world a better place? Draw a picture of your invention and label the parts.

- Extra! Extra! Read all about it! Write a news story to tell everyone about your new invention.

- Alexander Graham Bell, Orville and Wilbur Wright were three famous American inventors. What are they famous for? Go on a research hunt for information about these men. Use an encyclopedia, reference book, or the internet to help. Write four interesting facts about each inventor.

Ice Cream Larry
by Daniel Pinkwater
illustrated by Jill Pinkwater
Marshall Cavendish, 1999

What's summer without a nice refreshing ice cream story? Here's a cool story that will tickle your "funny bone" on a hot summer day. Larry, a lovable polar bear, becomes quite a "cele-bearty" when he eats an eighth of a ton of ice cream at Cohen's Cones during an overnight stay in their freezer. Instead of being in trouble because he has eaten so much ice cream, the bear catches the attention of the owner of Iceberg Ice Cream Company and becomes the "spokesbear" of the business.

- Arctic Almond, Berry-Berry, and Polar Pineapple were some of the flavors of the "Larry" ice cream bars. What new flavors can you think of? Write a list of five other new flavors of ice cream bars.

- Create an advertisement for one of your suggested flavors for the Larry Bars.

- The slogan for the Iceberg Ice Cream Company is: "Iceberg! Iceberg! We all scream for Iceberg!" Write another catchy new slogan that the company could use.

Cam Jansen and the Mystery of the Babe Ruth Baseball

by David A. Adler
illustrated by Susanna Natti
Puffin Books, 1982

Play ball! Baseball season is now in full swing, so it's the perfect time to enjoy this whodunit on the subject. Cam Jansen and her friend Eric Shelton are having fun at the community hobby show, when a valuable baseball autographed by Babe Ruth is stolen. Cam's photographic memory starts to click as she and Eric set out to investigate the crime. Can you guess who the "ball-napper" was?

- Babe Ruth's real name was George Herman Ruth. Write three facts that you have learned about this famous baseball player after reading the book.

- What Major League team do you like best? Tell why. Create a new logo for the team. Draw a picture of your design.

- Read *Baseball, Eyewitness Books* by James Kelley (Dorling Kindersley, 2000). Find out how a baseball bat is made and what's inside a baseball in this fascinating book of photos and interesting trivia about the popular sport. Learn all about some of baseball's champion players, equipment, uniforms, and World Series history.

Happy Birthday, America!

Put a sparkle in one of America's important patriotic holidays, the 4th of July, with these terrific books:

Fireworks, Picnics, and Flags

by James Cross Giblin
Clarion Books, 1983

For everything you've ever wanted to know about Independence Day and more, this is the perfect book for you! This book not only gives an interesting history lesson, but provides fascinating trivia about national symbols, such as the Liberty Bell and the bald eagle.

Celebration: The Story of American Holidays

by Lucille Recht Penner
Macmillan Publishing Company, 1993

Here's another handy book to put on the top of your holiday book list! This informative book features the history and background information about Independence Day and other red-letter holidays, such as Memorial Day, Labor Day, Veterans Day, Halloween, and Thanksgiving.

Celebrating Independence Day

by Shelly Nielson
Abdo and Daughters, 1992

This gem of a poetry book is perfect for America's top patriotic summer holiday. Some of the poems include *Flags for the Fourth, Pack-a-Picnic, Sparkler Dance,* and *Fantastic Fireworks.* The book's stunning artwork captures the spirit of a Fourth of July celebration.

Software

Let's go globe-trotting this summer! Summer is the season for traveling to marvelous vacation spots all over the world. Take your youngsters on a "trip" around the world with the help of their computers and the following software.

Destination Rain Forest
Imagination Express Series

Edmark: www.edmark.com
Mac/Win CD-ROM

This superb interactive software magically takes your youngsters on a journey to a lush, tropical rain forest, which will be a backdrop to creating great stories and poems on the subject. Your students will experience the thrill of being in an exotic rain forest as they hear the actual sounds of the forest animals and inhabitants. They will learn about another culture—the Kuna Indians—who live in the rain forest of Panama. A "talking" Rain Forest Fact Book is also featured in this program, which enables students to discover fascinating facts about the people and animals who live in the forests.

Travel the World with Timmy

Edmark: www.edmark.com
Mac/Win CD-ROM

All aboard for an exciting journey to Kenya, Argentina, and Japan as your youngsters travel the world to visit and learn about three countries. This software will increase your students' awareness of other cultures and languages through delightful activities such as stories, games, and arts and crafts.

Web Site

www.nationalgeographic.com

Want to take a quick "visit" to any country in the world? Click on over to the National Geographic Society's web site which features printable maps of any country. This site also provides classroom activities and lesson plans for teachers.

Cooking with Kids

Learning to prepare food and use utensils and appliances safely are life skills appropriate for all age levels. Creative snacks help us achieve these goals as well as practice good table manners. Celebrate spring with a few fun snack ideas.

Peanut Butter Fudge Crunch

March—Peanut Month

Ingredients
½ c. crunchy peanut butter
⅓ c. soft margarine
3 tablespoons milk
1 egg white
2, 3.9 oz. pkgs. instant banana pudding
1 lb. confectioner's sugar

Combine the peanut butter, margarine, milk, and egg white in a mixing bowl. Add the pudding and sugar. Mix well. Turn the mixture out onto wax paper. Top with a second sheet of wax paper. Flatten the mixture to about a 1" thickness. Cut and serve as is or refrigerate for about a half hour to firm; then remove the paper and cut to serve.

Shamrock Salad

March—St. Patrick"s Day

Ingredients
shredded lettuce
green peppers
cottage cheese
green food coloring

Sprinkle shredded lettuce onto a plate. Stir a few drops of green food coloring into the cottage cheese to tint. Spoon green cottage cheese over the lettuce. Remove the core from a green pepper and slice it to make shamrock-shaped pepper rings. Place one pepper shamrock onto the cottage cheese. Slice a second green pepper into sticks. Add a green pepper stick stem to the green pepper shamrock.

Shamrock Sandwich

March—St. Patrick's Day

Ingredients
wheat bread, sliced
green peppers
cucumbers
mayonnaise

Help the students peel and slice the cucumbers. Wash the green peppers and slice them into small strips. Let the students spread a thin layer of mayonnaise over one slice of bread. Have them arrange three cucumber slices and one green pepper strip into the shape of a shamrock on the mayonnaise. Top with a second slice of bread and cut in half to eat.

Rainbow Rolls

April—April Showers

Ingredients
frozen bread dough, thawed   food colorings

Divide the bread dough into several portions. Wear latex gloves to knead a different coloring into each portion. The students can help with this. Gloves prevent the hands from being tinted. Depending on the size of your class, you may need to use two or three loaves of dough. Let the students roll the colored dough into balls; then arrange the balls in the shape of a rainbow on a cookie sheet. Allow the rolls to rise, then bake as directed on the package. Serve warm with butter or jam.

Peanut Butter Crunch

March—Peanut Month

Ingredients
1 c. crunchy peanut butter
1½ c. instant powdered milk
6 T. powdered sugar
6 T. honey
2 tsp. vanilla
1 c. chopped peanuts

Place the first five ingredients into a bowl. Mix well. Have the students wet their hands, then roll portions of the mixture into small balls. Roll the balls in the chopped peanuts.

by Marie E. Cecchini

Cooking with Kids

Welcome summer with some kid-friendly snack ideas.

Raisin Party Treats

May—National Raisin Week

Ingredients
- 1   12 oz. pkg. chocolate chips
- ½ cup chopped walnuts
- mini marshmallows
- pinch salt
- 1 cup raisins

Melt the chocolate chips in the top of a double boiler. Remove from heat and allow to partially cool (about 5 minutes). Stir in the salt, raisins, and chopped walnuts. Blend well. Drop by teaspoonfuls onto wax paper. Top each mound with one colorful marshmallow. Allow to set until firm.

Crunchy Taco Salad

May—Cinco de Mayo

Ingredients
- lettuce
- cucumbers
- taco shells
- 1 16 oz. can pinto beans, drained
- carrots
- block cheddar cheese
- dressing of choice

Have students rip lettuce, dice cucumbers, shred carrots, and shred cheese. Put in a bowl. Add pinto beans and mix gently. Drizzle with dressing, then toss to distribute the dressing evenly. Have students use tongs to fill their taco shells with the salad mixture.

Ladybug Rice Cakes

June—Summer

Ingredients
- rice cakes
- strawberry jam
- raisins
- black string licorice

Let students spread jam over rice cakes. Cluster raisins at one end to represent the ladybug's head. Place a strip of string licorice down the center to separate the wings. Dot the wings with additional raisins.

298

Chocolate Delight
June—Dairy Month

Ingredients
- salt
- ice
- self-sealing plastic bags (sandwich size and food storage size)
- chocolate milk (prepared or mix your own)
- sugar
- packing tape or masking tape (optional)

Let each student fill a food storage bag about half-full with ice; then sprinkle the ice with about ½ cup salt. Set these bags aside. Help each student measure ½ cup chocolate milk and 1 tablespoon sugar into a sandwich bag; then tightly seal the bag. You may want to reinforce the seal with tape. Let students place these smaller bags in the larger, ice-filled ones. Help them seal these bags tightly. Again, you may wish to reinforce with tape. Have students shake and shake and shake the bags for about 5 minutes for the mixture to thicken into ice cream. Singing a few songs and shaking to the beat will make the time seem to pass more quickly. Remove the small bags from the ice, rinse, and snip off one corner. Let the students squeeze their chocolate treat into a cup; then eat with a spoon.

American Sundaes
July—Independence Day, Blueberry Month

Ingredients
- bananas
- strawberry yogurt
- blueberries

Peel and quarter the bananas. One banana will serve two children. Let each student place two banana quarters into a small bowl. Top the bananas with strawberry yogurt and sprinkle with blueberries for a red, white, and blue fruit treat.

Watermelon Pizza
July—Picnic Month

Ingredients
- 1" thick seedless watermelon slices
- fruit chunks and berries of choice
- chocolate or peanut butter chips (optional)
- clean craft sticks

Divide the class into groups of four. Present each group with a round slice of watermelon on a plate, assorted fruit chunks, berries, and candy chips. Let students use the craft sticks to dig small spaces into the surface of their watermelon slices. Place fruit chunks and berries into these spaces. To add candy chips, push the pointed end of each into the melon. Cut each watermelon pizza into four pieces and enjoy.

by Marie E. Cecchini

Holiday newsletter

Research has shown that children lose some of what they've learned over the summer. Parents can help keep their children's minds active by providing activities that develop their curiosity. Children should continue to read, read, read. Visit the library, share the newspaper, and read along with your child. Review math with cooking and baking activities to explore measurement, volume, and time. Provide note cards, postcards, and thank-you cards to encourage your child to keep writing. Take advantage of local activities and points of interest you haven't yet explored. Summer provides a more relaxed environment for learning. Make good use of this time.

Simple Science

Invite your child to help prepare for International Flower Day this July by planting a butterfly garden in your yard now. Butterflies are attracted to nectar-rich flowers and herbs such as cosmos, marigolds, zinnias, lavender, and oregano. Grow plants like these in a sunny location. Flowering plants need lots of sunlight to grow, and the cold-blooded creatures you are planning to attract enjoy resting on sun-warmed garden rocks. Nestle a shallow container between your plantings and fill it with water, which some butterflies like to sip. Most importantly, refrain from using pesticides. You don't want to kill what you're trying to attract. For information about specific butterfly-attracting plants, check the local library for a butterfly guidebook. Can your child tell why this project is called a butterfly garden? Does it really grow butterflies?

On the Move

Sidewalk chalk games are a popular outdoor summer activity. Challenge your child to a tic-tac-toe tossing game. All you need is chalk, small stones, and a place to draw. To prepare the board, draw a large square on a sidewalk or driveway. Draw the tic-tac-toe grid inside this square. The first player tosses a small stone. If it lands in a space, the space is marked with an X. If it lands on a line, no space is marked and it's the second player's turn. The second player proceeds in the same manner but marks the scored spaces with an O. The first player to fill three spaces in a row wins.

Creative Kitchen

Does your child experience crabby "nothing to do" days during the summer months? Perk up the day with a recipe suited for the occasion. In honor of Anti-Boredom Month this July, invite your child to make a crab salad using cottage cheese, fresh red peppers, stuffed green olives, and red food coloring. Tint the cottage cheese red with the food coloring, and slice the red pepper into strips. Reserve eight pepper strips, dice the rest of the pepper, and mix the pieces into the tinted cottage cheese. To assemble the crab, place a mound of the cottage cheese-red pepper mixture onto a plate. Stick the pepper sticks into this mound to create legs and pincers. Place two stuffed green olives into the cottage cheese at one end of the crab for eyes. This snack will surely turn a pout into a smile.

by Marie E. Cecchini

Communication Station

Help your child get started on a scrapbook-journal to chronicle the events and activities of the summer. Encourage him or her to include and label photos of family and friends, postcards from travel excursions, postcards received in the mail, pictures of newsworthy people cut from magazines and newspapers, and ticket stubs from special events and movies attended. Set aside pages for your child to write down any great adventures taken, jokes heard, or funny things that happen. Save a space to add a list of favorite songs heard and books read. This project will help your child keep writing and learn to organize. And, when asked in September, "What did you do this summer?" the answer will be readily available.

Poetry in Motion

Everything in nature is always in motion, constantly changing. Share the following poem about summer changes with your child.

Who Am I Now?

The creeping, crawling caterpillar
Inched up the plant,
Created an anchor,
Then hung to ornament.

It built a tiny dressing room
To try on something new,
And when the door reopened,
It spread its wings and flew!

Can your child tell what the caterpillar changed into? Challenge your child to look around and notice other summer changes; then write a "Who Am I Now?" poem or song about one of them. Can you guess the answer to your child's query?

From the Art Cart

Invite your child to explore the comics section of your local newspaper in honor of Cartoon Appreciation Week in May. Which ones are favorites? Why? Observe how the illustrations help the cartoonist tell the story while using few words. Encourage your child to invent characters and draw several comic strips about them. Make several copies of these comic strips and work together to compile them into comic books to send to family and friends who live far away.

Mathworks

Celebrate Fiction Is Fun Month in June by helping your child create a math storybook. Let him or her cut out several favorite pictures from a magazine, glue each at the top of a separate sheet of construction paper, and make up a story about what is happening in each picture. Help your child write a picture-story related word problem below each picture. For example, with a picture of a boy eating cookies, the problem might read, "Mom baked 12 cookies. Jason ate 5. How many are left?" Let your child solve the problem and write the answer on the back of each page. Encourage your child to challenge family members to read the book and solve the problems.

Reading Room

Encourage your child to continue reading throughout the summer by making periodic trips to your local library. Here are some titles you may want to try.

D.W. All Wet by Marc Brown, Little, Brown.

Farm Days by William Wegman, Hyperion.

Hotter Than a Hot Dog! by Stephanie Calmenson, Little, Brown.

My Backyard Garden by Carol Lerner, Morrow Junior Books.

The Pig in the Pond by Martin Waddell, Candlewick Press.

Say Hola to Spanish by Susan Middleton Elya, Lee & Low.

Clip Art for Spring

Happy Easter!

Happy St. Patrick's Day!

Just a Reminder:

APRIL FOOL!

Clip Art for Spring

NATIONAL GARDEN MONTH

April Showers

SPRING!

MOM

Mom, You're sweet!

MAY DAY

Happy Mother's Day!

Cinco de Mayo

Milk

Make Mine Milk!

Milk

Dairy Month

Dad, "frankly" you're the best!

Have a ball on Father's Day!

Happy Father's Day!

July 4th!

Summer Fun!

Flag Day!

Hooray!

Whooo's ready for summer?

S'more Summer fun!

So long!... Have a great summer!

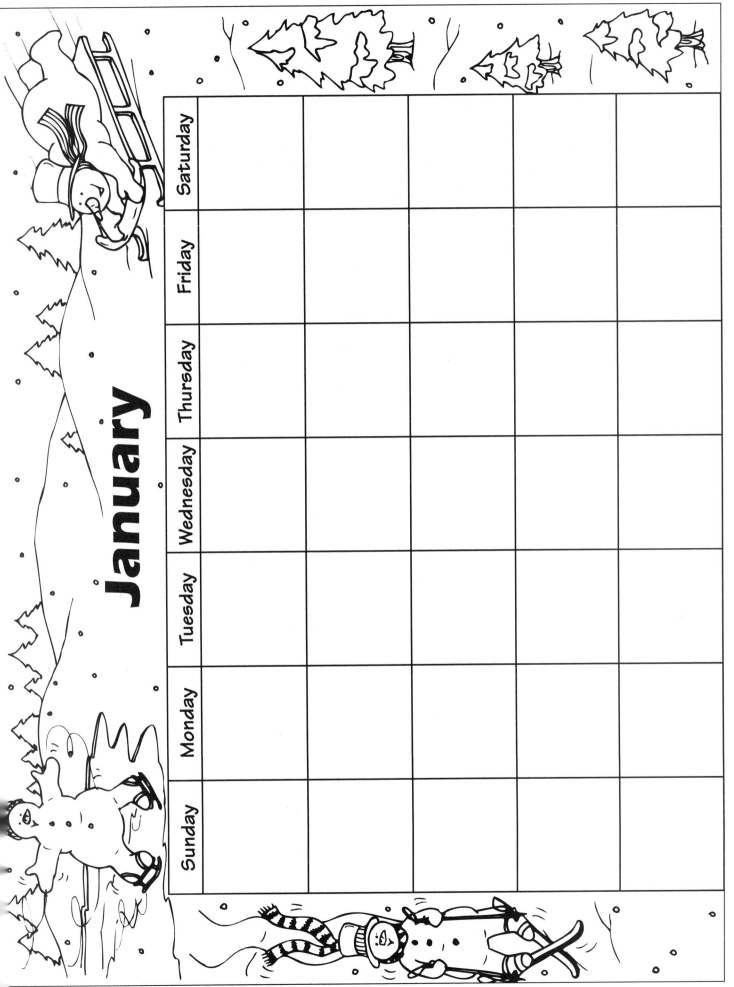

January

Sunday	Monday	Tuesday	Wednesday	Thursday	Friday	Saturday

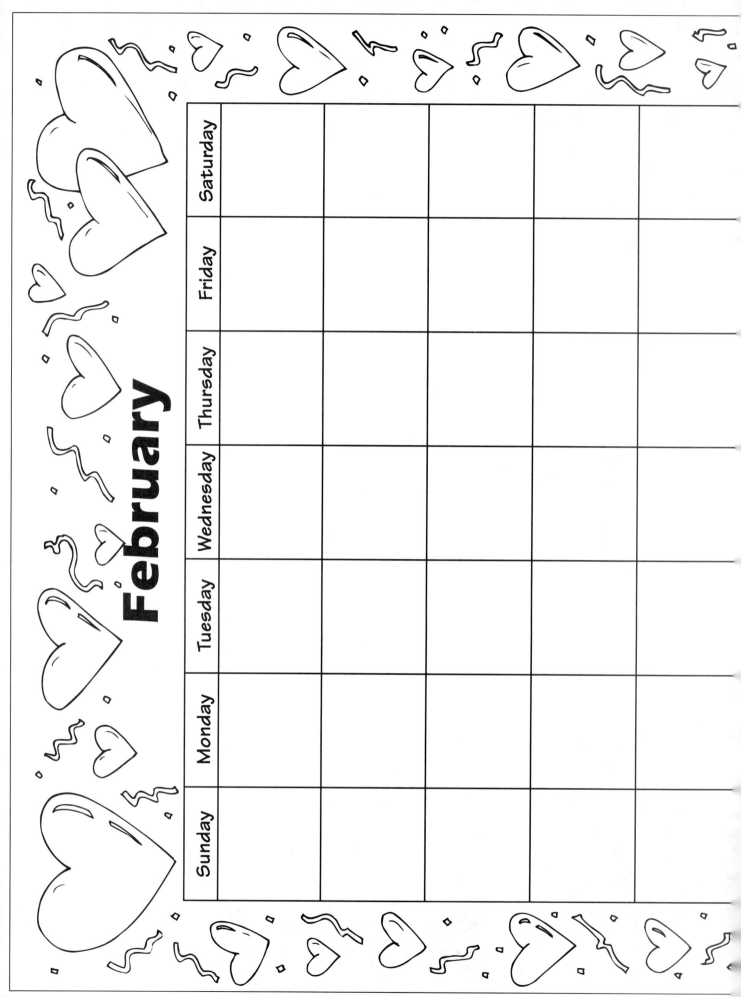

February

Sunday	Monday	Tuesday	Wednesday	Thursday	Friday	Saturday

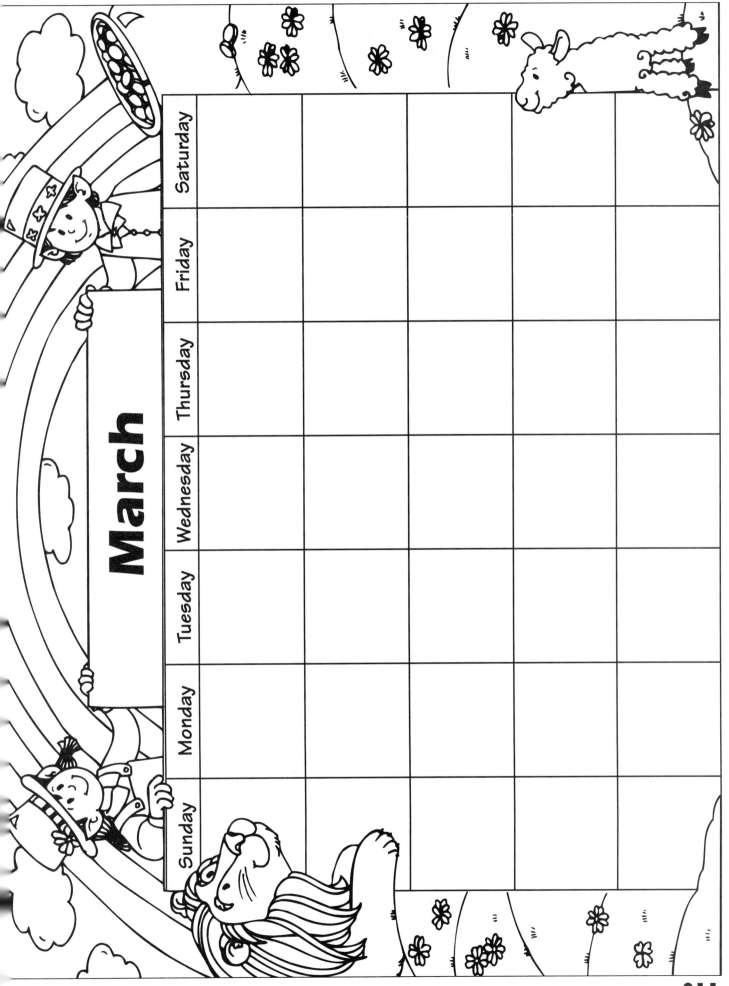

March

Sunday	Monday	Tuesday	Wednesday	Thursday	Friday	Saturday

April

Sunday	Monday	Tuesday	Wednesday	Thursday	Friday	Saturday

May

Sunday	Monday	Tuesday	Wednesday	Thursday	Friday	Saturday

June

Sunday	Monday	Tuesday	Wednesday	Thursday	Friday	Saturday

July

Sunday	Monday	Tuesday	Wednesday	Thursday	Friday	Saturday

August

Sunday	Monday	Tuesday	Wednesday	Thursday	Friday	Saturday

316

September

Sunday	Monday	Tuesday	Wednesday	Thursday	Friday	Saturday

October

Sunday	Monday	Tuesday	Wednesday	Thursday	Friday	Saturday

318

November

Sunday	Monday	Tuesday	Wednesday	Thursday	Friday	Saturday

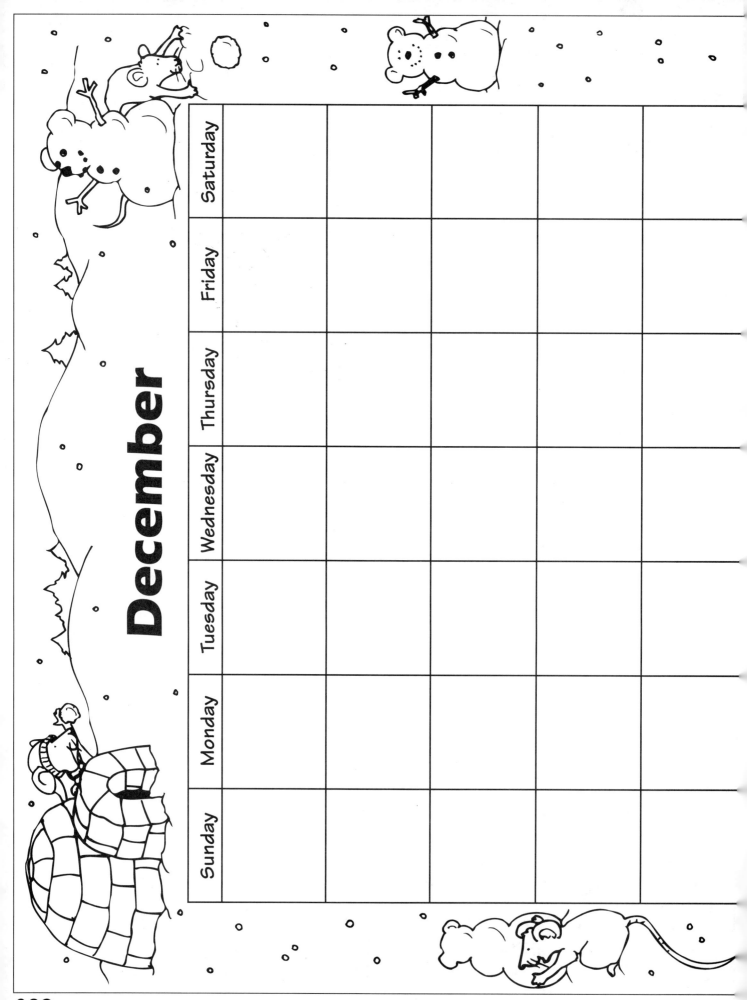

December

Sunday	Monday	Tuesday	Wednesday	Thursday	Friday	Saturday

320